Language and Discipline Perspectives on Academic Discourse

Language and Discipline Perspectives on Academic Discourse

Edited by

Kjersti Fløttum

Cambridge Scholars Publishing

Language and Discipline Perspectives on Academic Discourse, Edited by Kjersti Fløttum

This book first published 2007. The present binding first published 2008.

Cambridge Scholars Publishing

12 Back Chapman Street, Newcastle upon Tyne, NE6 2XX, UK

British Library Cataloguing in Publication Data
A catalogue record for this book is available from the British Library

Copyright © 2008 by Kjersti Fløttum and contributors

All rights for this book reserved. No part of this book may be reproduced, stored in a retrieval system, or transmitted, in any form or by any means, electronic, mechanical, photocopying, recording or otherwise, without the prior permission of the copyright owner.

ISBN (10): 1-4438-0046-5, ISBN (13): 978-1-4438-0046-4

Table of Contents

Preface and Acknowledgements vii

PART I: Introduction and General Issues 1

Chapter One 2
Introductory remarks
Philip Shaw

Chapter Two 14
Cultural Identities and Academic Voices
Kjersti Fløttum, Trine Dahl, Torodd Kinn, Anje Müller Gjesdal
and Eva Thue Vold

Chapter Three 40
The Rhetoric of Science in Practice: Experiences from Nordic Research
on Subject-Oriented Texts and Text Cultures
Kjell Lars Berge

PART II: Discipline Focus 65

Chapter Four 66
Authority and Expert Voices in the Discourse of History
Marina Bondi

Chapter Five 89
Different Strokes for Different Folks: Disciplinary Variation in Academic Writing
Ken Hyland

Chapter Six 109
The Prosecutor and the Defendant: Contrasting Critical Voices in French- and English-Written Academic Book Reviews
Françoise Salager-Meyer, María Ángeles Alcaraz Ariza and Maryclis Pabón

Chapter Seven 129
Cooperation and Conflict Between Authorial Voices and Model Readers
Through Rhetorical Topoi in Historical Discourse
Johan L. Tønnesson

PART III: Language Focus 149

Chapter Eight 150
The 'Iffiness' of Medical Research Articles: A Comparison of English
If and French Si
Shirley Carter-Thomas

Chapter Nine 176
A Genre Study of If in Medical Discourse
Elizabeth Rowley-Jolivet

Chapter Ten 202
Marking Evidentiality in Scientific Papers: The Case of Expectation Markers
Francis Grossmann and Françoise Wirth

Chapter Eleven 219
Academic Discourse as Social Control and System(s), seen through the use
of Demonstrative Noun Phrases in French Scientific Texts
Lita Lundquist

Chapter Twelve 243
Hybrid Voices: English as the Lingua Franca of Academics
Anna Mauranen

Chapter Thirteen 260
Similarities and Differences in French and English EAP Research Article
Abstracts: The case of ASp
John M. Swales and Sarah Van Bonn

List of Contributors 277

PREFACE AND ACKNOWLEDGEMENTS

This book, *Language and Discipline Perspectives on Academic Discourse*, represents the physical outcome of the symposium *Academic Voices in Contrast,* focusing on recent research within the field of academic discourse. The symposium, which took place at the University of Bergen, May 4–6 2006, was initiated and organised by the KIAP project (Norwegian abbreviation for *Cultural Identity in Academic Prose*). The main issue of KIAP has been the following: Can cultural identities be identified in academic prose, and if so, to what extent are these identities language- or discipline-specific in nature? This question has been answered through a contrastive study of a selection of linguistic features in English, French and Norwegian research articles within the disciplines of economics, linguistics and medicine (for more information, see www.uib.no/kiap/ and article by Fløttum et al. in this volume).

In the KIAP project, a special focus has been put on the study of the voice(s) of the academic author–in the doubly contrastive perspective presented above. To round off the project in a suitable manner, a narrow selection of distinguished scholars were invited to participate at the symposium. They were asked to address one or several of the following issues:

- "traditional" linguistic versus contextual approaches
- interlingual differences and reasons/explanations
- interdisciplinary differences and reasons/explanations

The symposium was a great success, contributing to the advancement of academic discourse studies, currently one of the most dynamic fields within text linguistic and discourse research. I am very pleased and grateful that all the invited speakers accepted to collaborate in the writing of this book: Thank you all for your valuable contributions!

I want to give special thanks to my friends and KIAP-colleagues, Trine Dahl and Torodd Kinn, and PhD candidates Eva Thue Vold, Anje Müller Gjesdal and Anders Alvsåker Didriksen, both for intellectual discussions and practical help. Finally I would like to thank Camilla Skogseth Clausen and Mikael Ladegård for various practical and technical assistance during the symposium, the University of Bergen for financial support of the symposium and the agency Kongress & Kultur and their manager Inger Lise Ravnanger for organisational assistance.

Kjersti Fløttum
Head of the KIAP project

PART I

INTRODUCTION AND GENERAL ISSUES

CHAPTER ONE

INTRODUCTORY REMARKS

PHILIP SHAW

1. Analyzing scientific discourse

Writers of research articles often use what might be called the 'Ascent of Man' trope in creating their research space. They arrange other approaches and findings so that they lead inexorably to their own, in the way that traditional views of evolution have seen the history of life as a line from amoebas to humans. This trope is effective rhetorically and also a useful mnemonic, which results in student essays full of sequences like the one for language-teaching methods: grammar-translation, audio-lingual, communicative. But Stephen Gould (1991:35) has argued that in fact "Life is a copiously branching bush....not a ladder of predictable progress." In the same way one might suppose that in many academic areas approaches and methods profitably exist simultaneously and help to illustrate different aspects of the object of investigation.

Scientific discourse is, as Berge says in this volume, a key discourse of modernity, and its study can lead to understanding of the modern intellectual environment and empowerment of those who seek to enter it. Linguistically-oriented students of scientific discourse are lucky enough to have acquired a new major contribution in the form of the KIAP project (Fløttum *et al.*, this volume). It enriches the ecology of the field in several ways, both empirically and theoretically. From an empirical point of view it provides a carefully constructed corpus large enough to allow comparisons of the chosen genre–the research article–across both languages and disciplines. Furthermore English is compared both with a 'large" and a 'small' language in terms of scientific publishing, and the disciplines chosen–medicine, economics, and linguistics– have been much studied in other connections, so that there is synergy with the work of others, such as Salager-Meyer on English, French and Spanish medicine (e.g., this volume), or Vassileva (2000) on linguistics in a variety of languages. The corpus has already been analyzed with statistical awareness, giving interesting results, and will doubtless be the basis for many other investigations. But KIAP is also interesting theoretically in that it aims to apply French/Scandinavian polyphonic linguistic theory (e.g., Nølke 2001) to identify the different voices in different subcorpora. Studies of academic discourse benefit greatly from sophisticated linguistic and discourse analysis, and in the spirit of the "branching bush of life", different approaches contribute different insights. This provides an opportunity to reflect on the methods and procedures available to linguistically-oriented studies of scientific discourse and its aims.

2. Dimensions of difference

Most such studies start from a corpus of texts delimited in some way by genre, discipline, language, users' competence type, medium and date. Both KIAP and many of the other investigations described in this book are based on single-genre corpora of scientific/academic articles, thus focusing on a key genre of the discourse of modernity. Scientific publication involves other genres represented here like the abstract, the academic book review, the medical case study, and the conference presentation, but the discourse of science is also represented in educational genres like the lecture, textbook and seminar, and crucially in genres like the popular-science book. These genres–*sakprosa* in Norwegian, rather lamely translatable as "non-fiction"–make the link to the broad taxpaying public who should benefit from the activities of science, and mediate between specialist and everyday discourse. Not represented here but by now widely described are the dissertation, which is liminal between a research and an educational genre (Stålhammar 2002; Charles 2003) and the minor academic genres–'occluded' ones like responses to job references (Swales et al 2000), and public ones like obituaries in journals (Kresta 1996).

Studies of scientific discourse have to take account not only of generic differences, but also of disciplinary ones. KIAP examines articles from a natural science (an applied one?), a social science, and something bordering on the humanities. Many other studies of scientific discourse, including most of those in this volume, have examined one or more of these disciplines but of course there have been studies of many others–from applied mathematics (Yakhontova 2002) and computer science (Posteguillo 1999) via wildlife behaviour and conservation biology (Samraj 2002) and crash safety (Räisanen 1998), to sociology (Brett 1994) and marketing (Hemais 2001, Lindeberg 1998), to name but a few. In this volume Hyland covers eight disciplines , 'hard' and 'soft', 'pure' and 'applied', and Bondi and Tønnesson tackle the quintessentially humanistic history.

Analysis of scientific discourse may be based on a single-language corpus and describe how genres are constructed or disciplines represented in that language. The language is inevitably often English or another of the historically dominant languages of international publication like French, German, or Russian, but many others from Swedish (Gunnarsson 1997), to Swahili (Mwansoko 2003) have been examined. In this volume Hyland and Bondi look at English, Lundquist at French (using part of the KIAP corpus), and Tønnesson and Berge at Norwegian. However a comparative approach is also frequently adopted, often contrasting the scientific discourse of English with that of another language (Russian/Ukraininan in Yakhontova 2002, Swedish in Melander *et al* 1997, Chinese in Bloch and Chi 1995, etc.). The majority of the writers in the present collection compare English and French, and some include Norwegian (KIAP) and Spanish (Salager-Meyer).

In English in particular, differences of competence type (native vs non-native) have been studied. Naturally enough, these studies used to be rather normative, following the commonsense idea that one should use a language the way the natives do, but the special status of English and the increasing predominance of users with non-native competence has meant that the usages of the two groups have come to be regarded as equally valid. Most writers in this volume study writers with native (as in KIAP) or unspecified competence, but Carter-Thomas and Rowley-Jolivet compare the English usage of French speakers with that of natively-competent users, and Mauranen describes some features of lingua-franca English educational discourse, in which the majority of speakers have non-native competence.

The written discourse of research has been much more widely studied than the spoken. It could be argued that this reflects its importance–it is written scientific discourse that is the shaper of modernity–but another factor is that linguistically-oriented investigations of scientific discourse are closely connected to their applications in language and writing instruction, and the need has often been for support in the written language. But on the educational (as opposed to research) side of the discourse, and in crucial conference interactions that construct the discipline, the spoken medium is dominant and is nevertheless widely considered to be under-researched. The advent of spoken corpora has made it much easier to deal with spoken academic discourse. In this volume Rowley-Jolivet draws on her corpus of medical conference presentations, contrasting them with written texts in the same discourse, and Mauranen looks at interactions in her ELFA spoken corpus.

Two other dimensions that have to be controlled in the construction of a corpus of academic discourse are date and writer gender. All the investigations in this volume are synchronic, representing more or less present-day scientific discourse, but there is a substantial diachronic literature. For example Salager-Meyer *et al* (2003) show that a tradition of fairly robust criticism of colleagues in medical research discourse started to change to a more guarded style in

English around 1930, but not in French, and not in Spanish until recently, perhaps under English influence. Writer gender is a dimension on which academic texts might vary, and KIAP does in fact take account of this. But corpus-based linguistic discourse analysis does not seem a productive instrument for identifying gender issues: at this level writers may be "doing science" in preference to "doing gender".

3. Some complications

3.1 Average and variance

A very attractive feature of the results reported by KIAP is the emphasis on the variation in the individual articles within each linguistic and disciplinary class. Within any set of texts grouped by an extralinguistic category the frequency of any particular feature will vary from text to text. The average frequency for the feature is only interesting if the standard deviation is reasonably low, that is if most text members are reasonably close to the average. But even where this condition is satisfied and the averages of two sets are significantly different from one another, the texts which differ markedly from the average of their set are interesting. Do they sound odd, old-fashioned, trendy, foreign? Do they sound like texts from a particular subdiscipline? Readers need to know not only the mean value for the marker examined but also the range of values which are likely to be acceptable.

3.2 Genre

Texts which appear to belong to the same genre may not be comparable. Because different disciplines belong to partly different big-D Discourses (Gee, 1996), both the system of genres and the hierarchy among them are different in different disciplines (Swales 2004). In some the article is the lower member of a set which includes scientific letters (Hyland 2000), in others it is the faster member of a set which includes books, and in others, at least in medicine it co-exists with parallel genres like the case study (Carter-Thomas, this volume). In some disciplines virtually all writing is for peers, in others there is a lot of disciplinary writing for other audiences (Hicks 2004). Furthermore in some fields (the natural sciences) a book is a low-status publication and it is articles that count, in others (history, literary studies) books are central (Swales 2004). In traditional structuralist terms, items that occupy different structural positions in their systems cannot be comparable, and in functional terms texts with (somewhat) different purposes belong to (somewhat) different genres. There might therefore be some risk of interpreting as a difference in the ideology of a discipline what is in fact a difference in the place of the genre compared.

3.3 Discipline

A more substantial problem might lie in the notion of discipline itself. Disciplines seem to be defined largely by the object they deal with, but within a discipline there can be very varied approaches or schools. If, for example, one adopts the distinction between cumulative nonomothetic disciplines like most natural sciences and interpretive ideographic ones like literary criticism, one will identify a division which divides disciplines like philosophy and sociology down the middle. Similarly the modes of enquiry of molecular biology and taxonomic botany (Swales 1998) have so little in common that it would be misleading to lump them under 'biology'. This means that one must be cautious when comparing members of a corpus that are supposed to be of different disciplines. It is striking for example, that MacDonald's insightful descriptions (1994) of the types of sentence subjects to be found in New Historicist literary criticism cannot be generalized to other literary essays, and that Samraj (2002) found quite different genre patterns in Wildlife Behaviour and Conservation Biology. One can well imagine that articles in sociolinguistics, transformational grammar, and second language acquisition are sufficiently different in discourse and structure to make it unwise to lump them under 'linguistics'. This means that it is important both to know whether one has selected a sample which is homogeneous with respect to school or subdiscipline, and, as mentioned above, to report on the internal homogeneity of the members of one's categories (as the KIAP project does). Of course analysis of the statistical significance of differences will prevent internally heterogeneous categories from being incorrectly reported as different from one another. However, if the insignificance of differences is actually due to two internally homogeneous categories being confounded, failure to consider this possibility by examining the school or subdiscipline of the texts making up one's corpus will result in missed generalizations.

An even more important problem with a linguistic approach to disciplinary discourse has been pointed out by Airey and Lunger (2006). They argue that the disciplinary discourse of physics includes not merely the spoken and written linguistic modes, but also the mathematical, the visual (graphs, etc.), the active (carrying out experiments), and the instrumental (the type of information that each instrument gives). Knowing physics, they argue, is knowing all these modes and integrating them. One can well imagine that ideographic philosophy, for example, is mainly constructed by written words, but the same is not true for all disciplines, where key aspects of the discourse may be constructed by other modes. Linguistically-oriented analysis of scientific discourse needs to recognise that it may be comparing the whole discourse of one discipline with part of that of another and that functions performed by words in one discipline may use another mode in another.

3.4 Language

If one works with a bilingual or multilingual corpus one obvious dimension for comparison of rhetoric or discourse is between texts in different languages. The difficulty is sometimes to interpret the results. Differences between corpora of articles in different disciplines, for example can arise from at least four different sources. The articles may not be comparable, because they are intended for different audiences and the genre ecology is different in the source academic cultures (Melander et al 1997). Thus writing in social science in other languages than English may derive from a different "literature" (Hicks 2004) than writing in English, that is, it may be addressed to a less specialized audience containing more practitioners. Alternatively, different types of publication may have different weights in different academic culture. Hicks quotes figures showing that 39% of publication in Australian social sciences and humanities was as "Books, edited books, book chapters, monographs and reports, creative works and 'other'" (2004:4), while in Spain this figure was 54% and in German sociology 58% of publication took these forms. A second possible source is that different schools or subdisciplines predominate in the disciplines in question in the two language communities. A third, very significant, source, is that the linguistic resources available in the two languages may be very different. This may be at a straightforward level, like the availability in French of the multiply ambiguous generic pronoun *on,* in Scandinavian languages of the everyday unmarked but referentially more restricted generic *man,* and in English only of the stylistically marked and rather infrequent generic *one.* But there are also more subtle links between linguistic resources and discourse. Von Stutterheim and Lambert (2005), for example have shown that speakers of languages which mark progressive aspect (English, Spanish) on the verb tend to produce process-oriented descriptions, while in languages without grammaticalized progressive aspect parallel descriptions are goal-oriented.

Finally one can assume that some differences between scientific writing in different languages are due to cultural differences between the scientific communities involved, some of which will be characteristic only of those communities and others of the traditions of the wider community, whatever that is. Norwegian marine biologists, for example, can be expected to have some shared characteristics typical only of their group, some typical of Norwegian scientists, and others typical of anyone who has been through the Norwegian school system, subjected to Norwegian mass media, etc.. In so far as school systems, media, etc. are similar across countries with the same official language (Salager-Meyer, pers. comm.), writers with a given first language might be expected to have similar rhetorical or discoursal preferences. But it is equally likely that writers with different first languages have the same rhetorical preferences (as some of the KIAP findings reported in Fløttum *et al.* (2006) suggest in relation to Anglo-American and Norwegian writers), and possible that the degree of integration to metropolitan culture varies across a multi-national language. Thus British academics may essentially share the culture of their US counterparts, but one can imagine that Brazilian and continental-Portuguese academic cultures are more independent of one another.

This is where the time dimension might be of interest. Most studies show that generally speaking developments have been parallel across disciplines and languages–towards a more theoretical and less descriptive rhetoric, towards increasing specialization, and towards greater embedding in the literature (that is, more references). But these processes have proceeded at different speeds in different disciplines and scientific cultures. Consequently a final potential source of difference between texts in different languages or disciplines is that the academic cultures involved are at different stages in a common process.

4. Types of investigation

Alongside variation in the dimensions that studies investigate, there is also, of course, variation in the features that they examine and the framework in which they interpret the results. Here there may be a conflict between reliability and validity and between depth and scope which means that different approaches must co-exist and illuminate one another. Focus on linguistic features of texts may not lead to enormous increases in understanding of the texts but it produces reliable numerical results which can be built on, while focus on higher levels of discourse produces analyses that may not be replicable but are insightful. Similarly studies of many texts in many disciplines produce superficial but wide-ranging contrasts, while carefully reading oneself into a discipline leads to examination of a very small area but produces a deep characterization.

Even among studies focusing on linguistic features, the choice of features to investigate affects the rhetorical elements that can be addressed. Analyses of pronouns, modifiers, or more functionally oriented classes like hedges throw light on the *ethos* and *pathos* elements–stance, reader/relations, etc. (for example Hyland 2000), while focus on noun phrases illuminates *logos* (for example MacDonald. 1994, Gunnarsson 1997). Focus on linguistic features may also work essentially top-down or bottom-up. Top-down, one knows from previous work or theory what forms are likely to be indices of the rhetorical functions one is interested in and examines their relative frequencies and placement in the parts of the corpus, while bottom-up one selects (admittedly on the basis of previous work, theory or intuitions) a form, and examines which rhetorical functions it is indexical of in the texts to be contrasted. In the present volume the KIAP corpus is used in a variety of ways. The Bergen team investigate, top-down, the frequency of a number of linguistic elements which in one way or another signal different voices in the text, enabling them to contrast polyphonic features across languages and disciplines. Grossmann and Wirth examine *en fait/in fact*, bottom-up, showing how the form realizes different aspects of *ethos* in different languages and disciplines. Lundquist also works bottom-up but looks at noun phrases with demonstrative determiners (compare Charles 2003) in French and shows how they reflect the content of their disciplines.

Hyland has adopted a top-down approach illuminated by practitioner interviews in many publications. In this volume he looks at signals of writer involvement and reader-writer interaction, adding to linguistic contrasts across disciplines interviews with discourse community members who can confirm and deepen the discourse analyst's insights into the *ethos* and *pathos* of their disciplinary writing. Hyland ranges over many forms and many disciplines. By contrast, Rowley-Jolivet and Carter-Thomas work in a somewhat bottom-up way on one form in one discipline. They both concentrate on medical discourse and on determining the frequency and functions of one form, conditional sentences. Their familiarity with the field enables them to compare usage within this discourse of one particular form and show how it is affected by genre, mode, language, and competence-type. These differences in usage then illuminate the ways in which the dimensions affect the disciplinary discourse.

Mauranen's paper also looks at linguistic features of texts, but in this case the texts are in spoken educational genres and the aim is to identify characteristic features of the code of academic English in environments where most speakers have non-native competence. Code features are affected not only by the discipline and the genre but also by other aspects of the communicative situation, in this case the competence-type of the interactants.

Another very common approach looks above linguistic items at the functional units that make up genres: move and steps in the tradition of Swales (1990, 2004), and more generally speech acts. It is often difficult to achieve reliable intersubjective agreement on the boundaries and even the classification of moves, but such analyses move nearer the actual acts intended by the writers of the texts examined and provide valid insights into the purposes of writers and the ideology of the discipline, particularly when supplemented by interviews. In this volume Swales and Van Bonn compare applied-linguistics abstracts in

French and English, showing how audience-type and 'national-science' cultural conventions are reflected even in articles in the same journal and by the same author. Salager-Meyer provides clear evidence that the strength and form of acts of negative evaluation vary across book reviews in three languages within the same discipline, presumably for a variety of linguistic and cultural reasons. Bondi takes up the KIAP theme of polyphony and looks at citations in the introduction to history articles, showing how their use reflects both the rhetoric and the content or *logos* of the discipline.

As Airey and Linder (2006) show for physics, a narrow deep analysis of one discipline moves away from linguistic expression towards the conceptual and methodological essence of the discipline, and away from reliable quantitative data towards, possibly non-replicable, valid qualitative insights. In this volume Tønnesson reports an investigation from the Norwegian *sakprosa* tradition into the multiple voices which interact to form historical discourse in a single Norwegian local history text, showing how the different voices weave a complex web to develop a broad picture. Local history is important because it is an interface between the professional historian and the local enthusiast and thus a link between the academic world and the communities it must ultimately serve. The methodology involves setting the text into the whole social and intellectual network in which it arises, with all its interactions of readers and writers, genres, publication types, political positions, etc.: something like the big-D Discourse of the discipline (Gee 1996). Analyses of this kind can only be done by a researcher with a good knowledge of the discipline and its context, combined with an awareness of rhetoric and discourse, a combination not always available in every discipline.

As we have seen, linguistically-oriented analyses of academic discourse tend to deal with indicators of *ethos* and *pathos* and not with the structure of ideas or topoi which are central to disciplines. I argue below that this is a reasonable task to carry out, but one must not fail to raise one's eyes to wider issues, as Berge points out in this volume. Academic texts are important because they are powerful and formative, and studies of the rhetoric of science must eventually address the big issues of relativism, ideology, and power.

The context of current investigations of academic discourse is an increased focus on international publishing and student movement in nearly all disciplines. International publishing and study abroad have always required researchers of most nationalities to write in a foreign language, first Latin, then French, German, or English, alongside their own, but current conditions mean that only international publishing is respected in many disciplines, and that only English is acceptable. Berge points out that this means that we might eventually find ourselves in a position where knowledge circulated freely among an international English-using elite, but was not easily accessible in the other national languages of Europe–an undemocratic and undesirable development in that academic discourse is the key source of knowledge and power in modern societies. This brings us to the final issue–what are linguistically-oriented analyses for?–which can only be touched on briefly.

5. Applications and implications

Most writers represented in this book have training in linguistics, pragmatics, rhetoric, and composition theory, and most have worked as teachers of academic writing or languages for specific purposes. Only a few have specialist training in the disciplines whose rhetoric they examine. This seems to me to point to the contribution that work of this type can most usefully make. Our potential contribution to an understanding of the *logos*, the ways of thinking of the disciplines, is limited by our superficial understanding of the texts. Our contribution to pure knowledge is likely to be to pragmatics or rhetoric, by testing and developing theories on the basis of new types of texts. Our contribution to scientific communication is likely to come from insights into *ethos* and *pathos*–stance, attitude, evaluation, voices–issues which are clear to us but occluded to specialists in other disciplines. Globalisation means that we often find ourselves making clear to people from other disciplines how these issues affect texts in a language foreign to them. An underlying theme of the papers in this book is that we have to balance the asymmetries of knowledge and linguistic power against the equality of rights of everyone inside and outside the academic communities.

6. References

Airey, John and Cedric Lunger. "Languages, Modality and Disciplinary Knowledge." Paper given at the 2nd conference on Integrating Content and Language in Higher Education, Maastricht, June 29th–July 1st, 2006.
Bloch, Joel and Lan Chi. "A Comparison of the Use of Citations in Chinese and English Academic Discourse." In *Academic Writing in a Second Language: Essays on Research and Pedagogy*, edited by Diane Belcher and George Braine, 231–275. Ablex: Norwood, NJ, 1995.
Brett, Paul. "A Genre Analysis of the Results Sections of Sociology Articles." *English for Specific Purposes,* 13 (1994) 1:47–59.
Busch-Lauer, Ines. "'A Pill for Every Illness'-- Englische und deutsche Ratgebertexte für Patienten." *Fachsprache,* 16 (1994): 127-139.
Charles, Maggie. "'This Mystery...': a Corpus-based Study of the Use of Nouns to Construct Stance in Theses from Two Contrasting Disciplines." *Journal of English for Academic Purposes,* 2 (2003): 313–326.

Fløttum, Kjersti, Trine Dahl and Torodd Kinn. *Academic Voices.* Amsterdam/Philadelphia: John Benjamins, 2006.
Gee, James P. *Social Linguistics and Literacies: Ideology in Discourse* (2nd edition). London: Taylor and Francis, 1996.
Gould, Stephen. *Wonderful Life: the Burgess Shale and the Nature of History.* Harmondsworth: Penguin, 1991.
Gunnarsson, Britt-Louise. "On the Sociohistorical Construction of Scientific Discourse." In *The Construction of Professional Discourse* edited by Britt-Louise Gunnarsson, Per Linell and Bengt Nordberg, 99–126. Longman. London and New York, 1997.
Hemais, Barbara. "The Discourse of Research and Practice in Marketing Journals." *English for Specific Purposes,* 20 (2001), 39–59
Hicks, Diana. "The Four Literatures of Social Science." In *Handbook of Quantitative Science and Technology Research* edited by Henk F Moed,. Wolfgang Glänzel and Ulrich Schmoch, 476–496. Dordrecht: Kluwer Academic, 2004.
Hyland, Ken. *Disciplinary Discourses: Social Interactions in Academic Writing.* London: Longman, 2000.
Kresta, Ronald. " 'Nachrufe' in englischen und deutschen Fachzeitschriften der Soziologie: untersuchungen zu einer vernachlässigten Textsorte." *Fachsprache*, 18 (1996): 118–137.
Lindeberg, Anne-Charlotte. "Promotional Rhetorical Steps and Linguistic Signalling in Research Articles in Three Disciplines." In *LSP. Identity, and Interface. Research, Knowledge and Society. Proceedings of the 11th European Symposium on Language for Special Purpose,* edited by Lita Lundquist, Heribert Picht and Jacques Qvistgaard, Vol. II, 689–698. Copenhagen: Copenhagen Business School, 1998.
MacDonald, Susan Peck. *Professional Academic Writing in the Humanities and Social Sciences.* Carbondale, IL: Southern Illinois University Press, 1994.
Melander, Björn, John Swales and Kirsten Fredrickson. "Journal Abstracts from Three Academic Fields in the United States and Sweden: National Culture or Genre Differences?" In *Culture and Styles of Academic Discourse,* edited by Anna Duszak, Berlin: Mouton de Gruyter. 1997.
Mwansoko, Hermas JM. "Swahili in Academic Writing." *Nordic Journal of African Studies* 12 /3 (2003): 265–276.
Nølke, Henning. "La ScaPoLine 2001: Version Revisée de la Theorie Scandinave de la Polyphonie Linguistique." In *Polyphonie linguistique,* edited by Margrethe Olsen, 43–65. Roskilde: RUC, 2001.
Posteguillo, Santiago "The Schematic Structure of Computer Science Research Articles". *English for Specific Purposes,* 182 (1999), 139–160.

Räisänen, Christine. *The Conference Forum as a System of Genres.* Göteborg: Gothenburg Studies in English, 1998.

Salager-Meyer, Françoise, Maria Angeles Alcaraz Ariza and Nahirana Zambrano,. "The Scimitar, the Dagger and the Glove: Intercultural Differences in the Rhetoric of Spanish, French and English Medical Discourse 1930-1995." *English for Specific Purposes,* 22 (2003): 223–247.

Samraj, Betty. "Introductions in Research Articles: Variations Across Disciplines." *English for Specific Purpose,* 21 (2002): 1–17.

Stutterheim, Christiane von and Monique Lambert. "Crosslinguistic Analysis of Temporal Perspectives in Text Production." In *The Structure of Learner Varieties,* edited by Henriette Hendriks. Berlin: de Gruyter, 2005, 202–230.

Stålhammar, Mall. "Abstracts of Doctoral Dissertations in the Humanities and Social Sciences." In *Porta Scientiae – Lingua specialis,* edited by Merja Koskela, Christer Laurén, Marianne Nordmann and Nina Pilke, Vol. 1:64–275. Vaasa: Vaasa University Press, 2002.

Swales, John. *Research Genres: Explorations and Applications.* Cambridge: Cambridge University Press, 2004.

—. *Other Floors, Other Voices: a Textography of a Small University Building.* Mahwah: Lawrence Erlbaum, 1998.

—. *Genre Analysis.* Cambridge: Cambridge University Press, 1990.

Swales, John, Henriette Jacobsen, Christina Kejser, Lena Koch, Joan, Lynch and Lone Mølbæck. "A New Link in a Chain of Genres ?" *Hermes* 25 (2000), 133–141.

Vassileva, Irena. *Who is the Author? A contrastive analysis of authorial presence in English, German, French, Russian and Bulgarian academic discourse.* St. Augustin: Asgard, 2000.

Yakhontova, Tatyana. " 'Selling' or 'Telling': the Issue of Cultural Variation in Research Genres." In *Academic Discourse* edited by John Flowerdew, 216–232. London: Longman, 2002.

# CHAPTER TWO

CULTURAL IDENTITIES AND ACADEMIC VOICES

KJERSTI FLØTTUM, TRINE DAHL, TORODD KINN, ANJE MÜLLER GJESDAL AND EVA THUE VOLD

1. Introduction

The present paper will address the question of whether it is possible to identify *cultural identities* in research articles written within different disciplines and different languages through a selection of various types of linguistic manifestations. The main focus will be on person presence as realised through different *academic voices*, representing what we call the *self-* and the *other-* dimensions. By *self* we refer to the author and by *other* to the reader and other persons related in one way or another to the community in question. This approach is linked to a rhetorical view of scientific discourse as something which is created in a particular multivoiced communicative situation. Our aim is to show that in order to determine the complex constellations of academic voices present "behind" various obvious person manifestations, it is necessary to take into account both linguistic cotext and extralinguistic context. The choice of contextual dimensions to consider constitutes an issue closely related to our conception of cultural identity in the discipline and language perspectives.

The issue presented above is related to the Norwegian research project "Cultural Identity in Academic Prose", abbreviated by the Norwegian acronym KIAP.[1] The KIAP project started out with the objective to give substance to the commonly expressed contestation of the conception of academic discourse as neutral and objective. We wanted to identify possible cultural identities as manifested in linguistic traces of academic voices in the genre of the research article. To accomplish our objective we have taken on a doubly contrastive perspective, analysing research articles written in three languages, viz. English, French and Norwegian, and within three disciplines, viz. economics, linguistics and medicine. Our investigation has been based on an electronic corpus

---

[1] KIAP was financed by the Research Council of Norway during the years 2002–2006.

consisting of 450 articles (about 3,000,000 words) taken from refereed journals, in the years 1992–2003. (See www.uib.no/kiap/ and Fløttum, Dahl & Kinn 2006, both containing a comprehensive list of references relevant to the issues dealt with here; in the present paper we only mention a few).

The focus of the KIAP project has been specified through three research issues, related to the manifestation of the authors (self-dimension) in the texts, to the presence of the voices of other researchers (other-dimension) and to the presentation of the authors' own research. This focus explains our choice of theoretical framework, which is based on a broad interpersonal and polyphonic perspective (see Nølke, Fløttum & Norén 2004), with genre theory as an overarching approach (see for example Swales 1990; Berge 2003).

In order to address the three research issues, we have selected different linguistic features which may realise the self- and the other-dimensions of person manifestation. The main features studied are the following:

- first person and indefinite subject pronouns
- verbs combined with these pronouns
- markers of epistemic modality
- argumentative connectives
- metatextual expressions
- the construction *let us* + infinitive
- polyphonic constructions (polemic negation and concession)
- bibliographical references

Throughout the project our main hypothesis has been that discipline is more important than language in the identification of cultural identities. Our investigations, both quantitative and qualitative, have confirmed this hypothesis in most respects: discipline wins over language. In very general terms, we may say that authors of research articles tend to write more like their disciplinary colleagues writing in other languages than like their language-community co-members writing in other disciplines–with respect to most of the features studied in KIAP.

In section 2, dealing with the notion of *cultural identity*, we discuss to what extent this general finding is modified by the differences revealed between disciplines and between languages. These differences allow us to portray "typical" researchers related to discipline and to language. The rest of the paper will be devoted to selected snapshots from our broad investigations leading up to the findings mentioned above. In section 3, we take a closer look at the referentially complex and rhetorically flexible pronoun 'we', providing room for a variety of different academic voices. In section 4, we turn to another complex pronoun as regards reference potential: the French pronoun *on* ('one'). This pronoun contributes to a remarkable play between different academic voices, representing both the self- and the other-dimension. Next, leaving direct person manifestation as realised by 'we' or by the French *on*, we narrow our perspective and look for the specific voice of the author (section 5). The focus in that section will be on more subtle traces, such as the epistemic modality marker *may* and its correspondences in French and Norwegian, i.e. *pouvoir* and *kunne*, respectively. In section 6, we address the multivoiced or polyphonic perspective, taking into account explicit voices as realised by the presence of bibliographical references (other-dimension) as well as implicit voices through polyphonic markers such as the negation particle *not* and the adversative-concessive connective *but* (self- and other-dimension). This polyphonic perspective has proved particularly fruitful in that it covers traces of both author and other researchers, i.e. both the self- and the other-dimension. In our final remarks (section 7), we point to some limitations of our study. We also raise the question whether the purpose of a research article is just as much interaction as persuasion.

2. Cultural identities in academic discourse?

The heading chosen for this section relates in a very obvious way to the title of the KIAP project (cf. section 1). The question mark added indicates first and foremost that the project right from the start clearly saw the challenges implicit in defining and delimiting the concept of *culture*, and then secondly, that it was necessary to think carefully about how the interpretation of our linguistically based findings could be linked in a sensible–and defensible–way to the cultural settings we proposed to discuss our data in relation to. As a starting point we stated that the concept of cultural identity, however defined, should be discussed in terms of possible tendencies in linguistic practices observed in the various subcorpora (consisting of various discipline and language combinations). We have thus looked for similarities within the groups and differences between them. The settings considered to be relevant for the project were as follows (see also Dahl 2004):

(a) A national/native language-based writing culture setting, developed within the general education system, which again is part of a wider society reflecting certain values.

(b) The academic world in general, reflecting values that transcend national boundaries, such as the creation of new knowledge, precision, honouring fellow members of the academy and persuasion in a very wide sense.

(c) The discipline itself.

(d) Genre and discourse community, a setting which cannot be seen as independent from the other three, but which may still bring in other factors not subsumed under those settings.[2]

Possibly with the exception of setting (b), the academic world, the settings all posed problems, in different ways. Setting (a), a national/native language-based writing culture setting, represented the most serious issue. With English as one of the languages to be investigated, how can it be claimed that usage within a language functioning as a native language in countries situated across the globe might be linked to a common writing culture? The same, to a somewhat lesser extent, also applied to French. Our answer to this question has been to appeal to what we see as common ideals for Anglo-American writers that seem to be valid to a considerable extent in English language cultures, and ideals shared by the francophone world for French.

Some support for this view may be found in intercultural studies. Such studies focus primarily on meetings *between* cultures and have developed concepts that explain differing behaviour within an intercultural group, where cultures are ranked relative to each other according to various dimensions. Cases in point are individualism versus collectivism (e.g. Hofstede 2001) and high and low context communication (Hall & Hall 1990). Our study is not, of course, based in an intercultural setting, since we investigate the three languages separately. However, when we discuss differences in linguistic practices between the languages, it might be tempting to look to some of these interculturally based concepts. In such studies, we find for instance that many, probably the majority, of English-speaking cultures score high on individualism, something which in texts may imply authors who are visible through e.g. first person pronouns. We also find that English-speaking cultures are characterised as more low context cultures (spelling things out rather than relying on implicit information) than for instance French-speaking cultures.

When it comes to setting (c), discipline, an issue of a different nature had to be considered: disciplines that share certain features are traditionally grouped as belonging within the same branch of science. Becher and Trowler (2001) have shown that many factors may come into play when academic institutions place their various departments in the institutional landscape, and in the course of history disciplines have also been moved from one "camp" to another, both due to institutional factors as already mentioned and also due to research developments. Many disciplines, including e.g. linguistics, draw on various

---

[2] A case in point is the different rhetorical preferences of various disciplines within the genre of the research article, perhaps partly due to the epistemology of the discipline, partly to discourse community size.

other disciplines for their research. So how do our selected disciplines fit into this picture? It should be said that medicine, economics and linguistics were chosen partly for personal reasons, partly because these disciplines have been focused on by others in somewhat similar investigations. However, the long and short of it is that perhaps neither medicine nor linguistics is a typical representative of the natural sciences and the humanities respectively. Linguistics in particular is difficult to place. It shares features with all three branches of science and is sometimes classified as belonging within the social sciences. Our study has confirmed the closeness between linguistics and our social science discipline, economics, for some of our features, but not for all.

Finally, our third challenge was linked to (d), genre and discourse community. We wished to include in our study both a very large and a very small language. However, this in turn implied that the respective discourse communities would differ enormously in size, something which other researchers have pointed to as having potential consequences for the genre issue (Fredrickson & Swales 1994; Melander 1998). Can it really be posited that the Norwegian research articles represent the same genre as the English ones? An additional problem here is that for two of the disciplines studied there is only one Norwegian journal available (for the third, linguistics, there are two). We have argued that the researchers who contribute to and read these journals also publish in international journals, and hence handle the generally accepted genre format. What we find is also that there do not seem to be great differences between Norwegian and English articles with respect to the features we have investigated.

Two of the settings–(a), related to language and (c), discipline–have of course been tightly integrated in our investigation as they relate directly to the two variables of the study. Setting (b) turned out to be useful with regard to the view of scientific communication as primarily persuasive, while setting (d) contributed to our understanding of for instance the medical texts and why they differed from the texts from the other two disciplines.

As indicated in section 1, our investigation has shown that it is possible to draw up profiles which are based on discipline and also, to some extent, language, so that academic authors can be said to be members of a group. Starting with the medical author profile, we may say that such authors are generally absent from the text of the research article. The following utterance may serve as an illustration of this: "Controls showed no staining in …". We do not very often find beginnings like "We have shown by the controls undertaken …" in the medical texts. The argumentation is mostly implicit, and the research is typically presented as completed. In our characterisation of author manifestation, we have established a categorisation consisting of three main author roles: the author as researcher, as writer or text guide and as arguer (see

Fløttum 2003a, 2004). In this perspective, medical authors typically assume the role of researcher.

Economist authors, on the other hand, are present in their texts through expressions such as "In section 3, we show that ...", but in a somewhat modest way being less directly argumentative than for instance linguists. Their argumentation is mostly implicit, and their research is being presented as conducted in the text itself, as a kind of "on-line" research. As regards author roles, economist authors manifest themselves as both researchers and writers (text guides).

It may not be surprising that linguist authors are the most clearly present of the three discipline profiles, as well as the most polemical authors. They argue explicitly through expressions such as "Contrary to the view ..., we argue ...". Like economist authors, they present "on-line" research. Linguist authors, then, assume all three author roles in their texts; they are researchers, writers (text guides) as well as arguers.

When it comes to language generalisations, it is more difficult to set up uniform profiles. However, there are some typical traits that may be mentioned with respect to the features studied in KIAP. First, authors of English articles are overtly present in their texts; they are reader-friendly (guiding the readers through the text by explicit indications about what is or what will be done) and relatively polemical. English single authors tend to be 'I'-users, like in the utterance "In this section, I will discuss ...". Authors of Norwegian articles are in many respects similar to authors of English articles in that they are present and reader-friendly. However, they seem to be more polemical, and they manifest a more collective voice. Thus, Norwegian single authors tend to be 'we'-users–often using the inclusive 'we' as in 'We see that ...' In contrast, authors of French articles are relatively absent. They provide little reader guidance and are covertly polemical. French single authors tend to be 'one'-users, like in "On peut constater ..." ('One can observe ...').

Having presented our basic conception of the notion of cultural identity as well as some of our observations related to disciplinary and language profiles, we now turn to the study of some selected linguistic features which have contributed to the characterisation of the above-mentioned profiles.

3. The use of 'we'

Personal pronouns are the clearest commonly used expressions of personal presence found in academic texts, and several researchers have studied the use of pronouns in such texts (e.g. Kuo 1999; Fløttum 2003a; Vassileva 2000; Hyland 2001a, b; Harwood 2005). The presence of the author(s) is above all manifested by first person pronouns, meaning 'I' and 'we'.

In section 2, we portrayed the medical, the economist and the linguist author as being typically present in their texts through different kinds of author roles, viz. primarily as researchers, as writers and as arguers. These portraits are based on a systematic classification of the more than 2500 examples of the use of *I* and the corresponding French and Norwegian first person singular subject pronouns found in KIAP Corpus articles with only one author. The study of the use of these pronouns yielded very clear differences between the three disciplines.

But about half of the corpus articles, and the large majority of the medical articles, have more than one author and do not employ 'I', but rather *we* and corresponding forms in the other languages. These first person plural subject pronouns are also found in articles with only one author–in fact, they are more frequent than singular 'I' even there. There are almost 10,800 examples of 'we' in the KIAP Corpus.

The extent to which authors are present in their texts and the ways in which this presence is manifested are two among many aspects of cultural identity, if this is operationalised for purposes of linguistic analysis as differential tendencies in language use. To account for authorial presence in texts, however, another sense of the word *identity* is needed, viz. referential identity: Who does the pronoun refer to?

Ideally, in the KIAP project we wanted to extend the study of author roles to the use of the pronoun 'we', to find out what roles the authors assign to themselves when they use this pronoun. In order to do this, it is first necessary to determine which examples refer to the author or authors. That is, we needed to divide the set of examples into sets of relevant and irrelevant ones. This, however, turned out to be a task quite fraught with problems: It is often very hard to decide who the pronoun refers to, and it quite frequently has a double reference. Table 1 provides an overview of the referential possibilities of 'we' (see also Kinn 2005).

Table 1. The referential potential of 'we'

	Exclusive 'we'	Inclusive 'we'
Non-metonymic uses	– authors alone – authors + 3rd person(s)	– author(s) + reader – author(s) + reader + 3rd person(s)
Metonymic uses	– one author alone	– author(s) alone – reader alone

As is well known, this pronoun can be used both exclusively and inclusively. Exclusive use means that the addressee is excluded, i.e. the reader of written texts. Inclusive use implies that the reader is included. Third persons may or may not be included in either case. That is, the pronoun 'we' may refer to *self* as well as to *others*. In addition to the exclusive–inclusive distinction and the possibility of inclusion of third persons, 'we' is frequently used metonymically, for instance, inclusive 'we' for the reader alone. This means that not only is it necessary in a reference-based classification of examples to distinguish between exclusive and inclusive 'we', but it must also be determined whether third persons are referred to, and whether there is an extra metonymic layer on top of the literal reference.

We will look at some Norwegian examples of the various types. Example (1), from an economics article with more than one author, illustrates straightforwardly exclusive use where several authors refer to themselves and themselves alone. This example would clearly be relevant in a study of author roles (here the authors seem to take on the arguer role).

(1) Igjen vil vi understreke at vi ikke argumenterer imot reguleringer av dette markedet. (noecon01; several authors)
'We want to emphasise again that we are not arguing against regulations of this market.'

In example (2), from a medical article with one author, 'we' seems to refer to the people at the hospital. This reference includes the author and is also an instance of exclusive 'we', but other third persons may well be included, and it is hard to decide whether the examples should be part of a study of author roles.

(2) Graden av reinnleggelse gir derfor ikke noe mål på kvaliteten av tilbudet vi har gitt, […]. (nomed29; one author)
'The degree of readmittance is therefore not a measure of the quality of the services that we have offered, …'

Exclusive 'we' can also be used metonymically, for instance as in example (3) from an economics article with one author. Here exclusive 'we' is used for 'I', what in English is often called an authorial 'we'. This appears to be more common in French and Norwegian than in English, but it is not uncommon in English either. Such examples should clearly be included in a study of author roles (the sequence *we argue that* ... is an explicit manifestation of the arguer role), but it is possible that they are more appropriately treated together with examples of 'I', rather than other kinds of 'we'.

(3) På bakgrunn av at […], argumenterer vi for at resultatene trekker i retning av forsiktighetsmotivert sparing. (noecon37; one author)
'On the background that …, we argue that the results pull in the direction of cautiousness-motivated saving.'

As mentioned, in inclusive 'we', the reader is included in the reference of the pronoun. Inclusive 'we' is very frequently used in connection with research that is represented as proceeding in the run of the text itself–on-line, so to speak (see section 2). Example (4) shows this. Here the reader and the author are referred to as common possessors of linguistic data presented in the article. Clearly this is a kind of author presence, viz. manifesting a mixed researcher and writer role, but it cannot be regarded as being on a par with the examples of exclusive 'we' above.

(4) I (7b) og (7c) derimot har vi et argument som uttrykker hvem som synger, [...]. (noling49; one author)
'In (7b) and (7c) [linguistic examples], on the other hand, we have an argument that expresses who is singing ...'

Inclusive 'we' can further be expanded to include third persons, like in the economics example (5), where reference is made to the community of economists interested in the poverty problem. It is not easy to decide whether this should be part of a study of author presence.

(5) Hovedpoenget mitt er [...] å indikere hvordan vi kan benytte denne litteraturen til å belyse hvorfor fattigdomsproblemet bør løses. (noecon20; one author)
'My main point is ... to indicate how we can use this literature to shed light on why the poverty problem ought to be solved.'

Example (6) is from a linguistics article with one author. This resembles example (4), where author and reader "have" linguistic data. In this example, however, it is arguably the single author who does the beginning (assuming the writer role by *We begin with* ...), but the reader is taken along in the process. That is, this is a metonymic use of inclusive 'we' for 'I'–unlike example (3), with exclusive 'we' for 'I'.

(6) Vi begynner med to NPer inneholdende substantivet *čaëk* 'te (diminutiv)' som attributt i genitiv: [...]. (noling06; one author)
'We begin with two NPs containing the noun *čaëk* 'tea (diminutive)' as a genitival attribute: ... '

Example (7), from an economics article, is also one of inclusive 'we' used metonymically, but this one appears to refer primarily to the reader alone. The authors are hardly reminding themselves of the facts, since they are obviously perfectly aware of them. It is the reader who is told what to remember.

(7) Nivået på ledigheten [...] var da [...] likt nivået ved fullstendig koordinering [...], men vi må huske på at det første tilfellet ikke bare er en situasjon uten koordinering av lønnsdannelsen, [...]. (noecon23; several authors)
'The level of unemployment ... was then ... equal to the level at full coordination ..., but we must remember that the first case is not just a situation without coordination of wage formation, ...'

In a study of the rhetoric of academic discourse, all aspects of the referential properties of pronouns are relevant. The various uses of 'we' open up for a multitude of possible voice-mixing and of rhetorically interesting moves. The author can be explicitly present, hide behind a plurality, include the reader in the research process, direct the reader by indirect means, etc. A full analysis of the rhetoric of pronominal usage depends on a sound referential analysis.

Some of our interpretations of pronominal reference above are undoubtedly open to discussion. Our main point is to demonstrate that any classification of uses of 'we' needs to be rather more sophisticated than one that assigns one and only one referential value to the pronoun in the case of metonymic uses–because the indirect reference involved in metonymy provides access to one referent by means of another. For instance, the distinction between example (3) with exclusive 'we' for 'I' and example (6) with inclusive 'we' for 'I' is only possible if it is acknowledged that there is reference to a 'we' in addition to an 'I'. And the distinction between example (1) with an ordinary exclusive 'we' and example (3) with exclusive 'we' for 'I' is only possible if the reference to 'I' in the latter is acknowledged in addition to the reference to a 'we'. In short, it has to be recognised that many examples of 'we' have a double reference.

4. Personal ambiguity: the French pronoun ON

As we have seen in section 3, pronouns constitute interesting markers of authorial presence in the research article and contribute to the complex plurality of voices implicit in the research article. This complexity is in part due to the wide-ranging referential potential and semantic fuzziness of deictic personal pronouns, as the study of 'we' has already demonstrated. Another pronoun characterised by semantic ambiguity is the French pronoun *on* 'one' (hereafter ON). This pronoun is characterised by a complex and flexible semantic content. While its basic semantic content is "one or several persons" with a vague reference, it can be used in senses corresponding to all the other personal pronouns in French. On the other hand, when used in its indefinite sense, ON corresponds closely to a passive construction. This situation is unique compared to the other personal pronouns in French, but also compared to the other languages studied in the KIAP project. It is therefore not surprising that our investigations have found that French research articles are particularly marked by a high frequency of the pronoun ON.

The frequent use of ON in French research articles is often explained by a tendency to avoid the first person singular, often seen as too personal and imposing (Loffler-Laurian 1980: 156). The interaction with other personal pronouns is no doubt an important factor conditioning the use of ON. However, the referential potential of ON also permits the representation of many and conflicting viewpoints. We will therefore argue that two of the main functions of ON in the research article is to represent different and conflicting voices and to contribute to the tensions and dynamics of the genre and that these functions will benefit from a multi-level textual analysis.

The complex semantic potential of ON means that it can be used for a variety of rhetorical purposes. As already mentioned, it can have different referents, ranging from 'I' and 'we' to 'they'. This means that ON can express different perspectives, including the author(s) but also others, like adherents and adversaries. It should therefore not only be considered as a manifestation of the author's voice on the micro-level, but rather as an important factor in the structuring of the text on the macro-level.

Because of the complex referential potential of ON and the wide range of possible interpretations, its meaning is discourse-based and needs to be decoded on the basis of its context, including the genre in question. In order to examine the functions of ON on the macro-level, i.e. how it contributes to the representation of different voices and perspectives, we need to begin by an analysis on the micro-level, the immediate cotext of ON. Several interpretive criteria have been proposed in previous works (see Fløttum 2003a, 2006b; Fløttum, Jonasson & Norén forthcoming), including linguistic markers such as adverbs, tense, mode and the semantics of verbs. On the basis of such criteria, an appropriate interpretation can be assigned to a given occurrence of ON, although its fuzzy semantics leaves the question unanswered in many cases. Analyses of the KIAP Corpus based on the criteria mentioned above have led Fløttum (2006b) to propose a classification of potential referential values of ON in the research articles, of which we present a modified version in Table 2.

This table is a non-exhaustive illustration of the values of ON in the research article, with particular emphasis on the self- and the other-dimension (see section 1), referring to the author and other textual actors respectively. As can be seen, the reference of ON ranges from the completely personal and exclusive ON (corresponding to 'I', 'we'), representing the self-dimension, that is, the author(s) alone, to the clearly impersonal, distant and even antagonistic (corresponding to 'you' and 'they'), representing the other-dimension, that is the readers or extra-textual actors (both adherents and adversaries). Between the two extremes we find the self & other-dimension, which we have divided into two sub-groups: the first representing author, reader and a more or less restricted discourse community, the second representing the generic value, or people in general.

Table 2. The referential potential of ON

Actor(s)	Referent(s)
Self	Author(s)
Self & Other I	Authors and readers. Discourse community (more or less restricted)
Self & Other II	People in general, indefinite reference
Other	Textual actors other than the author(s)

This classification has the advantages of showing the functioning of ON on a textual level, and how the recurrence of ON can contribute to the construction of textual actors. It also shows how analyses of ON on the micro-level contribute to the analysis of ON on the macro-level. But conversely it seems likely that the macro-level, i.e. the genre conventions governing the representation of textual actors, contributes in its turn to the analyses of the micro-level, and that a multi-level analysis should take into account the continuous interaction of the different textual levels.

In order to illustrate a possible multi-level analysis of ON, we will now go on to look at some examples taken from the KIAP Corpus. They represent different aspects of the referential potential of ON, ranging from ON representing the author alone (the self-dimension) to ON excluding the author (the other-dimension). Due to limitations of space, the descriptions will be rather cursory.

ON as S*elf*

(8) Quelques remarques finales. On voudrait tout d'abord noter qu'après tout il y a une relative légitimité de la notion de langue. (frling12)
'Some final remarks. One would first of all like to note that there is after all a relative legitimacy to the notion of language.'

In example (8), it seems appropriate to interpret ON as corresponding to the self-dimension as it is written by a single author. First of all, the metatextual elements support this interpretation. The preceding sentence situates the extract at the end of the article and indicates a final evaluation of the arguments presented. The sequencing of the conclusion itself is marked by the element *tout d'abord*. Secondly, the personal interpretation is indicated by the modalisation of the sentence. The modal auxiliary *vouloir* contributes to the modalisation of the content. The source of the modalisation must be attributed to the author and indicates a position vis-à-vis the statement. Therefore, as this verb represents the author as the instance responsible for the modalisation of the text, it also associates the utterance to the self-dimension. Furthermore, in this context, the elements *après tout* and *relative*, although not inherently modal, indicate a certain hesitation and are instances of hedging.

We will now move on to an example where the reference is expanded to include the reader.

ON as *Self & Other*

(9) En second lieu, on notera que certains groupes prépositionnels apparaissent en position de sujet ... (frling08)
'Secondly, one will note that certain prepositional groups appear in subject position ...'

In this example, ON seems to be used as a tool to involve the reader in the text; the author is guiding the reader(s) through the text and its argumentation. This interpretation is indicated first of all by the metatextual elements referring to the construction and sequencing of the text. These elements are *En second lieu*, referring to sequencing of the arguments and thus reminding the reader that there is a list of arguments in favour of the author's position. Also, the author draws attention to a fact (*certains groupes prépositionnels apparaissent en position de sujet ...*), which is a way of outlining the arguments to the reader. ON seems to blur the borders between the contributions of the author and the reader. Although the author is in fact presenting the facts, the use of ON, with its fuzzy reference, also involves the reader in the process of reasoning. In fact, this kind of ON may even be interpreted as slightly "paternalistic", as it includes the reader in an argument that in fact is the responsibility of the author. To complicate matters even further, in instances like this, ON could even be seen as a sort of imperative, indicating to the reader when, how and where to focus his or her attention.

In the next example, ON represents the other-dimension alone, and the others are constructed as adversaries of the author.[3]

ON as *Other*

(10)   Ou encore croit-on qu'on puisse régler le problème du "sens du sens" par une bonne définition? C'est pour le moins peu vraisemblable. (frling12)
'Does one really believe that one can resolve the problem of the "meaning of meaning" by a good definition? This does not seem very likely.'

In (10) the distance to the author is primarily marked by the sentence following immediately afterwards, where the author clearly expresses disagreement with the point of view associated with ON. Also, the semantics of the verb *croire* marks a critical distance vis-à-vis the represented solution of the problem of meaning, as this verb seems less "scientific" than a verb such as *penser*.

As we have seen, the semantic potential of ON has multiple functions in the French research article. It contributes to a textual "play" or a *mise-en-scène* of textual actors and can represent both the self- and the other-dimensions. Therefore, this pronoun can be considered as an important factor in the textual dynamics in the sense that it represents the textual actors who push the argumentation forwards, but also as a factor of coherence since the recurrence of ON creates a kind of semantic continuity although its referent may change. However, it should be emphasised that these macro-level functions can only be identified through analyses of the micro-level cotext.

5. Marking epistemic modality: the case of *may* and its counterparts in French and Norwegian

From explicit author manifestation in forms of personal pronouns like 'we', and to some extent French *on*, we will now turn to some slightly more subtle traces of the author in the text, namely the epistemic modality marker *may* and its counterparts in French and Norwegian, i.e. *pouvoir* and *kunne*, respectively.[4]

---

[3] Since the two occurrences of ON seem to have the same reference, they will be treated together.

[4] This is of course not to say that these three auxiliaries are equivalents in all respects; the linguistic relations within and between languages are much too complicated for that. For

Epistemic modality markers are linguistic expressions that reveal the author's judgement of the truth value of the information conveyed. When writing research articles, authors constantly have to decide with what degree of certainty they want to present their claims. By choosing epistemic *may*, the writer presents the content of his or her proposition as *possibly true*. Epistemic *may* is a tentative expression; signalling a certain degree of uncertainty on the part of the author. As a hedging device, it serves to shield the author from potential criticism, and the presence of such markers is considered a characteristic trait of academic discourse.[5]

Through a survey of epistemic *may* and the corresponding auxiliaries in French and Norwegian, we seek in this section to illustrate some of the differences and similarities that can be found between cultures and disciplines when it comes to the expression of uncertainty and tentativeness. We will first address the question of frequency, before we go on to examine in some more detail what kind of pragmatic functions epistemic *may*, *kunne* and *pouvoir* are used in. The findings presented here are taken from a larger study on epistemic modality which was carried out on a subcorpus of the KIAP Corpus, including articles from all three languages, but only two of the disciplines, namely medicine and linguistics.

The modal verb *may* is considered a typical and dominant marker of epistemic modality, partly because of its frequency and partly because much research on modality has focused on modal verbs. In several studies on hedging in English academic discourse (many of which have focussed on medical discourse), *may* has been shown to be the most or one of the most widely used markers of epistemic modality (Vihla 2000: 218–219, Varttala 2001: 104, Hyland 1998: 149). In our corpus, *may* is the most frequent marker of epistemic modality in the medical texts, but in linguistics, it comes in fact only fourth– preceded by *seem*, *suggest* and *assume*.[6] Although epistemic *may* is not as popular with linguists as it is with medical researchers, it remains a very frequent marker of epistemic modality. Can the same be said about its counterparts in Norwegian and French?

Table 3 gives the relative frequencies of epistemic *may*, *kunne* and *pouvoir* in the present tense (raw numbers in parentheses). For the French verb *pouvoir*, the conditional was also included, because an exploratory analysis suggested

---

example, *can* is another counterpart of *pouvoir* and *kunne*, but not included here since it is not used epistemically (except in interrogative and negative constructions).
[5] There appear to be considerable cultural differences, though, and it is not so sure that hedging is a characteristic trait of academic discourse in general. For example, earlier KIAP studies (Vold 2006a) indicate that markers of uncertainty are significantly more frequent in English and Norwegian research articles than in French ones.
[6] For a full list of the markers and their relative frequencies, see Vold (2006a).

that the epistemic use of this form was more frequent than the epistemic use of present tense forms. Past tense forms have not been included, which means that, for practical reasons, *might* has also been excluded, although this form does not always function as the past tense of *may;* it often functions as a modal auxiliary in its own right. *Might* is included in the larger study, which is presented in Vold (2006a and b).

The figures indicate that in all three languages, the medical researchers use the epistemic sense of these modal verbs more often than the linguists.[7] The difference between disciplines is particularly notable in the English corpus, where the medical researchers use epistemic *may* two to three times as often as the linguists. The most striking difference, however, is between languages. The frequency of Norwegian epistemic *kan* is even higher than for epistemic *may*: it is 0.7 in the linguistics papers and 1.0 in medicine, which makes it the most frequent marker of epistemic modality in the Norwegian part of our corpus–in linguistics as well as in medicine. While *may* and *kan* are frequently used to mark epistemic modality, French *peut* is hardly ever used epistemically, despite the fact that the epistemic sense is a well-known and established meaning of the verb *pouvoir* (see e.g. Le Querler 1996, 2001; Sueur 1979), just as it is for *may* in English and *kunne* in Norwegian. The same type of use is formally or theoretically possible in all three languages, but the degree to which the epistemic sense is in fact used varies considerably.

Table 3. Frequencies of epistemic *may, kan, peut* and *pourrait*[8]

Discipline	epistemic *may* f/1000 (no)	epistemic *kan* f/1000 (no)	epistemic *peut* f/1000 (no)	epistemic *pourrait* f/1000 (no)
linguistics	0.46 (79)	0.70 (64)	0.06 (4)	0.03 (2)
medicine	1.23 (73)	1.00 (43)	0.09 (6)	0.31 (19)
Total	0.66 (152)	0.80 (107)	0.08 (10)	0.16 (21)

The rare use of epistemic *pouvoir* is somewhat surprising, compared with the corresponding frequencies of epistemic *may* and *kunne*. There is one exception to this general picture, however. If we look at the conditional, *pourrait*, which is in fact a combination of two potential epistemic modality markers, namely the

---

[7] This does not mean that the medical researchers *in general* hedge more than the linguists; the linguists have higher frequencies of other markers.
[8] *Peut* and *pourrait* are here used as canonical forms for the present tense and the conditional, respectively. *Peut* covers all present indicative forms (*peux, peut, pouvons, pouvez, peuvent*), and *pourrait* all conditional forms (*pourrais, pourrait, pourrions, pourriez, pourraient*).

modal verb *pouvoir* and the conditional suffix, which in some cases mark uncertainty (cf. e.g. Dendale 1993, 1999; Kronning 2002), we see that this form is frequently used epistemically in the medical papers, but–with the exception of two instances–it is not used at all in the linguistics papers. In the medical part of the corpus, *pourrait* constitutes in fact the second most frequent marker of epistemic modality, preceded only by the semi-auxiliary *sembler*.

The medical researchers' frequent use of epistemic *pourrait* and hence the striking difference between disciplines may stem from an influence from English. Since English is the lingua franca of all medical research, the French medical researchers probably read a lot of medical literature in English. The use of French *pourrait* in the medical papers is in many respects similar to the use of *may* and *might* in the English medical papers. In both corpora, the epistemic sense of these modals is in fact the most frequently used sense. The epistemic sense of *pourrait* accounts for nearly 60% of the occurrences, although the verb *pouvoir* has numerous other–and in everyday language much more frequent–senses, and the epistemic sense of *may* and *might* accounts for approximately 70% and 80% of the occurrences, respectively.[9] This suggests that in medical discourse (be it English or French), these modal verbs are used first and foremost as epistemic modality markers, and other senses are rare in comparison. So in this respect, the French medical authors tend to write more like their disciplinary colleagues writing in other languages than like linguists writing in French.

If we take a closer look at the epistemic occurrences and their context, we see that epistemic *may*, *kan* and *pourrait* are used in much the same way in all three languages, as far as their pragmatic or communicative functions are concerned. Epistemic *may*, *kan* and *pourrait* are all used with the following functions:

– suggest possible explanations (example 11):

(11) Les mécanismes à l'origine de ces manifestations sont peu clairs : il **pourrait** s'agir d'anomalies des cellules T helper dont le profil de sécrétion cytokinique **pourrait** être altéré, ou d'anomalies des cellules T suppressives ; il **pourrait** également s'agir d'une conséquence d'anomalies génétiques du chromosome 6 retentissant sur la présentation de l'antigène et entraînant des modifications de facteurs macrophagiques régulant les cellules B et la production d'anticorps. (frmed07)

---

[9] This contrasts with the figures for the linguistics papers, where instances of epistemic *may* and *might* account for respectively 28% and 46% of the total number of occurrences.

Cultural Identities and Academic Voices 31

'The mechanisms ... are not very clear: it might be anomalies of the T helper cells of which the cytocine secretion profile could be altered, ...: it might also be a consequence of genetic anomalies of chromosome 6 ...'

– present hypotheses and conclusions in a cautious manner (examples 12 and 13):

(12)   Det er imidlertid påfallende at det ikke fins et eneste belegg med bevart *ne* pluss *-gi* i rent negerende betydning, mens overgangstypen *ne* pluss *-a*, *-at* er sikkert belagt. Det **kan tyde på** en prinsipiell forskjell mellom de to negasjonstypene, (noling08)
'It is however striking that there is not a single attestation ... This might indicate a fundamental difference between the two negation types, ...'

(13)   The strength of the association between second teenage birth and adverse outcomes was virtually unaltered by adjusting for confounding variables. This **suggests** that there **may** be a causal relation between second teenage birth and these outcomes. (engmed01)

– signal limitations of the study (example 14):

(14)   The results of this investigation do not necessarily apply to younger women or women without heart disease. We studied a specific combination estrogen/progestin, and our results **may** not apply to other regimens, such as unopposed estrogen. Although the HERS trial was large and conducted in 20 centers across the United States, the population enrolled **may** not be completely representative of women with heart disease. In addition to meeting inclusion and exclusion criteria, all HERS participants were volunteers and **may** consequently differ in quality of life from the general population of women with heart disease. (engmed11)

Epistemic *may*, *kan* and *pourrait* are thus used in much the same contexts and serve to fulfil similar pragmatic or communicative functions in all three languages. There are some disciplinary differences, though–the most notable being that the latter function (signalling limitations) is more important in the medical papers than in the linguistics papers, probably because the experimental nature of much medical research calls for some indication of possible sources of error in the experimental situation. It also reflects the fact that a paragraph on limitations forms an almost obligatory part of an IMRAD paper, whereas the signalling of limitations is much less standardised in linguistics.

As can be seen from the above examples, *may* and its counterparts are sometimes combined with other epistemic modality markers, thus further weakening the claim. In the English medical corpus, *may* is combined with other epistemic modality markers in 26% of the instances. In the large majority of cases, like in example 13, the lexical verb *suggest* is the other marker. The sequence *suggest* + *that*-clause containing *may* occurs very frequently and seems to be a very typical, almost standardised way of presenting hypotheses or conclusions in medical papers. With such standardised expressions, the epistemic modality markers involved may lose some of their pragmatic value, in the sense that they will be perceived as the unmarked form (see Lewin 2005: 172). In the linguistics papers, *may* is combined with other epistemic modality markers in 22% of the cases, but there is more variation as to what other markers are used. In the Norwegian corpus, epistemic *kan* is combined with other epistemic modality markers in 40% (linguistics) and 36% (medicine) of the instances. What markers epistemic *kan* co-occurs with varies, although *mulig* ('possible') is particularly common. The high frequency of compound hedges in Norwegian does not necessarily mean that Norwegian authors are even more tentative and cautious when presenting their claims than English authors: it may simply reflect a difference in the extent to which we use fixed combinations of words. French epistemic *pourrait* on the other hand, virtually never occurs in combination with other epistemic modality markers, and in this respect, the use of epistemic *pourrait* in the French medical papers differs from the use of epistemic *may* and *kan* in the English and the Norwegian medical papers.

As the examples show, the use of epistemic modality markers signals an openness on the part of the author towards other points of view. In some cases (like in example 14), the markers are used in "answers" to questions that the author believes may be asked. He or she is thus anticipating potential criticism. These critical voices or alternative points of view are implicitly present in the text. From this perspective, epistemic modality markers can be seen as linguistic manifestations of polyphony, which will be the subject of the next section.

6. Polyphony: explicit and implicit voices

In the sections above, we have seen that the study of different pronouns and epistemic markers provides evidence for the conception of the research article as particularly multivoiced, giving room for many different and complex academic voices. By adopting linguistic polyphony theory (in the ScaPoLine version; see Nølke et al. 2004) as the main theoretical point of departure, we have been able to unify most of our analyses in a homogeneous framework, oriented towards the self- and other-dimensions. The polyphonic perspective has proved particularly fruitful in that it covers not only these dimensions (traces of both author and other researchers) which are explicitly manifested, but also implicit voices (where the source of the actual voice is not cited or made explicit in some other way). Thus, the presence of voices can be explicit or implicit.

Before looking at a couple of examples, we will give a short and simplified introduction to the ScaPoLine theory. It offers a wide scope, in the sense that it describes and explains a series of linguistic phenomena. Elements from different levels in the linguistic description contribute to the polyphonic structure of an utterance: pronouns, connectives, sentence adverbs, negation, presupposition, information structure, reported speech and many more. The fact that the theory has a wide scope represents clear methodological advantages. A common terminology in itself makes it easier to undertake comparative studies and may make them more valid and more powerful.

This approach of linguistic polyphony is based on a conception of language as fundamentally dialogical in nature (inspired by Bakhtine, see for example Bakhtine 1970; see also Bondi & Silver 2004). It constitutes a fruitful alternative to the well-established idea of the uniqueness of the speaking subject. In a polyphonic conception of meaning, it is essential to demonstrate how the presence of several voices, or points of view, are signalled in discourse. In this linguistic version of the theory, the object of study is the polyphonic structure, uncovered by an investigation of signals given in the utterance. In its turn, the polyphonic structure gives us instructions as regards possible interpretations of the utterance related to its discourse context and which allow us to talk about different polyphonic configurations.

In order to be persuasive, the author of a research article must often take into account a series of voices in the immediate and more distant context. This might be done by giving the floor to other voices–explicitly, attributed to distinct or to more fuzzy sources, or implicitly, indicated by specific signals, without any clear attribution of source. Explicit polyphony is often realised by reported speech; the implicit way of giving the floor to other voices may be realised by a series of linguistic markers (see Fløttum 2005a).

Let us now return to the self- and other-dimensions. In the present paper we relate the self-dimension to the author. As regards the other-dimension, at least in the context of academic discourse, we often think of reference practices and citations or reported speech, i.e. explicit polyphony, where the source of the voice or the point of view presented is spelled out (see Fløttum 2003b; Salager-Meyer 1999). The analyses of the bibliographical references have given interesting results related to differences between disciplines and languages (Fløttum et al. 2006). In the KIAP Corpus, bibliographical references are much more frequent in the articles of medical authors than in articles of linguists and particularly economists. As regards the language dimension, bibliographical references are more frequent in English and Norwegian articles than in French articles (for explanations of these observations, see Fløttum et al. 2006). The following is a typical example of explicit polyphony expressed by bibliographical references:

(15) Blanchard and Watson (1986) and Blanchard and Quah (1989) found evidence that demand shocks were the main source of US fluctuations, but Shapiro and Watson (1988) and Gali (1992) found that supply shocks predominated. (engecon22)

However, traces of others may be found in many other linguistic, and more subtle, configurations. The explicit and the implicit are often interwoven (Fløttum 2006a), as, in fact, in the example above. To grasp the meaning of this sequence, it is not sufficient to interpret the function of the four explicit voices represented by the given references. We have to take into consideration another level of polyphony, implicit but clearly signalled by the adversative *but*, indicating a concessive relation between the two points of view presented. The connective *but* gives us an instruction about the authors making the concession that point of view 1 is accepted ('Blanchard and Watson (1986) and Blanchard and Quah (1989) found evidence that …'), but not judged valid in the context and reasoning in question. The valid point of view here is point of view 2 ('Shapiro and Watson (1988) and Gali (1992) found that …'), the one on which the argumentation of the authors is based. As regards the source of point of view 1, the utterance alone cannot tell us what it is. However, given the context of the whole article, we may imagine that other researchers are responsible for it. It could even be the authors' (the self's) point of view at another and maybe earlier stage in their work. The whole utterance can be interpreted as a mild form of polemic.

Let us look at another example:

(16) The antebellum US may have been the quintessential example of a 'large' country in world trade, **but** that does **not** necessarily imply that the optimal tariff was high and the welfare gains from it would be large. (engecon43)

In this example (taken from a single-author article), an underlying or implicit point of view ('that necessarily implies that …') is refuted by a second point of view, marked by the negation *not*. While the author is responsible for the latter (indicated by *not*), the source of the former is not given. However, the context indicates an interpretation which attributes this point of view to other researchers. To the extent that negation is used polemically, to refute underlying points of view, it indicates author manifestation as well as the implicit presence of other voices (Fløttum 2005b).

Example (16) also contains the polyphonic marker *but,* indicating, as already noted, a concessive relation between the two points of view which are related to each other. The polemical tone already present by *not* in this example is emphasised by this connective.

While the negation 'not' in its polemic meaning always points to an "opponent" (to whom the refuted point of view is attributed), the concessive *but* always points to a source whose point of view is accepted, but not judged valid in the here and now of the text. These are important observations for the interpretation of the text as a whole, and in relation to its context. In KIAP, in addition to the referencing practice of explicit polyphony, we have focused on implicit polyphony, as manifested by these markers (*not* and *but* and their counterparts in French and Norwegian). As regards differences between our nine subcorpora, we have observed that negation is clearly used more in linguistics than in economics and medicine, and that it is used more in Norwegian than in English and French. The same picture holds for adversative conjunctions.

The polyphonic approach has revealed that there is more to the presence of self than constructions with first person pronouns in research articles and that there is more to the presence of others than a straightforward identification of bibliographical references in the form of reported speech. By this analysis we have shown that a text which is monological in its form may have an implicit but clearly polyphonic structure, the author (the self) integrating voices of others. Our hypothesis has been that the identification of different voices and their sources reveal relations (such as refusal or acceptance) between the authors and the voices they are integrating in their own message, and that this interaction is essential to the interpretation of the text as a whole.

The relevance of the polyphonic perspective in the present context is that the authors set up polyphonic 'plays', signalling the presence of both their own voice and the voices of others. Different voices are given the floor. These plays are created by the authors in their own way and represent a subtle and complex mode of interaction.

7. Final remarks

We have pointed to the importance of taking different contextual dimensions into account in order to determine how the notion of cultural identity may be understood in the setting of the research article. We have also shown that the immediate cotext and the larger extralinguistic context together contribute to the identification and interpretation of the complex constellation of academic voices present–be they implicit or explicit. However, it is evident that the selection of linguistic features studied in this paper has limited the "cultural identities" we have identified and related to a set of author profiles. We have nevertheless been able to point to relatively clear typical traits of the nine discourse communities studied. The different academic voices identified (in all their complexity) constitute an essential trait of the different "cultures".

In section 2, we stated that scientific communication is primarily persuasive. However, the study of academic voices undertaken here, based on the KIAP Corpus of research articles, of the self- and especially the other-dimension, may lead to a different conclusion. It seems reasonable to raise the question of whether the research article is more interactive than purely persuasive. The interactive perspective is evident by the frequent use of 1) pronouns including the reader or other researchers, 2) bibliographical references bringing other researchers into the text, 3) epistemic markers showing the reader that what is presented may need further investigations to be presented to others as the "truth", and 4) polyphonic expressions mixing self- and other-dimensions. The frequent use of these features indicates the importance not only of a persuasive purpose and of positioning oneself, but also the importance of indicating that one is or wants to be part of a community.

8. References

Bakhtine, Mikhaïl. *La poétique de Dostoïevski*. Paris: Seuil, 1970. (First edition in Russian: Moscow 1929.)

Becher, Tony and Paul R. Trowler. *Academic Tribes and Territories. Intellectual Enquiry and the Culture of Disciplines*. 2nd ed. Buckingham: The Society for Research into Higher Education & Open University Press, 2001.

Berge, Kjell Lars. "The scientific text genres as social actions: text theoretical reflections on the relations between context and text in scientific writing." In *Academic Discourse. Multidisciplinary Approaches*, edited by Kjersti Fløttum and François Rastier, 144–157. Oslo: Novus, 2003.

Bondi, Marina and Marc Silver. "Textual voices: a cross-disciplinary study of attribution in academic discourse." In *Evaluation in Spoken and Written Academic Discourse*, edited by Laurie Anderson and Julia Bamford, 121–141. Roma: Officina, 2004.

Dahl, Trine. "Textual metadiscourse in research articles: a marker of national culture or of academic discipline?" *Journal of Pragmatics* 36 (2004): 1807–1825.

Dendale, Patrick. "Le conditionnel de l'information incertaine : marqueur modal ou marqueur évidentiel ?" In *Actes du XXe Congrès International de Linguistique et Philologie Romanes*, vol. 1, edited by Gerold Hilty, 165–176. Tübingen: Francke Verlag, 1993.

—. "Devoir au conditionnel : valeur évidentio-modale et origine du conditionnel." In *La modalité sous tous ses aspects*, edited by Svetlana Vogeleer, Andrée Borillo, Marcel Vuillaume and Carl Vetters, 7–28. Amsterdam: Rodopi, 1999.

Fløttum, Kjersti. "Personal English, indefinite French and plural Norwegian scientific authors? Pronominal author manifestation in research articles." *Norsk Lingvistisk Tidsskrift* 21 (2003a): 21–55.
—. "Bibliographical references and polyphony in research articles." In *Academic Discourse. Multidisciplinary Approaches*, edited by Kjersti Fløttum and François Rastier, 97–119. Oslo: Novus, 2003b.
—. "La présence de l'auteur dans les articles scientifiques : étude des pronoms *je, nous* et *on.*" In *Structures et discours*, edited by Antoine Auchlin et al., 401–416. Québec: Ed. Nota Bene, 2004.
—. "The self and the others – polyphonic visibility in research articles." *International Journal of Applied Linguistics* 15 (2005a): 29–44.
—. "MOI et AUTRUI dans le discours scientifique : l'exemple de la négation NE...PAS." In *Dialogisme, polyphonie: approches linguistiques*, edited by Jacques Bres, Patrick Pierre Haillet, Sylvi Mellet, Henning Nølke and Laurence Rosier, 323–337. Bruxelles: De Boeck-Duculot, 2005b.
—. "Interrelation de voix internes et externes dans le discours." In *Le sens et ses voix. Dialogisme et polyphonie en langue et en discours*, edited by Laurent Perrin, 301–322. Metz : *Recherches Linguistiques* (28), 2006a.
—. "Les « personnes » dans le discours scientifique : le cas du pronom ON." Paper presented at the *XVIe Congrès des Romanistes Scandinaves*, Copenhagen 24.–27.08.2005. Published 2006b at http://www.ruc.dk/isok/skriftserier/XVI-SRK-Pub/KFL/KFL01-Floettum/
Fløttum, Kjersti and François Rastier (eds.). *Academic Discourse. Multidisciplinary Approaches*, Oslo: Novus, 2003
Fløttum, Kjersti, Trine Dahl and Torodd Kinn. *Academic Voices*. Amsterdam/Philadelphia: John Benjamins Publishing Company, 2006.
Fløttum, Kjersti, Kerstin Jonasson and Coco Norén. *ON – pronom à facettes*. Forthcoming.
Fredrickson, Kirstin M. and John M. Swales. "Competition and discourse community: introductions from *Nysvenska studier.*" In *Text and Talk in Professional Contexts. Selected Papers from the International Conference "Discourse and the Professions"*, Uppsala, 26–29 August, 1992, edited by Britt-Louise Gunnarsson, Per Linell and Bengt Nordberg, 9–21. Stockholm: ASLA, 1994.
Gjesdal, Anje Müller. *L'emploi du pronom "on" dans les articles de recherche. Une étude diachronique et qualitative*. Master thesis. Bergen: Department of Romance studies, University of Bergen, 2003.
Hall, Edward T. and Mildred R. Hall. *Understanding Cultural Differences*. Yarmouth, ME: Intercultural Press, 1990.

Harwood, Nigel. "'We do not seem to have a theory ... The theory I present here attempts to fill this gap': Inclusive and exclusive pronouns in academic writing." *Applied Linguistics* 26 (2005): 343–375.
Hofstede, Geert. *Culture's Consequences. Comparing Values, Behaviors, Institutions, and Organizations Across Nations*. 2nd ed. Thousand Oaks/ London: Sage, 2001.
Hyland, Ken. *Hedging in Scientific Research Articles*. Amsterdam: John Benjamins Publishing Company, 1998.
—. "Bringing in the reader. Addressee features in academic articles." *Written Communication* 18 (2001a): 549–574.
—. "Humble servants of the discipline? Self-mention in research articles." *English for Specific Purposes* 20 (2001b): 207–226.
Kinn, Torodd. "Plays of we-hood: What do we mean by we?" *Akademisk Prosa / Skrifter fra KIAP* 3 (2005): 129–142. Bergen: Department of Romance studies, University of Bergen.
Kronning, Hans. "Le conditionnel « journalistique » : médiation et modalisation épistémiques." *Romansk Forum* 16 (2002): 561–575.
Kuo, Chih-Hua. "The use of personal pronouns: Role relationships in scientific journal articles." *English for Specific Purposes* 18 (1999): 121–138.
Le Querler, Nicole. *Typologie des modalités*. Caen: Presses universitaires de Caen, 1996.
—. "La place du verbe modal pouvoir dans une typologie des modalités." In *Les verbes modaux*, edited by Patrick Dendale and Johan van der Auwera, 17–32. Amsterdam: Rodopi, 2001.
Lewin, Beverly A. "Hedging: an exploratory study of authors' and readers' identification of 'toning down' in scientific texts." *Journal of English for Academic Purposes* 4 (2005): 163–178.
Loffler-Laurian, Anne-Marie. "L'expression du locuteur dans les discours scientifiques – "je", "nous" et "on" dans quelques textes de chimie et de physique." *Revue de Linguistique Romane* 44 (1980): 135–157.
Melander, Björn. "Culture or genre? Issues in the interpretation of cross-cultural differences in scientific papers." In *Genre Studies in English for Academic Purposes*, edited by Inmaculada Fortanet, Santiago Posteguillo, Juan Carlos Palmer and Juan Francisco Coll, 211–226. Castelló: Universitat Jaume I, 1998.
Nølke, Henning, Kjersti Fløttum and Coco Norén. *ScaPoLine. La théorie scandinave de la polyphonie linguistique*. Paris: Kimé, 2004.
Salager-Meyer, Françoise. "Referential behaviour in scientific writing: a diachronic study (1810–1995)." *English for Specific Purposes* 18 (1999): 279–305.

Sueur, Jean-Pierre. "Une analyse sémantique des verbes *devoir* et *pouvoir*." *Le Français moderne* 2 (1979): 97–120.

Swales, John M. *Genre Analysis. English in Academic and Research Settings.* Cambridge: Cambridge University Press, 1990.

Varttala, Teppo. *Hedging in Scientifically Oriented discourse. Exploring Variation According to Discipline and Intended Audience. Electronic doctoral dissertation* (Acta Electronica Universitatis Tamperensis 138), (2001): http: //acta.uta.fi/pdf/951-44-5195-3.pdf.

Vassileva, Irena. *Who is the Author? A Contrastive Analysis of Authorial Presence in English, German, French, Russian and Bulgarian Academic Discourse.* Sankt Augustin: Asgard Verlag, 2000.

Vihla, Minna. "Epistemic possibility: A study based on a medical corpus." In *Corpora Galore: Analyses and Techniques in Describing English: Papers from the Nineteenth International Conference on English Language Research on Computerised Corpora (ICAME 1998)*, edited by John M. Kirk. Language and Computers 30 (2000): 209–224. Amsterdam: Rodopi.

Vold, Eva Thue. "Epistemic modality markers in research articles: a cross-linguistic and cross-disciplinary study." *International Journal of Applied Linguistics* 16 (2006a): 61–87.

—. "The choice and use of epistemic modality markers in linguistics and medical research articles." In *Academic Discourse across Disciplines*, edited by Ken Hyland and Marina Bondi. Bern: Peter Lang, 2006b.

CHAPTER THREE

THE RHETORIC OF SCIENCE IN PRACTICE:
EXPERIENCES FROM NORDIC RESEARCH
ON SUBJECT-ORIENTED TEXTS[1]
AND TEXT CULTURES

KJELL LARS BERGE

1. Background: The Scandinavian subject-oriented texts projects and the study of scientific writing

During the 90's three extensive projects studying the development and characteristics of the text cultures of non-fictional writing or "subject-oriented texts" ("sakprosa" in Nordic languages) was carried out in Norway and Sweden. All three projects followed a consistent multi-disciplinary approach, in spite of the fact that the composite field of discourse analysis showed itself to be attractive for many of the involved researchers. These projects had *three* dominant characteristics in common (Berge 2001):

Firstly, one wished to study systematically different text cultures in a society where subject oriented texts constituted and defined the culture. Consequently a society was to be understood with reference to its communication patterns. This goal was animated by the ambition to study the constitution of text cultures regarding non-fictional texts as a study of the development and establishment of modernity in Sweden and Norway. As a result, the projects chose the 18th Century as their starting point in time. This is the century when the principles of freedom of writing is beginning to be implemented in the Nordic kingdoms, a free press producing journals and newspapers is developed, permanent publishing houses are being established and scientific academies advocating free

---

[1] The Scandinavian word "sakprosa" is translated to "subject-oriented texts". This is a translation recommended by AILA (the International Association of Applied Linguistics) when the Nordic projects were presented at the AILA-conference in Tokyo in 1999.

thinking and interest-free research are promoted. Finally literacy increasingly becomes a common resource for the masses as a result of the development of a relatively advanced school system, democratic institutions and a liberal economy. As a consequence the Nordic countries are today characterised by a strong democratic tradition, emphasis on education and written culture, an innovative and enterprise-oriented business culture, and well as substantial welfare states. A common perspective of all three projects was that this historical result might partly be explained by the development, distribution of, access to and broad use of subject oriented text cultures in Scandinavia since the 18th century. In fact the term "sakprosa" is a word invented in Scandinavia (by the Finnish linguist Rolf Pipping), and was originally (1938) established as a term referring to objective, value-free, precise and clear language, as opposed to the subjective, personal, metaphorical and emotional language of the belle arts and political discourse. There is an ideological relation between the philosophy of language of the inventor of the "sakprosa"-term and the logical positivism tradition. This approach implied that the Nordic projects were interested in the relation between the use of texts and norms for text production on the one hand, and the advanced distribution of power typical of modern societies on the other. Consequently, influential non-fictional texts such as manuals for political work in mass organisations dominating politics and cultural life in the 19th and 20th century, and all-embracing text cultures such as state bureaucracies, were viewed as relevant research phenomena for the projects. A special feature of the Nordic situation as compared with other countries, is that the Nordic nations have relatively small populations, and that these populations share a strong egalitarian ideology. Consequently the public spheres in these societies traditionally have been quite "transparent", establishing the ground for a close relationship between the intellectual elites and scientists on the one hand and the rest of the general public on the other.

Secondly, the aim was to develop theories and methods necessary for a comprehensive study of subject-oriented text cultures and texts. The characteristic features of cultures where subject-oriented texts were created were studied. The types of textual practices dominant in the various subject-oriented text cultures were also studied, as well as the texts themselves. The dominant focus was on textual structure, however, though language styles and registers of the texts were also investigated.

Thirdly the projects desired to study the relation between textual practices and text norms on the one hand and a sample of important institutions constitutive of modern societies on the other, such as the already mentioned bureaucracies and the complex textual practices of mass-recruiting political organisations. In the research projects there was a significant interest in the text cultures of modern science. As is common in the in the Nordic language tradition, the term "science" here, refers to the natural sciences, the social sciences, as well as typical humanities academic disciplines. In contemporary science an overwhelming part of the knowledge used in the government of complex societies and states, in the development of industries and trade, in medicine and health care and in intellectual reflection and debate has been developed since the 17th Century. This "scientification" of all parts of society is not only due to the writings of the scientists themselves. Very few people have actually read Galileo's, Pasteur's, Einstein's or even Darwin's scientific works. The dominance of science in modern societies may of course be explained by the intensive and long-lasting schooling of the population. In two important contributions to the Nordic projects professor Per Ledin of Örebro University demonstrated that the development and popularity of journals and magazines from the beginning of the 19th century onwards, could be explained by these popular text cultures' dominant scientific approach to the reality of natural facts and human experiences. In these written texts the man in the street learnt that home remedies of different kinds, from the treatment of illnesses to the acculturation of the agricultural tradition, could not be trusted, but had to be replaced with knowledge developed by advanced science. This was a type of knowledge that for most people was incomprehensible and unattainable. Even the powerful political right-wing movements of the 20th century in reacting to the modernization of society, were immersed in scientific thinking, clearly demonstrated by the scientific argumentation behind racist politics in Germany, South-Africa and elsewhere in long periods of the century.

In this article I intend to present some prominent tendencies in the study of academic and scientific texts and text cultures by the Nordic projects. An important point of reference for the projects' studies of academic text cultures was the discipline of the rhetoric of science. This is a discipline that is well established in the international research community, especially in the United States. Within the rhetoric of science field there is a strong tradition of studying the relation between the dominant goal of science - the quest for unbiased truth - and how such truth is established through various forms of semiotic mediation, such as written texts (text books, articles), oral presentations, illustrations, animations, films etc. The discipline is also concerned with how the truth of scientific utterances is accepted and established as a fact in the research community. Thus, the study of the rhetoric of science is concerned with persuasive communication, and is also interested in the relation between text and power in any specific text culture. To have power in the scientific community is to be able to persuade the community of the correctness or probability of one's own truth claims.

This approach to scientific text cultures and academic writing is however not without some specific intellectual and moral problems. Many scientists may well understand a rhetorical approach to scientific communication as being in conflict with the ethos of scientific work. It might be viewed as an invitation to epistemological relativism and an end to scientific communitarianism, to claim that the question of truth in science can be explained by reference to persuasion. Issues of this kind were intensely discussed during the so-called Sokal-debate. Given the ideological link between the original intended content of the word "sakprosa" and logical positivism, it might also be regarded as a paradox that the rhetorical tradition should be regarded as a relevant theoretical framework for Nordic projects studying subject oriented texts. However, these projects did not question the notion that a constitutive feature of science is the search for unbiased truth. And the reality of natural and mental worlds irrespective of our ideas regarding them, was certainly not questioned. However, the researchers associated with the projects were interested in finding out how truth claims in various fields of sciences were presented and represented as texts. They were also interested in how persuasive work was done in ways that are in accordance with ethical standards of specific scientific text cultures. But before we venture further into how the rhetoric of science was studied in the Nordic projects, it will be relevant to discuss how scientific textual practices may be understood as rhetorical activities without being inconsistent with the ethos of an unbiased science.

2. Textual reality, truth and epistemology: Is the rhetoric of science consistent with scientific realism?

As previously mentioned, the rhetoric of science is a controversial discipline, especially among certain representatives of the natural sciences and philosophers who defend an orthodox scientific realist position. Some of these representatives spot in this new discipline a new version of an outrageous idealism, such as the one advocated by the Irish philosopher Berkeley who insisted that "To be is to be perceived or to perceive" ("Esse est aut percipi aut percipere"). In response to those who sceptical about a discipline such as the rhetoric of science, though, the slogan would be "to be is to be uttered in language or to utter in language". In fact, one of the most prominent spokesmen of the rhetoric of science, Allan Gross, has used formulations that may be interpreted as close to an idealistic position in proposing for instance that "rhetoric is constitutive of scientific knowledge" (Gross 2006: 5).

What is at stake here is that the rhetoric of science does not accept without further ado one of the basic premises of the realist position, the so-called "correspondence conception of truth": i.e. that any utterance or text that is independent of the semiotic resources used for creating it, is true if it *describes* facts that are true. Or to use a formulation typical of the realists: "A statement S

is true if *S* describes the facts". Thus, in the realist tradition, any utterance or text is supposed to be a mirror image or icon of a non-textual reality, both natural and mental. The realist position gives privilege to utterances and texts that are *descriptions*. As we have indicated, it is typical of the rhetoric of science that it is concerned with how texts and utterances attain the position of such a descriptive "statement". The rhetoric of science understands this process as persuasive. For any competent language user to understand any utterance, text or "statement" as "true" he or she has to be *convinced* that it is "true" by means of the utterance or text. For a scientific realist the task of science is to check whether a "statement" that is proposed as "true" is "true" independent of the claim that it is "true". If I in a text propose as a macro-proposition that "the Israeli army is killing civilians in Lebanon" its truth may be ensured by investigating whether the Israeli army is actually killing civilians in Lebanon or not, irrespective of my descriptions of the situation in Lebanon in some utterance or text. The rhetoric of science then, accepts that science is governed by the quest for unbiased truth. It is not the position of the rhetoric of science that any sort non-textual reality is created by an utterance or text. A still weaker version of the idealist and constructivist positions may be relevant for rhetoricians who study scientific texts. An acceptable position to take would be to propose that any non-textual reality is given meaning or is understood via the utterance or text. The rhetoric of science then, does not accept that natural facts and mental states may be grasped individually and presented collectively without the help of semiotic devices such as language. The relevance of the rhetoric of science is thus based on the fact that even if science is defined by the quest for unbiased truth, or by checking that statements proposed as true are true or false, irrespective of propositions claiming they are "true", most people – scientists or not – are not able to replicate or repeat the necessary investigations. Therefore the scientific presentation of texts claiming to be "true" has to be based on a mutual agreement of *trust*. By means of any scientific text knowledge about, insights in and understandings of, any given reality is made probable for those who are not in the position to do this reality description work themselves. The task of the rhetoric of science is then to describe how such persuasive work is done through different forms of semiotic mediation. The task of rhetoric is *not* to assess whether what is presented as probably "true" is – in fact – true or false, or whether the mutual agreement to trust what is presented as "true is " in fact true, has been violated or not, but to investigate, describe and explain the textual strategies typical of the scientific truth-seeking culture in question, and its representatives. Such textual strategies may of course be very different in disciplines such as biology or social anthropology. In the Nordic research projects studying subject matter oriented texts, the epistemological position of the rhetoric of science was in this way considered consistent with the position of scientific realism (and therefore also with logical positivism), even if it challenged the dominant view of language and other semiotic means (such as graphs, illustrations and photographs) as iconic and descriptive in these traditions. A wide range of semiotic means is used, and must be used, in order to convince the scientific community of the probability of scientific truth-claims. The task of rhetoricians studying scientific texts and utterances, is thus to describe and explain how this work of making something appear scientifically probable is being done in different scientific communities.

3. Why study the rhetoric of scientific texts? An expansion of arguments

Even if the critical researcher should accept this modified view of the rhetoric of science as making it consistent with the basic tenets of scientific realism, it is not obvious that rhetoric should be regarded as a valuable and relevant theoretical and methodological tradition in the study of subject oriented texts. Of course "rhetoric" used to be synonymous with the textual practices of democracy in ancient Athens, as well as the long lasting pedagogical tradition that resulted from this. In the scientific literature, however, "rhetoric" has come to refer to several different types of phenomena.

Firstly, "rhetoric" is viewed as a particular kind of communication amongst many others, all characterised as persuasion. It was this understanding of rhetoric which made it unacceptable for Plato as an instrument for the development of epistemic knowledge. For him to be preoccupied with rhetoric meant to be engaged in that which might be presented as "true" though persuasive discourse, to the neglect of what is in fact "true". As we have seen, Plato's opposition between "true" knowledge, independent of persuasion – "episteme" – and knowledge made probable through persuasive communication – "doxa" - is still relevant for discussions of whether rhetoric is an appropriate approach to the study of scientific texts and communication.

Secondly, "rhetoric" may be understood as a medium of enculturalisation (analogue to the German word "Bildung") by means of communication. In this tradition one wishes to focus on rhetoric as a prototypical curriculum for the teaching of speaking, writing and communication, a field that is covered today by applied linguists. An interesting characteristic of the relatively new interest in how scientists construe and represent their work in articles, reports, papers, posters, oral presentations and books, is that it is often driven by a pedagogical interest in the teaching and learning of scientific writing. A lot of research into scientific texts and text production within an applied linguistics framework may be explained by the functional value of teaching students how to practice science using language as a tool. It is a common experience of most post-industrial welfare states that the new generation of young people attending the universities in huge numbers has problems in cracking the behavioural codes of science. Consequently, many universities include practical training in scientific writing and argumentation in preparatory courses. Since these courses create a demand for research-based knowledge regarding how scientists actually write, funding for research into scientific writing is made available. This research is seldom critical of the types of academic texts studied, and it only studies cursorily the wider context of culture in which scientific texts are produced. This strategy may also explain why the study of scientific texts in an applied linguistics framework seldom raises the epistemological questions that are the essential focal point of the rhetoric of science tradition.

Thirdly, "rhetoric" may be understood as coding specific types of genre knowledge. In this way "rhetoric" is understood as a textual norm system in specific text producing cultural institutions in the course of history. Historically, the rhetorical progymnasmata tradition has been considered irrelevant and useless for the development of textual norms in scientific writing. A rhetoric of science must consider the relevance of classical rhetorical theories and handbooks for the study of scientific communication, as well as taking into consideration the fact that researchers who established the Renaissance empirical tradition systematically distanced themselves from rhetorical models. In this respect, the applied linguistic approach may be considered closer to research communities' own appreciations of what they are doing when they are communicating scientifically.

Fourthly, "rhetoric" may be viewed as a textual science in itself, delivering a comprehensive text theory and methods for the study of texts. The classical tradition has transmitted a fairly extensive literature classifying and describing the communicative practices of rhetoricians in Greece and Rome. Quite a lot of these texts are pedagogical prescriptions for how to speak to an audience, and how one can teach young people to behave properly in communication, a condition for a future position as a respected citizen. Still, some of the classical texts aspire to a more comprehensive theory of what rhetoric is. The classical work in this tradition is of course Aristotle's "Rhetoric". This work presents a definition of rhetoric that is a defence of the criticism raised by Plato, as well as a description based on this definition. Even in the introduction Aristotle presents his basic view of rhetoric as a specific field of human behaviour, which has its own rules and conventions:

> "Rhetoric is the counterpart of Dialectic. Both alike are concerned with such things as come, more or less, within the general ken of all men and belong to no definite science. Accordingly all men make use, more or less, of both; for to a certain extent all men attempt to discuss statements and to maintain them, to defend themselves and to attack others. Ordinary people do this either at random

or through practice and from acquired habit. Both ways being possible, the subject can plainly be handled systematically, for it is possible to inquire the reason why some speakers succeed through practice and others spontaneously; and every one will at once agree that such an inquiry is the function of an art." (http://www.public.iastate.edu/~honeyl/Rhetoric/)

Since all men "attempt to discuss statements and to maintain them, to defend themselves and to attack others" the task of rhetoric as a science is "to inquire the reason why some speakers succeed through practice and others spontaneously". Rhetoric as a science then, describes what the elements of rhetorical behaviour are, and explains on the basis of this description why some are better at convincing other people than others. It is on the basis of this establishment of rhetoric as a science that it still has relevance in modern text research and discourse analysis. Many text researchers attracted to rhetoric still use the terms and definitions developed by Aristotle as methodological tools. Since Aristotle studied only the genres of Athenian democracy, it is of course disputed whether the same methodological tools are relevant for the description of other genres developed in completely different cultures with other communicative functions, such as that of scientific writing.

It is interesting that in the five criteria used to determine if scientific texts have rhetorical features - suggested by the influential rhetorician of science Lawrence Prelli - arguments are employed for a rhetoric of science that moves beyond the classical tradition. In Prelli's book *A Rhetoric of Science. Inventing Scientific Discourse* published in 1989, scientific discourse is defined as "symbolic inducement": The rhetoric of science enables the strengthening, clarification, evaluation, mediation in relation to other disciplines and non-researchers, and the creation of new scientific paradigms, i.e. models of explanation and constitutive features of scientific agreement. In this way the rhetoric of science enables understanding of constitutive and necessarily true premises or propositions, for instance by means of selective samples, examples, text books, exercises etc. In this way, the rhetoric of science makes clear premises and conclusions that enable possible criticisms. Prelli's second criterion is that "scientific discourse is situational discourse". Science takes place inside a more or less established culture with norms that regulate who may express themselves and in what way. Thus, the scientific community is a historic construction. Further, the rhetoric of science presupposes a certain ethos that is taken more or less for granted, articulated in Merton's five criteria of scientific culture: *communality, disinterestedness, organized scepticism, originality, humility*. Prelli's third criterion for a rhetoric of science is that "scientific discourse is addressed discourse". The rhetoric of science is dialogical. It is discussion-oriented within a scientific community. The fourth decisive factor of a rhetoric of science according to Prelli is that "scientific discourse is reasonable discourse". The rhetoric of science enables conclusions that are reasonable from the point of view of the paradigm that the participants in any given rhetorical situation adhere to, as well as communication between paradigms, making translation between them possible. The fifth and final criterion of a rhetoric of science in Prelli's contribution is that "scientific discourse is invented discourse" The establishment of paradigms implies persuasion, according to Prelli. This example of a definition of the rhetorical characteristics of science by a prominent rhetorician has clearly illustrated that to define a new type of text-oriented discipline on the ground of the oldest one of this kind, rhetoric, demands certain adjustments relative to features of the text culture being studied. Any text researcher or discourse analyst might present four of five criteria without any reference to the rhetorical tradition. Still, the fifth criterion is a genuinely rhetorical one. By means of this criterion Prelli makes reference to the specialised rhetorical tradition of "topics", which means, amongst other things, those themes which are presented as relevant, how these themes are understood etc. This modified use of rhetoric is also advocated by Allan Gross in his book *Starring the Text. The Place of Rhetoric in Science Studies* (2006).

Finally, the scientific literature views "rhetoric" as an instrument for ethical reflection on text. This position is inherent in the classical tradition. In fact, Aristotle's *Rhetoric* is both a reply to, and an attack on, Plato's refusal of rhetoric as a relevant and decent tool for the quest of knowledge, and a criticism of the tendencies to use rhetorical knowledge cynically in Athenian society as a means for making white black, and vice versa. By presenting rhetorical knowledge as a kind of practical knowledge everyone has access to, and as knowledge that has been made crucial for the development of important institutions in Athenian democracy such as the courts and popular assemblies, Aristotle demonstrates the need for an ethical reflection on the features and qualities of such knowledge and the way it is manifested in communication. By showing these features and qualities explicitly and discussing them openly Aristotle establishes the ground for a sound and decent discussion of the norms that should constitute the necessary premises for ethical rhetorical practice. By establishing such constitutive rules it should be possible to distinguish in a fundamental manner between rhetoric and propaganda, or between reasonable points of view and aggressive or unfounded agitation.

The relevance of rhetoric for the study of scientific texts and text cultures in the Nordic subject oriented texts, then, was not rhetoric as a general theory and method for the study of textual communication. Actually, only two arguments for the relevance of rhetoric were considered relevant in this context. First, rhetoric and the rhetorical tradition were necessary as a model for the study of scientific textual practices when understood as persuasive communication. As mentioned, the point of view advocated was that the scientific text made qualified knowledge of reality probable for those who are not in a position to do such reality description work themselves. Thus, of special interest in the rhetorical tradition was the science of proofs, indices and topics. Secondly, rhetoric and the rhetorical tradition were relevant as an instrument for ethical reflection on how scientific texts were executed. Important questions here were: What were the ethical norms for scientific utterances and texts in specific scientific text cultures, how and why were they established as they were, and in what way did representatives of specific scientific text cultures acquire these more or less articulated norms?

In this way the rhetoric of science was able to help broaden some general themes inherent in the three research projects, both the fact that the development of scientific text cultures are a precondition for modernity, and the fact that these text cultures have immense power in contemporary society. Let us take a further look at these two research themes in the context of the three subject-oriented research projects, in the light of the rhetoric of science:

As an autonomous text culture, science is characterised by being both a precondition for modernity, and one of modernity's most characteristic features. By studying how science is mediated semiotically we are studying aspects of the dominant doxa of modern society. Thus, when we study how scientific text cultures have evolved and are evolving, we are witnessing the development of modern society. This point has been made by a number of scholars; most prominently by Jack Goody with his studies of the impact of literacy on the evolution of society and culture, and by Charles Bazerman in his studies of the development of the experimental article in the natural sciences. It is typical of scientific text cultures that they present a worldview that for the most part is inconsistent with everyday experiences of most human beings. Science does not believe what is told. Scientific argumentation is based on this presumption. Scientific argumentation and persuasion is therefore characterised by being a de-naturalised type of language use, and by a type of enculturalisation that uses normative resources that are quite different from those used in every-day spoken interaction. Scientific texts reflect a distrust in common human communication, substituting the conventions of everyday speech for new textual norms. It is a common experience in most studies of scientific text cultures in the Nordic research projects to discover that textual norms are adapted to the dominant doxa of the particular scientific discipline. We shall return to some examples of such experiences at the end of this article. These textual norms are established on the basis of what is considered to be the "truth" in actual scientific text cultures. Since this quest for "truth" always demands a consequent scepticism towards established truths – formulated most prominently in Karl Popper's falsification principle, stating that every genuine test of a scientific theory is an attempt to refute or to falsify it – these norms are always considered to be changeable. Textual interaction in science, then, is prototypically viewed in accordance with its instrumental features. Thus, a scientific community in principle is never a tradition-oriented community, but a community devoted to modernity and intellectual change. If a scientific text does not fulfil its task as an indication of the doxa of a specific scientific text culture, it will inevitably be considered irrelevant, and its norm resources dysfunctional.

Perhaps paradoxically, this fact is the reason for the stable and robust text norms operative in the most established sciences, such as medicine and the natural sciences. The strict conventionalisation indicates of course that the doxa of medicine and the natural sciences is something settled and not to be negotiated. These text cultures have developed advanced text norms, often grammaticalised in handbooks. The manual of the Norwegian-language journal for doctors - *Tidsskrift for den norske lægeforening* - comprises 150 pages with detailed instructions for authors. The prototypical natural science article follows the standards of the IMRAD-norm, thoroughly studied in the literature on scientific writing. The situation is quite different in many of the more artistically oriented human sciences. Of course textual norms are developed in such communities as well, but they are seldom legislated in the way that the norms of natural sciences are. In human sciences disciplines individualisation is the norm, and one is sceptical about the standardisation that characterises the natural sciences. In fact this apparent liberalism reflects the obvious instability of the doxa of the humanistic scientific traditions. A Norwegian study of the development of the text norms of literary science (Bakken) that we shall present later in this article, demonstrates that codification of norms happened mainly at the level of topics and of linguistic style and register. Text norms for composition at more global textual levels were not developed at all.

Since the breakthrough of liberal politics in the 80's the outcomes of scientific work are more and more becoming accepted as commodities. It is becoming increasingly more accepted that state-funded universities capitalize their products and ideas. Scientific articles printed in journals or downloaded from quality sites on the web are commercially traded as products. Increasingly, single scientists' excellence is being assessed in terms of their capacity to produce texts that are published in prestigious journals or book series. Traditional authorship is becoming neglected in favour of a system where important participants in research projects are presented as the co-producers of articles. At the University of Oslo one article was written with 150 researchers named as co-authors. This ongoing industrialisation of scientific writing has already had its local scandals. In Norway it was discovered that one of its most prominent and respected medicinal researchers had faked the data used in articles by him (often with many co-authors mentioned) published in attractive journals such as *The Lancet* and *Nature*. We can observe in this commodification of scientific writing a tendency towards what we might label "scientific fetishism". This tendency is indicated by the fact that the IMRAD-model, originally developed in the natural sciences as a text norm adapted to the doxa of these sciences, is even being imitated in sciences that investigate cultural facts and use the interpretation of human behaviour as a basic method. An example of this trend is the development of scientific writing in linguistics. As shown in one of the Norwegian subject oriented research projects, linguists are trying to imitate the IMRAD-model and the doxa that comes with it, even though this entails that characteristics of the available data are being violated. Interestingly enough, these writing strategies result in complicated textual patterns that attempt to compensate for the incompatibility between textual norms and doxa.

4. Studying scientific text cultures: Fundamental methodological concerns

A common denominator in the Nordic subject-oriented research projects was that the study of texts and the normative resources used in creating them should be accompanied by studies of the relevant cultural and situational contexts, as well as the interactions between institutional qualities of these contexts, the texts themselves and the text norms typical of these contexts. This approach was chosen not least in order to underline that the texts were not understood as a superficial expression of these cultures, but as a constitutive feature of such cultures. Without advanced text cultures – which do not necessarily have to be mediated by written texts – it would not be possible to establish complex institutions at all. This understanding implicated that methodological strategies would be inspired not only by semiotics, text linguistics and discourse analysis, but also by anthropology, thus constituting a textual anthropology.

The methodological program for one of the projects was presented by summing up some of the fundamental positions of a possible text anthropology:

Firstly, textual categorisations need to be understood from within the activities in which they are used. Text categorisations are indexes of various activities in a specific culture where texts are produced. These categorisations could be conceived of as a map covering all the genres used in the culture, as well as all kinds of texts used, and the semiotic systems used as resources for creating them. This meant that scientific activities had to be studied not from a universal point of view, but as textual practices typical of the specific science in question. Therefore all sciences can, and should, not be studied according the same scientific standards and models, or from the point of view of specific scientific disciplines. There is a strong tendency in new types of public management to assess all scientific activities using highly institutionalised medicine as a standard. This political position indicates insensitivity towards the variation typical of activities in different fields. It was necessary to document this variation.

Second, different sciences were considered to be different text cultures. These cultures could be more or less institutionalised. Of course some sciences have a long history of institutionalisation, while others are only recently established and consequently underdeveloped. This last type of situation is typical for much research in the field of discourse analysis, while physics is of course a typical discipline with a very long tradition. Research in certain areas of the sciences has been industrialised, with most of the research taking place in private enterprises, and some important sciences are a constitutive part of the international war industry, while others exist only in the seminars of professors and students and in the articles they produce, without any broad recognition in society. These huge differences need to be considered when acknowledgement interests, truth concepts, probability criteria, textual strategies and textual norms of various text cultures are investigated.

A third methodological insight was that the borders between different scientific text cultures could vary considerably. Many well-developed sciences are characterised by an extreme specialisation that makes it impossible for only a small and exclusive group of researchers to understand and assess the quality of the work being done. The evolvement of semiotic resources is a constitutive feature of such specialisation. The development of advanced pictorial and visual resources for creating meaning, together with access to advanced computer and communication technologies has established the ground for even more complexity and specialisation. This advance is of course typical for many of the research fields in contemporary medicine. On the other hand, for some sciences the borders between the scientific text cultures could be considered open, and the sciences involved characterised by theoretical and methodological multi-disciplinarity and innovation. An example of a scientific text culture of this type was the so-called Tartu-school in semiotics. This tradition was established after the death of Stalin at the University of Tartu in Estonia in the then Soviet Union. The Tartu-school developed an original mix of ecological biology, Saussurian and Hjelmslevian linguistics, and information theory. Another prominent example of interdisciplinary interaction and invention is the field of ethnomethodology, which established a genuine study of spoken interaction for the first time in history. In this way a reaction to, and revolt against, the dominant doxa of mainstream sociology led to a paradigm shift in linguistics.

As mentioned at the beginning of this article, the research projects' interest was in an investigation of the unique qualities of texts produced in different scientific text cultures. A fundamental point made was that a text is a finite realisation of some meaning potential in a specific situation. The text creates new meaning, but it is normally constructed in such a way that this meaning should be understood. Any text is an utterance, and is therefore unique. At the same time it utilises normative resources that are more or less conventionalised in the culture of origin. The variation with regard to how different researchers or research groups position themselves and their model readers in different scientific text cultures is an important arena for research. In another article in this volume, professor Johan Tønnesson demonstrates how the writing of history implicates the evaluation of various sources, each presented as different voices in historians' texts. This positioning may vary from writer to writer, from researcher to researcher, and it may also be governed by disciplinary textual norms. Any scientific writer has to adapt himself or herself to the specific text norms of the research community on hand. An important task in the project was of course to make explicit these norms and assess their degree of standardisation and grammaticalisation. We shall return to examples of this work at the end this article.

The list of methodological positions is longer than stated above, but the rest of these are not directly relevant to the arguments put forward in this article. More important for discussion of methodological strategies in the three Nordic projects are the characteristics of the doxa of any specific science on the one hand, and the strategies chosen for sampling of text cultures and texts on the other. Let us first present differences in the scientific doxa.

An important experience emerging from the three Nordic projects is that different branches of science require different approaches to the study of the rhetoric used by them. As mentioned earlier in this article there is a strong relationship between the paradigmatic positions of science, what kind of topics may be discussed, and the relationship between these topics and understandings of reality, i.e. the doxa, and the way norms for textual strategies are constituted. An important difference is apparent between sciences that study natural laws and social conventions that determine behaviour on the one hand, and sciences that study unique phenomena on the other. The first kind of scientific paradigm is normally referred to as "nomothetic", while the other, regarding unique phenomena, is called "idiographic". In addition, a distinction is made between nomothetic sciences that study natural laws that make prediction possible, and nomothetic sciences that study cultural norms that may explain observable meaningful behaviour. Established knowledge of the first kind is based on the expectation that its formulated laws and rules are unconditionally true in all situations, while established knowledge of the other kind is based on the expectation that the norms and conventions described present probable explanations to observed behaviour in a specific society. In a nomothetically oriented discipline like linguistics many conflicts between researchers might be explained by the distinction between these two types of nomothetic science. In idiographic science on the other hand, phenomena are studied in their specific context of situation, and the strategy is to explain the behaviour in that context, and not in wider cultural contexts or in terms of natural laws, of course. Radical idiographic sciences such as deconstructivism in the discipline of literary criticism give up explanation altogether, and substitute it with a descriptive and argumentative exegesis of individual interpretations. The rhetoric strategies in sciences with such huge paradigmatic differences of course vary greatly from science to science, as we shall soon demonstrate with examples. The basic text types: explanation, description, argumentation, and narrative are represented in scientific texts according to the constitutive differences created by the two types of nomothetic science on the one hand, and idiographic science on the other. According to one study (Aas) produced by one of the Norwegian subject oriented research projects, a crucial difference between writing in mainstream natural sciences and post-modern literary criticism showed itself in the way interpersonal resources were used. In the natural science texts the researcher was committed to a non-cultural reality, and to how insights from this reality could be utilised to the greater advantage of the community. Thus, the scientist also had a social commitment. These combined commitments were observable in the use of modality in the texts studied. The natural scientist prototypically uses a vague and negotiable deontic, epistemic modality, underlining what "probably" is true, and what "probably" might be utilised of the presented findings. The interpersonal strategies in post-modern literary criticism are somewhat opposite. New interpretations are presented as more relevant than others, and these interpretations are understood as a part of an ideological debate regarding different understandings of the cultural world. Since the researchers are not committed to an external reality, only to interpretations of disputed cultural facts, interpersonal relations are characterised by non-negotiable positioning and a strong obligation to the addresser's positions. The doxa presented in these different scientific practices are, respectively, a naturalistic and an idealistic discourse. It may be a paradox for some that the argumentative, descriptive and explicative parts of the post-modern literary critics text are characterised by strong truth propositions, non-negotiable meanings, and few concessions, while the natural scientists rhetorical strategies are much more open to different interpretations. The naturalistic doxa presented in the rhetoric of the representative for nomothetic science is characterised by uncertainty, doubt and insecurity, while the idealistic doxa of the representative for idiographic science is characterised by its opposite.

In the rhetoric of science tradition the conventional data selection strategy has to been to study canonical, outstanding contributions to science, such as Newton and Darwin's seminal works. In the Nordic projects, however, mainstream everyday scientific practices have been the object of study. Thus, the data that has been collected has been viewed as representative of the researchers themselves. These materials have not been statistically selected, as in the KIAP-project presented elsewhere in this volume. In this way the sample selected consists of utterances defined as typical texts by the researchers themselves. When the rhetoric of an individual researcher has been investigated, the motive for this has been that the researcher in question has a prominent position amongst his colleagues in terms of constituting a special school or tradition. These methodological strategies are of course motivated by main objective of the project previously presented in this article: to study the evolvement and institutionalisation of scientific text cultures in Nordic societies. It is also motivated by an interest in how scientific text cultures becomes accepted and embraced by all members of the society, thus constituting a contemporary societal power hegemony. This research focus explains the interest in the scientification of everyday life by means of weekly magazines, official information services and the popular mediation of science. In many of the studies in the Nordic projects the focus has been on apparently "trivial" scientific texts such as the composition and use of text books at all levels of the educational system, almanacs and discourses on contraceptives and birth control (Melander & Olsson). Another consequence of this approach is that it has been of special interest to study socialisation processes where people internalise scientific knowledge in different cultural contexts, such as schools, universities and people's colleges. Even though the primary purpose of this research on uses of scientific literacy in all parts of society has not been a pedagogical one, the applied linguistics and writing research traditions have been of great interest in developing these projects.

5. How to study the rhetoric of scientific texts? Some analytic dimensions represented by Nordic project examples

The results of the Nordic subject-oriented projects studying scientific texts strongly emphasize that different kinds of science and different scientific activities imply quite different approaches to the study of scientific rhetoric. "Science" is text culture consisting of different discourse communities with different communicative goals, different textual traditions, different genres, different truth-concepts, different types of interaction with society, as illustrated in John Swales' textographic study of scientific practices in an university building in his book "Other Floors. Other Voices". Let us now have a look at some analytic dimensions studied by a few of the research projects directly initiated by, or associated with one of the Norwegian subject-oriented projects.

The first example demonstrates how a prominent criminology professor establishes a common ground in a scientific text by positioning the model-reader in relation to a specific paradigm, closing access to other alternatives. The second example is drawn from a study of how argumentative structures in the disciplines of medicine, history and linguistics are realised, and how these realisations relate to, and configure, the specific doxa of the discipline. The third example illustrates the rhetorical strategies of two paradigms of the same scientific tradition in conflict. This example is taken from a study of how the discipline of literary criticism has been established at Norwegian universities.

5.1 Paradigmatic positioning in criminology

In his book "Thomas Mathisen on trial" (Norwegian: *Kan Thomas Mathisen forsvares?*) Magne Gjerstad analyses the Norwegian criminology professor Thomas Mathisen's book "Prison On Trial". Gjerstad follows a three-step strategy as he dissects Mathisen's rhetorical strategies.

Gjerstad's first move is to define the position of the text studied in what he calls "the textual hierarchy of scientific texts". With the help of a thorough analysis of the position of the book as a university text book at home and abroad, in translation, and through reviews in relevant national and international journals, and even more important its position in international citation indexes, Gjerstad is able to show that Mathisen's book has acquired a prominent place in the text hierarchy of the social field of criminology. The aim is *not* to try to define the book as a canonical text, comparing it with the seminal works of outstanding scientists as they are normally studied in the rhetoric of science, but to demonstrate that the position of the book in the text hierarchy defines its power in the criminology text culture. If the position of the text in the text hierarchy may be understood as empowered, the text is relevant for rhetorical analysis. In this way Gjerstad does not accept the communicative rationality proposed by the norms of the scientific society. The book is not considered as empowered because of its inherent scientific qualities, but because of its position in the hierarchy of texts.

The next move is to show how Mathisen establishes the text's scientific ethos by making an analogy between the conventions studied in social sciences as well as their functional explanations, and the predictions and laws in natural sciences. Gjerstad tries to show that Mathisen's deductions and statistical reasoning do not possess the truth-value Mathisen ascribes to them, but rather that Mathisen's inferences are based on selective samples, controversial interpretations and abductive reasoning presenting probabilities.

The final move is to unveil what Gjerstad calls "the identity work" in the rhetoric of the text. Gjerstad shows how the author establishes textual roles and positions for different participants and the relations between them. This investigation is based on a polyphonic analysis of the different participants in the text, whether they are institutions, persons representing institutions, or persons; whether they are given voices, or are represented through other voices etc. Gjerstad manages to show that Mathisen establishes a gap between the social scientist's understanding of the social world, and non-scientists – or so-called "ordinary people's" - understandings of the same world. The ideology of the criminological text repeats the classical distinction between doxa and episteme, and the acknowledged interest of Mathisen's text is to demonstrate that a non-scientific understanding of how prisons function is false, and has to be substituted by an understanding based on science proper. Gjerstad also proposes that Mathisen simplifies the stances of participants given roles and voices in the text, using an obviously patronising strategy.

Needless to say, Gjerstad's rhetorical scrutiny of Mathisen's prominent and much-respected text was, and is still, controversial. The author who was studied, professor Thomas Mathisen, reacted strongly to the analysis, and wrote a comprehensive reply to it. A long and heated public debate followed. Much of the anger in the debate could be explained by Gjerstad's obvious interest in unveiling what he considered to be Mathisen's problematic ethical standards. Mathisen on his side refused to accept Gjerstad's authority and insisted that a rhetorical analysis of scientific texts had to be based on a professional knowledge of the discipline, a knowledge he could not, and did not want to, assign to Gjerstad. Gjerstad's analysis and the debate following it demonstrate both the interesting and problematic qualities of a rhetoric of science that criticises fundamental positions of respected scholars. Gjerstad's strategy in many ways resembles Robert de Beaugrande's harsh criticism of Noam Chomsky's rhetorical positioning of controversial, however seminal, contributions to linguistics. In both Gjerstad's and de Beaugrande's cases the problematic aspects of their analytical strategies are due to their apparent dislike of the epistemological position of their respective research objects. They do not accept the fundamental scientific values advocated by their research objects through their texts. This position makes reflective dialogue almost irrelevant, and impossible to achieve. Still, the analytical strategies they present both initiate a more profound discussion of the epistemology in question, as well as establishing a discussion on how strong proponents of specific paradigms should present their opponents positions.

5.2 Text structures and scientific doxa in articles in medicine, linguistics and history

A significant contribution to Nordic studies of scientific writing is Kjersti Breivega's PhD-thesis "Scientific Argumentation Strategies" (Norwegian: *Vitskaplege argumentasjonsstrategiar*), published as a monograph in the Norwegian *Sakprosa*-series. In this study Breivega detects a fundamental difference between what she calls "humanistic" and "natural scientific" genres, by studying the distribution of argumentative superstructures as well as more global strategies which cover the interaction of argumentative as well as descriptive and narrative superstructures constituting different superstructural configurations. Somewhat superficially presented, humanistic articles are characterised by one global argumentative strategy where a problem at a lower level in the text structure is solved at a higher level through salient dynamic argumentation, characterised by explicit enunciative traces of the author and declarative performatives. The natural science genre is characterised on the other hand by two superstructural configurations at the same level, one static descriptive configuration and one dynamic argumentative configuration. In this way research data and the interpretation of them is systematically held apart.

An important observation made by Breivega is that the use of genres normally correlates with the object of study of the discipline. Texts written in the textual culture constituted by historical science systematically use the humanistic genre, while articles in the field of medicine routinely utilise the natural science genre. The relation between text structure and doxa seems determinative. Still, the relationship between doxa and text structure is contingent. Breivega observes that amongst the three disciplines she studied, sciences that investigate cultural facts may adopt the textual norms of the natural sciences, while the opposite does not occur. Researchers in the field of linguistics may utilise both textual norms while researchers working with cultural data in medicine, for instance psychiatrists, never use the textual norm of the humanistic tradition.

Breivega explains these findings by referring to the textual traditions in the different disciplines, and that the text norms constituting distinct genre-formats at a superstructural level, have attained an autonomy that leaves researchers working inside the different sciences insensitive to the relationship between scientific paradigms and their doxa and rhetorical strategies. Essentially, one writes as one is supposed to and has been socialisised to through one's university training. From a rhetorical point of view a functional explanation is also relevant. The text norm the researcher selects in writing his or her text is the one that is understood as the most convenient resource for an article capable of persuading the participants of the relevant text culture. When researchers who analyse cultural data utilise the text norms of the natural sciences, adapted to describe and explain naturalistic data, as linguists occasionally do, and psychiatrists always do, this may imply that the text norms of the natural sciences are considered more empowered, and therefore more prestigious than others. The text norm of the natural sciences tradition may be understood as a prescriptive model for other scientific writing. It may also implicate that researchers using this text norm want to redefine what has normally been understood as cultural phenomena as natural facts, indicating a shift from a hermeneutic tradition in favour of a naturalistic one. This is of course typical of the prominent tradition in linguistics, especially since the breakthrough of chomskian linguistics.

Thanks to Breivega's study two interesting ethical problems relevant to the rhetoric of science have been explicated. First of all that textual variation is due to different doxa, and that this ecological variation inside the complex field of science must be recognised and respected. At the same time, the study indicates that there seems to be a genre hierarchy at stake attributing different status to different texts. Breivega seem to support the impression presented elsewhere in this article, that the scientification of society together with the commodification of science at universities as well as in society at large, has led to a strengthening of the cultural status of the natural science genre, and a weakening of the status of the humanist tradition. In popular opinion, natural science articles objectively describe the facts of life, while humanist articles interpret them subjectively. This opposition establishes important political issues regarding the position of research in society where the rhetoric of science may present important insights.

5.3 Paradigms in conflict: the textual norms of two competing schools in literary criticism

As mentioned earlier, the Nordic projects studying the subject oriented text cultures in Norway and Sweden, were focused on describing the historical development of different text cultures, including those of science. In the international literature the historical development of the text norms and registers of the experimental article has received a prominent place. Less studied – if studied at all - is the development of text norms and registers in the humanistic disciplines. It is probable that this reality might be explained by our prior conclusions that the genres of natural sciences lie at the top of the status hierarchy. The development of modernity is characterised by the fact that the natural sciences and the technologies that partly result from research done in these disciplines, have taken over the position of the humanistic disciplines, especially regarding rhetoric. The disciplines of the human sciences are becoming redefined from their being the main instrument for enculturalisation of human beings, to having the status of sciences that are supposed to deliver arguments in favour of distinct national or regional cultures. It is in this historical context that the discipline of literary studies or literacy science (as it is called in Scandinavian societies) has been developed and established. This establishment started in the end of the 19th century, and the approach in the first decades was dominantly historical. The aim of these sciences was to document literary texts construed in different nations or regions in the course of time. Thus, the discipline was originally known as "literary history". In the 1930's an alternative tradition appeared advocating a completely different doxa, based on the autonomy of the literary work, combined with the assumption that some literary works represented eternal, and therefore universal, aesthetic values and ideas. It is important that this alternative aesthetic-philosophical school was not an import of international trends, but originally developed in Norwegian scientific communities. In both these traditions the artefacts studied were considered valuable texts. The selection of texts from the era of Romanticism on, was more or less reserved for the belle arts of poems, dramas, novels and short stories. These were written and published mainly in book format, and selected, printed and distributed by publishers and sold in quality-oriented book stores

In Jonas Bakken's PhD. thesis "The Rhetoric of Literacy Science" (Norwegian: *Litteraturvitenskapens retorikk*) he studied whether the hypothesis holds that different text culture communities dominated by different doxas develop different text norms. As the KIAP-project articles in this volume demonstrate, the variation of a number of stylistic features' co-varies with the science of the text more than with the language used. Bakken criticises this approach, as well as the idea that there should be a necessary relation between doxa and text norm, a hypothesis presented and discussed by Breivega. Instead he opts for a rhetorical approach where the text norms utilised in the different scientific text cultures are explained by the hypothesis that a researcher will unconsciously adopt the textual strategy that is the most persuasive in a given cultural context. Consequently, the scientific writer is adapting to the established text norm. This is of course a functional explanation of a specific behaviour. But as Bakken shows, intentional explanations are also possible: a researcher may use an alternative textual norm that suits his aims in a specific context, representing in that way a deviation from conventional practice. Bakken's analysis of the two text cultural communities fighting for hegemony in literature research indicate that this model is a relevant description of what happens when text norms are developed and utilised. It is then possible to have conflicting text norms in the same field of science, reflecting fundamental differences in doxa. That this is a relevant approach for the rhetoric of a number of sciences that study man and culture is obvious. Most of these sciences are involved in serious epistemological debates and conflicts, and one may therefore assume that there are variations in rhetorical strategies. Studies such as Bakken's also present the evidence necessary for the study of textual cultures and the interactions within, as well as between them from a power perspective. In the Norwegian case, conflict between different schools, representing different doxa and utilising partly different text norms and registers, went on for decades at all possible levels of the university system. Seen from this angle, in these particular cases scientific articles were used as weapons in an intellectual and academic battle. It was only at a superficial level that these articles demonstrated testable descriptions of a reality external to the texts, or open and reasonable forms of argumentation.

6. Lessons learnt from Nordic research on subject-oriented texts: challenges and further research

In this article I have presented studies of scientific and academic writing and texts in a context of Norwegian and Swedish research on subject oriented texts from a rhetoric of science position. I have demonstrated that rhetoric of science does not necessarily represent either a subjective idealism or a radical constructivism, but is consistent with the basic propositions of scientific realism and the ethos of mainstream science, as formulated by Merton. However, these Nordic studies of scientific text cultures and academic texts demonstrate clearly that there is a massive degree of diachronic and synchronic variation in how different scientific disciplines represent themselves in texts and how they interact with researchers who are competent - and therefore considered participants - in these specific disciplines. This variation reflects different concepts of truth, different doxa, different communicative goals, and different practices. The experience of these Nordic research projects on subject-oriented texts shows that in Nordic countries as well as internationally, research on this variation is limited and incoherent. The lessons to be learned from this experience are that this research must be developed and a text-anthropological strategy must be adopted, where more global and local contextual studies are combined with studies of communicative practices, as well as of the utterances and texts that are the outcomes of such practices. In the Anglo-American cultural sphere researchers such as John Swales, Charles Bazerman, Carol Berkenkotter and Catharine Shryer have delivered important contributions to this potential new discipline. But even in this important and dominant cultural sphere it is relevant to note that the research is sparse.

But why should we study the rhetoric of science from an text-anthropological angle? It is of course important as a traditional documentation project, or as a field of research that delivers the raw data for practical and instrumental uses in the acculturation of new students or researchers. As demonstrated in this article, the Nordic project has developed a another aim which is unique to them, however influenced by and established within the broader rhetoric tradition: the analysis of rhetorical strategies of researchers as a basis for ethical reflection on the influence and power of science, scientific communication and thought, both in scientific text cultures themselves, as well as in society at large. The advanced democracies of the west are now in a post-industrialist epoch, with the concurrent development of a so-called "knowledge society". In such a knowledge society, science is even more important than before as a way of thinking, and as a way of acting. This acknowledgement is fundamental for the education and research policies of all Nordic countries. The power of science has of course been considerable for many centuries, but in post-modern society science has transgressed its borders, and established itself as the most influential source and background for political as well as intellectual debate. Science has become commodified and society has become scientified. Through the educational system in all post-industrialised societies our children are preoccupied with science for at least 13 years of their lives, if not more. A broad text-anthropological discipline that interacts with the rhetoric of science-tradition could deliver a fundamental means for understanding, reflection upon and active criticism of this kind of society. That is the fundamental lesson to be learnt from these three Nordic research projects on subject-oriented texts, and that is probably the best argument around for the centrality of the study of the rhetoric of science.

7. References

Aristotle. *Rhetoric.* http://www.public.iastate.edu/~honeyl/Rhetoric/
Bakken, Jonas. *Litteraturvitenskapens retorikk* (The rhetoric of literacy science). Ph.D-thesis. Oslo: University of Oslo, 2006
Bazerman, Charles. *Shaping Written Knowledge.* Madison: University of Wisconsin Press, 1988.
Berge, Kjell Lars. "Det vitenskapelige studiet av sakprosa" (The scientific study of subject oriented texts*). In* Berge, K.L, Breivega, K. R., Roksvold, T & Tønnesson, J., *Fire blikk på sakprosaen.* 9-74. Oslo: Sakprosa 1, 2001.
Breivega, Kjersti R. *Vitskaplege argumentasjonsstrategiar* (Scientific argumentation strategies). Oslo: Sakprosa 8, 2003.
de Beaugrande, Robert. "Performative speech acts in linguistic theory: The rationality of Noam Chomsky". In *Journal of Pragmatics.* 29. 1-39, 1998
Gjerstad, Magne. *Kan Thomas Mathisen forsvares?* (Thomas Mathisen on trial). Oslo: Sakprosa 5, 2001.

Goody, Jack. *The Logic of Writing and the Organization of Society.* Cambridge: Cambridge UP, 1986.

Gross, Alan. *Starring the Text. The Place of Rhetoric in Science Studies.* Carbondale: Southern Illinois Press, 2006.

Ledin, Per. *Veckopressens historia.* Del II (The history of the weekly journals, Part II). Stockholm: Svensk sakprosa 29, 2000.

Melander, Björn and Björn Olsson, eds. *Verklighetens texter* (The texts of reality). Lund: Studentlitteratur, 2001.

Prelli, Lawrence J. *A Rhetoric of Science. Inventing Scientific Discourse.* Columbia: University of South Carolina, 1989.

Schryer, Catherine. "The Lab v. the clinic: Sites of competeing genres." In Freedman, A & Medway, P. *Genre and the new Rhetoric.* Taylor & Francis: London. 105-124, 1994.

Swales, John. *Other Floors. Other Voices. A Textography of a Small University Building.* London: Lawrence Erlbaum, 1998.

Aas, Hedda. *Meningsskaping i vitenskapelig tekst* (Meaning making in scientific texts). Oslo: University of Oslo, 1999.

PART II
DISCIPLINE FOCUS

CHAPTER FOUR

AUTHORITY AND EXPERT VOICES IN THE DISCOURSE OF HISTORY

MARINA BONDI

1. Introduction

The interplay between averral and attribution (Sinclair 1987) can be seen as a key aspect of academic discourse as such. Averral is the default condition of a text, where the reader can assume that the responsibility for each proposition lies with the speaker or writer. Attribution, on the other hand, is the case where a proposition is indicated as deriving from a source.[1] Building on this distinction, Groom (2000) distinguishes issues of *identification*, the ways in which a writer makes clear who is responsible for a given proposition through averral and attribution, from issues of *position*, expressing the dominant voice in the text, or the ways in which a writer develops a credible authoritative persona whose voice is dominant. Our own interest in this paper will be rather on issues of position.

Academic discourse studies have often placed great emphasis on citation practices in research and on the tools of reporting (Swales 1981, Thompson and Ye 1991, Tadros 1993, Hunston 1993, 1995, 2000, 2004, Thompson 1996, Hyland 1999, 2000, Thompson 2000, 2005, Fløttum 2003, Bondi 2005), while comparative studies have revealed significant variation in the use of attribution across disciplines or disciplinary fields (Parry 1998, Hyland 2000, Fløttum 2003, Thompson 2005, Dahl 2004, Charles 2005, Groom 2005). Not enough attention, however, has been paid to different types of textual voices, and to disciplinary variation in constructing the writer's identity (Ivanič 1998). Hyland (2001, 2002) and Fløttum (2005) provide interesting cross-disciplinary studies of forms of self-mention, but their main focus is on self-mention, writer visibility and interaction with the reader. Our purpose will be to explore

---

[1] For a definition, see also Tadros (1993), Hunston (1993, 2000).

different ways in which the writer constructs his/her own authoritative persona through specific forms of averral and attribution in historical article openings.

The role of attributed discourse in history has attracted the attention of many: Schreibner (2001) has explored the "quotation fever" of historians in relation to the epistemology of the discipline, whereas Hunston (1993) has offered useful suggestions as to the tendency of historians to choose attributing verbs that signal complex relationships between the historian and the attributor. The openings of historical research articles, in particular, seem to find their starting point in moves that–rather than placing the article in the context of a debate within the discourse community–make intensive use of reported discourse in forms of dramatization of the voices of sources (Silver and Bondi 2004). Assuming that disciplinary peculiarities can be usefully studied from the point of view of cross-disciplinary studies (Fløttum and Rastier eds. 2003; Hyland and Bondi eds. 2006), our focus will be on authority and expert voices in the discourse of history, but we will use the discourse of economics for comparative purposes, with a view to illuminating variation within the humanities and social science.

This study proposes an overview of the types of voices involved in the presentation of historical research and discusses them with reference to the role they play in the construction of the writer's identity. We will take a broad view of the writer's voice, including in this perspective not only the most overt interactional features, i.e. those bringing the writer's "management of the unfolding of the text to the surface" (Thompson 2001:61), engaging writers and readers explicitly in the process, but also the more discrete interactive features, i.e. language choices that show "the writer's awareness of a participating audience and the ways he or she seeks to accommodate its probable knowledge, interests, rhetorical expectations and processing abilities" (Hyland 2005: 49) The voices involved in historical discourse–whether writer's discourse or attributed discourse–reveal different degrees of awareness of the events reported in the text, thus contributing to a multiplicity of perspectives on the events. Focusing on the interplay between textual voice and time setting, we will see how information is often provided not only for the sake of reconstructing temporal sequences, but also to establish the writer's own authority and position.

In particular, focusing on averral, we will notice how the Writer establishes a position by evaluating both entities or events in the world of the narrative and the sources used to reconstruct events. Different lexicalizations will be shown to express modal evaluation–the writer's taking responsibility for the predication and the predicate's characterization in terms of certainty–and affective evaluation–categorizing phenomena and evaluating them in terms of desirability. We will also show how the peculiar temporal perspective of historical discourse allows the writer access to further knowledge, e.g. in speculation about future events. Focusing on attribution, on the other hand, we will look at writers showing forms of alignment and disalignment with the voice of experts, i.e. sources that are given voice in the text. The voices of experts (Expert voices) will be shown to have a significant role in the construction of the writer's argument.

The basic theoretical framework for a description of academic voices in the discourse of history is presented in Section 2. After introducing methods and materials in Section 3, we will deal with writer roles and types of evaluation in Section 4, while focusing on the role of expert voices and their dialogue with the writer in Section 5.

2. Academic voices in the discourse of history

The choice of history as the subject matter of our analysis is clearly linked to its very specific status in the field of disciplinary discourses: keeping in mind the basically argumentative nature of academic discourse, history stands out for the obvious tension between narrative and argument in the basic structure of its discourse. If temporal notions definitely play a major role in historical discourse (cf. Eggins et al. 1993, Martin 1993a, b, Coffin 1997, 2003, Veel and Coffin 1996, and particularly Martin 2003), especially through the representation of time sequences and time settings ("packaging time", Martin 2003: 28), it is the interpretative dimension of historical narratives that we are particularly interested in.

Coffin (1997) distinguishes three types of stance in narratives:

- **Recorder stance**, characterizing factual chronicles, devoid of explicitly attitudinal lexis;
- **Interpreter stance**, typically expressing judgements of behaviour (in terms of fortune, abilities, courage etc);
- **Adjudicator stance**, expressing moral judgements (in terms of truthfulness, ethics…), which she sees as often avoided in academic history.

If it is true that Recorder position is often deployed to convince readers of the plausibility of interpretation, a dialogic view of argument suggests adding yet another dimension, which may be called the dimension of academic argument (with reference to the dialogic, rather than monologic structure of argument). The writer does not only interpret events: he or she also argues for his or her own position in the context of a disciplinary debate, in a complex dialogic pattern with the reader. History is not just account and interpretation of events, but also dialogic argumentation of the interpretation put forward.

Looking at academic history from the point of view of discourse, therefore, we can think of history as basically recount or narrative, but at the same time also interpretation of narrated events and dialogic argumentation of the interpretation. Adapting Coffin (1997), we can say that the writer him/herself will accordingly appear in different roles–as **Recounter**, as **Interpreter** and as **Academic Arguer**, as set out in Table 1[2]:

Table 1. History: Textual dimension and Writer's roles

Textual Dimension	W's Role
Recount/narrative	(W as Recounter)
Interpretation of narrated events	(W as Interpreter)
Dialogic argumentation of the interpretation	(W as Academic Arguer)

Starting from a view of language use as being always interactive, we accept that meanings emerge from use in contexts that are shaped by the cultural, historical and institutional forces that characterize those contexts. The distinction between Interpreter role and Academic Arguer role is thus more one of degree of explicitness than of kind. The Writer is presenting his or her own arguments in ways that are aware of a reader in both cases, but overtly highlighting different aspects of his role of historian.

According to Bakhtin (1981), any act of speech is intrinsically dialogic, not only because it presupposes interaction with an addressee, but also because it includes a multiplicity of voices. Bakhtin's emphasis is on the heteroglossia and internal stratification of any language, on the dynamic process of taking and using another person's words or thoughts as a natural element of communication, and on the different degrees of distance that one may assume as to one's own discourse. Writers often include potential objections to their own claims in patterns of temporary agreement with theses, which are then refuted, or revised in subsequent claims. They signal sequences of concessions and contrasting statements through a combination of contrastive connectors with markers of epistemic or attitudinal evaluation .

Our own focus here, however, is on the ways in which writers may present their persona at the beginning of the text through careful display of their own evaluative authority or by positioning themselves at some distance from the temporal perspective or the evaluative position of other voices in the text.

---

[2] For a different classification of author roles (researcher, writer, arguer and evaluator), see Fløttum, Dahl and Kinn 2006.

Textual voices can be classified, according to their status in discourse, into two basic categories:

a) **Discourse Participants** (DP), when reference is made to the writer, the reader and the discourse community at large (whether by general attribution or citation of specific bibliographical references);
b) **Discourse Actors** (DA), when the voices projected are those of historical characters or sources (acting as "witnesses" and "expert witnesses" in the reconstruction of events).

Building on this distinction, other elements can be considered. A key issue in historical discourse turns out to be access to knowledge. This is determined by the time axis/es that the single textual voice can relate to. Historical discourse is typically characterized by two time reference axes:
a) the time of **Discourse** - the "now" of the writer and the reader;
b) the time(s) of the **Story**–the "now" (or the variety of time settings) characterizing the specific issue/event dealt with. [3]
A preliminary overview of academic voices is offered in Figure 1, showing the close link between the types of voices, the role in discourse and the time axis.

Figure 1. Academic voices: status in discourse and time axes

Discourse Participants		Discourse Actors	
Time of Discourse	Writer	Historical characters	Time of the Story
	Reader		
	Discourse Community: other historians, called into argumentative dialogue	Expert Voices: other historians, journalists, diarists etc used as verbal sources	

In term's of Sinclair's (1981) planes of discourse, Discourse participants (DP) and Time of Discourse will characterize the "interactive plane", reflecting the ongoing interaction, whereas Discourse Actors (DA) and Time of the Story will characterize the "autonomous plane", reflecting the world represented in the text.

---

[3] The feature is quite obviously typical of any narrative and has been widely studied by scholars with an interest in fictional narrative. Chatman talks of "story-time–the duration of the purported events of the narrative" and "discourse-time–the time it takes to peruse the discourse" (1978: 62) A similar distinction is made by Weinrich (1964/2004: 38-39) between *erzählte Zeit* (story time) and *Erzählzeit* (narrative time).

In terms of access to knowledge, though, the Writer and the Reader have a privileged point of view in time. Their access is not limited to the time of Discourse: through their sources, they can get access to the time of the Story and, through their background knowledge, their awareness of the specific past examined extends to later knowledge, up to the present of discourse. Their expert sources, on the other hand, have direct knowledge of the time of the story, but their access to knowledge is restricted to the past. Both Writer and Expert can thus display some kind of expertise, but the Writer exerts a degree of control over time sequences and over Expert Voices themselves: Writers can choose what to quote, how to interpret the quote, how to position themselves regarding the quote, etc.

Following Silver and Bondi (2004: 144), on the basis of these parameters, we can distinguish two basic types of openings– "Phenomenic" and "Epistemic– with their combinations.

We label **Phenomenic** those openings which narrate an event/ phenomenon and remain within a closed temporal framework, where the reader is offered "immediate" contact with the object of study. They often include voices of Discourse Actors. The time setting and the temporal reference axis is given by the object of study (historical episode: time of the Story)

In **Epistemic** openings, instead, clear reference is made to how a particular case or event could be situated into a larger interpretative/ theoretical debate, i.e. the event examined is placed within a specific interpretative framework or within the context of disciplinary debate. The voices of Discourse Participants are dominant. The time setting and the temporal reference axis is given by the Writer's present (time of Discourse).

If we look at historical openings in a cross-disciplinary perspective (cf. also Bondi and Silver 2004, Bondi forthcoming), we notice a great variety of forms of attributed discourse. On the whole there is a dominant role of Discourse Actors as against Discourse Participants and recourse to metadiscursive contextualization (debate within the discourse community) is limited. Purely epistemic openings do occur, but they are not the most frequent choice. Once again, cross-disciplinary variation can give some quantitative indication. As I have shown elsewhere using the corpora that constitute the basis for this study (Bondi forthcoming), Epistemic openings - i.e. openings that place the paper in the context of disciplinary debate or development - are largely dominant in economics (62.7%) and openings with an epistemic element of some sort account for a good 85% of the openings (319/375). In history, on the other hand, only 40.3 % of the openings in the corpus (113/280) can be accounted for as somehow containing epistemic elements and a mere 11% (31/280) is limited to the voices of Discourse Participants (writer, reader and discourse community). History tends to mix voices and include both DA and DP (cf. "weaving voices",

Silver and Bondi 2004) to a greater extent. As we hope to show in Section 5, it also tends to cut across discourse planes in interesting ways.

3. Materials and tools for analysis

The present study is based on a small corpus of historical openings, i.e. the opening section up to and including the second paragraph of each article. The choice of studying the first two paragraphs was meant to offer material that showed the starting point of the article, but also the direction taken, the dynamics of the beginning section of the text. We thus chose to start from positional rather than functional units, on the belief that the linearity of texts is a major constraint and that initial choices will play a major role in the development and interpretation of any text.

In order to highlight features of disciplinary discourse, a comparable corpus of openings in economics was also used, on the assumption that comparison will illuminate peculiarities. The two corpora are thus taken to be representative of research writing in different disciplines. They are about 100,000 words each and include all research articles published in the years 1999 and 2000 in the journals listed in Table 2 below.

Table 2. Composition of the two small corpora used for the study

Corpora	Journals	Total No. of openings	Total No. of words
History	Labour History Review (LHR) Historical Research (HR) Gender & History (GH) Journal of European Ideas (JEI) Journal of Medieval History (JMH) Journal of Interdisciplinary History (JIH) Journal of Social History (JSH) Studies in History (SH) American Quarterly (AQ) American Historical Review (AHR)	280	95,682

Economics	European Economic Review (EER) European Journal of Political Economy (EJoPE), International Journal of Industrial Organization (IJoIO) International Review of Economics and Finance (IRoEF) Journal of Corporate Finance (JoCF) Journal of Development Economics (JoDE) Journal of Socio-Economics (JoSE) The North American Journal of Economics and Finance (NAJEF)	375	100,572

The study combines qualitative and quantitative analysis and draws on a number of major approaches for its basic methodology. In particular, it draws on Discourse and Genre Analysis for issues of contextual interpretation, as it considers both the macro-field of social action (academic discourse) and the characteristics of the functional generic structure of the research article and its introduction (Swales' CARS model)[4], with a view to disciplinary variation in introductions (cf. Samraj 2002). The notions are used as an interpretative key to our focus on article openings as a privileged site for the construction of the writer's persona. From Corpus Linguistics, we borrow tools for the analysis of the lexical features of openings. Especially when focusing on evaluative lexis, we make use of some of the functions of *Wordsmith Tools* (Scott 1998), in particular word-list frequencies and key-words (see also Scott and Trimble 2006), as well as concordances and collocations.

More specific tools for language analysis are needed for the two key language areas under investigation: evaluative meanings and temporal notions. The notion of Evaluation (Hunston and Thompson eds. 2000) becomes specifically relevant for the study of authorial stance. Hunston's approach draws together different types of evaluation (Hunston 2000):

a) **Status**, including what others call Epistemic stance or modal evaluation, is primarily concerned with propositions and with the writer taking responsibility for the predication or characterizing the predicate in terms of likelyhood;

---

[4] The model is based on a three-step structure: 1) Establishing a territory (Claiming centrality and/or Making topic generalization(s) and/or Reviewing items of previous research); 2) Establishing a niche (Counter-claiming or Indicating a gap or Question raising or Continuing a tradition); 3) Occupying the niche (Outlining purposes or Announcing present research, Announcing principal findings, Indicating RA structure) (Swales 1990:141).

b) **Value**, including what other call Attitudinal stance or affective evaluation, is primarily concerned with entities and with the writer categorizing phenomena / evaluating them in terms of desirability.

Drawing on both aspects of evaluation, our analysis centres on how how the writer constructs his/her authoritative position and on how other textual voices can be used to co-construct the writer's position in the text. Forms of attribution can also be analyzed in terms of modal and affective evaluation along two lines: the writer's evaluation of the textual voice and the textual voice's evaluation of the attributed proposition.

Tools from Systemic Funtional Linguistics analyses of historical discourse also become relevant in the study of temporal notions. The realization of temporal notions (**Time Setting**) is central to many accounts of narrative and historical discourse (Eggins et al 1993, Martin 1993a, 1993b, Coffin 1996, 1997, Veel and Coffin 1996, and especially Martin 2003). Martin (2003), in particular, distinguishes time setting from mere time sequence, which is often marked by temporal connectors or simply left implicit and inferable from the succession of events. Time setting is based on periodization typically signalled by time adverbials whose main purpose is to identify phases in the text: "We hop through the past instead of walking through each event one after another" (Martin 2003: 24-25). In moving from personal recount to institutional history, there is a shift from mere sequencing of events to phasing of events, which allows narration to focus on agency and aims at producing generalizations about people or events. Phases are identified (and often nominalized) as historical periods: the dynamism of events is thus given a superimposed macro-structure which turns sequences of events into a hierarchy of time units enclosed in other time units. (Martin 2003: 28).

Our focus will be on instances of references to the future in the course of the narrative: while keeping to the time setting of the event under examination, the writer may often refer to future events. Forms of "Future in the Past" may be either attributed to characters or sources (reporting what they expected, predicted, desired etc.) or simply averred, i.e. statements about what the Writer knows actually happened or turned out to be true. Unattributed forms of "Future in the Past" can be used to highlight Writer's expertise and knowledge of future events, as well as to support his/her interpretation of events.

4. Writer roles and types of evaluation

4.1 The Writer as Interpreter

The interpretative dimension of history, as defined in Section 2, can be seen at play in the two main areas of evaluation: Status and Value. Example 1 offers ample evidence of the clear link between the two. The writer does not simply sequence events (recounting), but rather interprets them. The text moves from recounting to interpreting right from the very first clause, which is an example of the simplest pattern of evaluative grammar (Hunston and Sinclair 2000): the War of Austrian Succession is identified as *a unique experience*. The Value thus attributed to the event–signalling its importance and historical relevance–constitutes a significant interpretative claim on the part of the historian, which is clearly justified in the rest of the first paragraph by numerous references to the Writer's knowledge of previous and successive events. The second paragraph goes back to the central setting of the narrative and works out a similar pattern for the sequence of steps conjuring up the army.

(1) The War of Austrian Succession was a *unique* experience for the American people for it was *the first time* that the British government raised large numbers of American troops to serve in the West Indies. Before the War of Austrian Succession, with the exception of attacks against the French in Canada, such as the Walker expedition to Quebec in 1711, American soldiers had almost exclusively been employed by American provincial governments in operations against Indians.1 All of this *would change* in the War of Austrian Succession: 3,000 American troops *would be dispatched* during the War of Austrian Succession to the West Indies to serve with regular British military forces in order to attack the Spanish. The Vernon-Cathcart expedition against Cartagena on the Spanish Main, in 1741, was thus *the first time* in which large numbers of Americans *would serve* outside the mainland of North America. Moreover, the Vernon-Cathcart expedition to the West Indies *would place unusual demands* on the American colonies. And the American people, especially their elected colonial assemblies, *would respond* to some of the burdens of the expedition by placing local American interests before the requirements of imperial warfare.

The plan for the assault on Cartagena, which was formulated by the British government in the last months of 1739, called for a force of eight regiments of British soldiers to be sent from the British Isles to the West Indies. At the same time an additional force of approximately 3,000 troops *was to be* recruited in the North American colonies and sent to the West Indies. The forces from Britain and North America *were to* rendezvous at Jamaica where, in conjunction with British naval forces, they *were to* undertake an attack on Cartagena.2 The decision to raise a force of Americans *to be* employed in operations in the West Indies apparently grew out of the belief, in London, that 'every part of our Dominions, in proportion to their strength and numbers should contribute to the promoting of the common cause',3 and that there 'is a very great number of good men in our colonies in America which may be used with very great advantage against either France or Spain'. (HR 2000)

The whole of the first paragraph above is determined by the need to emphasize the uniqueness of the experience. This is done, not only through Value-attributes like *unique, first, unusual*, but also by careful use of Status-attributes. The systematic choice of modal *would* qualifying all processes after the second sentence somehow dramatizes for the reader the perception of change. Combined used of tense, aspect and modality helps demonstrate the important role of the War as a major divide and at the same time keeps the reader firmly rooted in the time setting established: anything that comes before the beginning of the War is past perfect; the development of the war is "future in the past". The choice of *would* still gives events the status of fact (at least in the awareness of the reader and the writer), but also emphasizes that the events are all future for anyone living before the War, and therefore new and unique experience.

The time sequence of events can still be inferred from the text, but the Writer's choice has been not to focus on the narrative sequence (as with a series of simple pasts, for example), but rather on the time setting and the argumentative sequence. The specific Status created by the time/ tense/ aspect combination is clearly functional to supporting the interpretation offered by the Writer. Keeping the time perspective so clearly rooted at that specific point in time (the outbreak of the war), the writer helps the reader identify the two periods (before and after the outbreak) as radically separate and dramatizes change.

The writer's interpretation of the importance of the war in the previous example may well be a major argumentative claim, which distinguishes his/her position from other historians. There are, however, no explicit signals of this distinctiveness. Many openings, on the other hand, clearly show that the writer is not only involved in justifying a claim, but in dialogically arguing the claim, so as to place it in the context of a debate, signalling for example the originality and importance of his/her own interpretation, rather than of the subject matter.

4.2 The Writer as Academic Arguer

If the Example 1 above foregrounded the role of the Writer as Interpreter, other examples might foreground the Writer as Academic Arguer, involved in a debate within the discourse community. This is typically the case when opening moves establishing "the territory" and "the niche" (Swales 1990: 141; 2004: 226-233) are realized by reviewing items of previous research and counter-claiming or indicating a gap.

Example 2 provides such an instance of movement from interpreting to arguing. It also shows how evaluations of Status and Value can be attributed both to the subject matter under investigation and to other interpretations of the subject matter. The opening starts by identifying a phenomenon to be explained (the development of larger and more differentiated types of housing in the first quarter of the XVIII century) and reports previous interpretations of the phenomenon in terms of a quest for gentility. The interpretation in terms of class distinctions is given a Status of probability (*probably true*), but the theory proposed by the writer–an interpretation in terms of gender distinctions–is given greater value in terms of desirability, presented as it is in terms of moving *beyond* (conventionally "positive") and being *more subtle*.

> (2) *Introduction*. Beginning in the first quarter of the eighteenth century many colonial elites built homes modeled on England's lower gentry. These dwellings were different in both size and function from earlier houses. Not only were they larger, but they divided up hitherto undifferentiated space into separate rooms where specialized social interactions took place and where the public part of the house could be segregated from the private. *Scholarly discussion* about the new spatial arrangements in the great house *has focused upon* an aspiring, nouveau-riche elite's quest for gentility.
>
> Ornate rooms signaled wealth and taste, and therefore social superiority, as the wealthy invested their objects and their homes with meanings, expressed through an encoded polite behaviour, which, *it has been argued*, sharpened class distinctions. *Such a process is probably true, but this essay moves beyond* gentility *to argue that* the spatial resources made available by the building of eighteenth-century mansions permitted the formation of multiple gendered publics. It assumes that colonial mansions were both mirrors of and metaphors for colonial society and asks what publics were created through differential access to and use of space, how these publics bound people together into both more local and more widespread communities of interest and ultimately power, and how these publics became more gendered over time. To explore this *more subtle use of space* this essay utilizes the theoretical insights of Jürgen Habermas, Karen Hansen, and Hannah Arendt on the construction of public spheres to show the process through which real as opposed to theoretical publics evolved. (JOSH 1999)

The Writer's authority is often displayed through attributions of Value and Status. Value-words like *unique* (Example 1) or *subtle* (Example 2) signal the importance or significance of the Writer's position and may contrast it with other interpretations. The role played by evaluative lexis in this strategy can be seen by focusing on Value-words in openings and studying how they feature in frequency lists and in key-words (see 4.3. below). Status qualifications, while clearly oriented to constructing the world of the text, may also contribute to constructing the Writer's authority. Reference to future in the past (as with *would* in example 1) and careful control of changes in time settings may help writers display knowledge about future events, thus showing their expertise and differentiating from their own sources (see 4.4).

4.3 Value: Signalling Importance/Significance

Value statements like those in Example 1 and 2 seem to characterize openings. From a functional point of view, they can be justified by the presence of functional moves like "claiming centrality", "counter-claiming" or "indicating a gap" (Swales 1990: 141; 2004: 226-233).

The impression of their importance can be supported by a preliminary overview of the role of Value-words in the frequency lists provided by *Wordsmith tools* (Scott 1998). We can see that openings are characterized by many intrinsically evaluative words, mostly "comparatives" : *more, new, most, such, first, only, other* and *important* (76 occurrences) are all among the first most frequent 100 words. Going down the list we find many other word forms: *great* (55), *interest* (47), *particular* (47), *importance* (40), *particularly* (35) *significant* (33), *considerable* (26), *significance* (25). As the figures suggest, these are all fairly frequent: we can count on roughly 1-2 occurrences each per 10 openings.

Comparison of the frequency list of historical openings with the list of economic openings produces Key-words, as defined by Scott (1998; see also Scott and Tribble 2006: 55-88): word forms that are significantly more or less frequent in one corpus or text as against a reference corpus or text. The higher frequency of words like *history* or *historians* in the historical corpus will hardly be surprising, of course, because clearly determined by the object of the texts. The presence of an evaluative word like *significance*, on the other hand, is not determined by the subject matter, but could be related to preferred patterns of evaluation. The word is indeed identified as a positive key-word in comparison to economics (26 vs 3 occurrences), whereas another evaluative word - *expected* - is classified as negative key-word, significantly less frequent in history than in economics (10 vs 54 occurrences).

The presence of *significance* and *expected* in statistically significant variation across the two comparable corpora suggests that there may be a preference for different parameters of evaluation (Thompson and Hunston 2000: 23-24) in the two corpora: history seems to privilege relevance, whereas economics favours expectedness.

The parameters, in their turn, could be variously related to the aims of the discipline. History aims at interpretation and often recurs to value-laden words to draw attention to the significance of events. Economics, on the other hand, aims at predicting events and in thus more interested in Status, in how predictable and expected things are.

4.4 Status: displaying privileged knowledge

As we have already said, evaluation of Status can also contribute to creating Writer's identity. Statements about the likelihood of events are not infrequent in history, of course, and they allow the writer to attribute different degrees of certainty to events. What makes the use of *would* in Example 1 stand out as an interesting feature of Writer voice, however, is not simply the attribution of Status: it is the peculiar interplay between Status and time setting.

References to "Future in the Past" can be seen as interesting tools for displaying the Writer's expertise and knowledge of development in history: the Future in the Past allows Writers a double temporal perspective which Discourse Actors don't have: it is prospective from the point of view of the Story, but retrospective from the point of view of Discourse. The text highlights (or temporarily adopts) a double temporal perspective which dissociates the Writer's knowledge from the awareness of historical characters: the reader is reminded that the Writer knows things that were not known at the time of the Story. Future projection thus helps Writers interpret causes and circumstance of the story *ex post*, at the same time also allowing readers to interpret the Writer's argumentative position more clearly.

Would is obviously only one of the tools of future projection, but it's the most frequent signal and we will therefore–within the limited framework of this study–restrict our attention to this single form. *Would* is the most frequent modal in historical openings (with 119 occurrences) (12 ptw). In economics, for comparison, the most frequent modal is *can* (260 occurrences) (26 ptw) and *would* (99 occurrences) has a frequency of 10 ptw.

What is most interesting, however, is to look at the concordances of *would*. The first thing we might notice is fairly obvious: *would* often signals futurity in history, whereas it almost invariably signals hypothesis in economics. In historical openings, every other occurrence of *would* (64/119) is an instance of Future in the Past. Of these 30 are unattributed (Writer voice) and 34 attributed to Discourse Actors. In economic openings, on the other hand, only a very limited number of occurrences are instances of Future in the Past (11/99) and only 2 of these (2/11) are expressions of writer's averral. Besides confirming the importance of narrative in history and of speculation in economics, the data draws attention to the frequency with which openings adopt this double temporal perspective highlighting Writer expertise.

An analysis of concordances and collocates of *would* also shows other interesting features of attributed forms. Markers of attribution in this context are characterized by great lexical variety, both in their verbal forms (*saying, orchestrated, arguing, ensured, considered, doubt , grasp, promising, stated, feared, knew, plotted, guaranteed, predicted, neared, asked, thought, contended, predicted, envisioned…*) and in their nominal forms (*quotations, ackowledgement, prophecy, implication, belief, pursuit…*). Attribution markers often combine with oblique modals/ auxiliaries or negatives/ denials (*would have expected, had expected, could envision, had hoped, giving up hopes that…*) and are clearly divided into both epistemic (e.g. *expect*) and volitional (e.g. *promise*, *fear*) forms: in both cases they tend to be non-factive, they show a pragmatic preference for counterfactual attributions and signal a much lower degree of certainty than Writer's *would*.

The tendency to associate future statements attributed to characters/and experts with counterfactuality goes together with the tendency to emphasize factuality in Writer's averral: the juxtaposition of the two is highlighted in openings where it helps establish Writer's authority and credibility through contrast with Discourse Actors.

5. Writer's dialogue with expert voices

The greater variety of types of voices in the discourse of history can be related to the key role of sources in the epistemology of the discipline. This suggests paying particular attention to the Writer's stance towards the sources, and in particular towards their interpretative function. Expert voices called in to set the scene for historical discourse do not just *recount*, they *interpret* events and data and therefore Writer voices can argue with them.

History makes intensive use of reported discourse in forms of dramatization of the voices of sources/ protagonists, especially in Phenomenic openings (Example 1 above), or in openings that start by focusing on an event but go on with an epistemic contextualization of the possible interpretations of the event (Phenomenic^Epistemic openings, like 2 above).

What becomes particularly interesting is to study patterns of divergence and convergence of voices, in particular Writer's voice and Expert voice. Expert voices are often introduced as direct witnesses of the time, but their introduction in the wider debate is also often an opportunity to highlight the need for the interpretative skills of the Writer and open up dialogue with other voices, typically the discourse community.

Example 3 below shows how Expert voices can clearly dominate an opening: almost all of the first paragraph is taken up by a quotation form Matthew Prior's *Chronica Maiora*, as the fullest and the earliest account of Richard's election. The account itself is quite clearly not a simple recount but an interpretation of events.

(3) During a parliament meeting at Christmas 1256 at Westminster, important news was conveyed. The *fullest* account is given by Matthew Paris in his *Chronica Maiora*:

German envoys arrived, announcing that Earl Richard of Cornwall, King Henry III's younger brother, had been chosen, unanimously and spontaneously, as King of the Romans, that is ruler of Germany and Emperor-elect. This caused some concern, not the least so to Earl Richard himself. He was reluctant to accept the honour, and was only swayed by the advice he received from some of those present. He was told to muster his courage and face the challenges ahead of him. Richard was warned not to follow the example of Robert Curthose, once duke of Normandy, who had refused the crown of Jerusalem when it was offered to him. For this act of pride he had been punished, as fortune deserted him ever afterwards. Moreover, unlike Richard's two predecessors, Henry Raspe and William of Holland, he had not been imposed by the Pope, but had been chosen willingly and freely by the Germans. In fact, his future subjects had already collected a treasure for him and he would be surrounded by friends and relatives. Eventually, Richard accepted his election, promising that he would not rule to acquire worldly gain or glory, but only to set right the affairs of his new realm.1

This passage, the *earliest* narrative account concerning Richard's German career, has *frequently been dismissed as unrealistic, fanciful, and of little historical value*.2 After all, as we will see, Richard's election had been *neither* unanimous, *nor* spontaneous, and Matthew's version of events thus stands *in striking contrast to the surviving documentary evidence*. However, *if* viewed in relation both to the themes and aims of the *Chronica Maiora*, as well as to political events in England, *a different interpretation becomes possible. This account allows us to glimpse* not only the literary techniques employed by Matthew Paris, but also the ambitions and undertakings of the English court, and how it tried to present them. (JOMH 2000)

The second paragraph of the opening is mostly devoted to evaluations of the account itself. It opens with the negative evaluation offered by the discourse community (*unrealistic, fanciful, of little historical value*). The Writer shows temporary agreement (*after all*) with this negative evaluation, by simply denying the unanimous and spontaneous nature of the election, while rapidly taking a different stance (signalled by *however*) and revealing the possibility to get at a different interpretation of the text. The movement from Expert voices to the discourse community and back to the Writer's interpretation of sources allows the Writer to construct his position vis à vis the discourse community and to emphasize the subtlety and originality of his interpretation. This is realized by gradually building up patterns of convergence between Writer voice and Expert voice, while building explicit conflict between Expert voice (and by inference Writer voice) and the discourse community.

The argumentative voice of the Writer may at other times be much less explicitly community-oriented: Writer as Interpreter dominates over Writer as Academic Arguer. Expert voices may then be called in to co-construct the Writer's argument. In Example 4, for instance, there are less explicit signals of alignment/disalignment. But again the interpretation of events makes use of Expert voices. The Writer's evaluation of Expert voice is immediately positive and later only strategically critical: the Expert voice is introduced in terms that are highly appreciative of its authoritativeness (*prestigious, perceptive, well-known*) and that therefore create a solid basis for the interpretation proposed. The second paragraph builds on this by adding three supports for the claim reported: evidence for the claim (*a substantial body of evidence in corroboration of this point*) is provided directly by the Writer's voice. This acts both as an implicit criticism of the prestigious Expert voice (*might have cited*) and as a key element in the construction the Writer's position and authoritative persona. this time vis à vis the protagonists themselves, the Expert.

> (4) In January of 1929, as the Weimar Republic neared the crisis that would shatter its fragile stability, an essay in the *prestigious Deutsche Rundschau* called attention to a distinctive aspect of the era's public culture. Written by a *perceptive* and *well-known* conservative journalist named Paul Fechter, the essay noted the growing prominence of the concept of *Raum*, or space, in German cultural, social and political life. "*Raum* has become current to a heightened degree in the last few years," Fechter wrote. "One finds discussions of *Raum* problems, *Raum* formation, *Raum* systems, etc. One begins to sense that it is more than the divinely ordained residing place of our small life, that in the one word *Raum* a sum of the most wonderful things and concepts has been summarized".
>
> Fechter *might have cited a substantial body of evidence in corroboration of his point*. Spatial analytical perspectives centered upon theories of *Raum* were increasingly prevalent in disciplines ranging from international law to political science, history and sociology. In popular political journals, particularly among the adherents of the volkish "conservative revolution", *Raum* was a standard rhetorical component of analyses of contemporary German political and economic life. And, bridging the gaps between many disciplines, the vigorous school of German Geopolitik was utilizing concepts of *Raum* to spawn a host of new, pseudo-scientific subdisciplines, ranging from "geojurisprudence" to "geomedicine". [HOEI 1999]

Expert voices are thus shown to play a major role in the construction of the writer's argument as well as persona, by creating patterns of conflict and convergence. In Example 3, through a sequence of three types voices (Expert-Discourse community-Writer), an initial situation of conflict preludes to the Writer moving from partial agreement with the discourse community to partial divergence. The Writer's evaluation of Expert voice constructs the Writer's position vis à vis the discourse community (Writer as Academic Arguer). In Example 4, the initial situation is one of convergence between Writer and Expert and the change introduced is just a partial divergence in terms of the evidence available for the interpretation provided. The Writer's evaluation of Expert voice constructs the Writer's position vis à vis the reader.

In both cases sources become textual voices that are used to co-construct the writer's position in the text and textual dialogue cuts across the basic distinctions operated in terms of the interactive and the autonomous plane of discourse. The relationship between the two is one of inclusion, as might be visualized in Figure 2 below.

On the interactive plane, which will always see Reader and Writer interacting in text, the Writer's (dominant) voice will be seen particularly through expressions of writer's evaluation, thus highlighting a view of History as (narrative) interpretation; whereas explicit reference to the Discourse community (and the wider discourse context) will highlight a view of History as (narrative) academic argument.

Figure 2. Textual voices and their interaction

INTERACTIVE PLANE	Writer-Reader interaction	Time of Discourse
Discourse participants → ↓	Writer's dominant voice ↕	→ History as Interpretation
Writer + discourse community ↔	Discourse actors: characters and experts	
→ History as Academic Argument	AUTONOMOUS PLANE	Time of the Story

On the autonomous plane, there will be different types of textual voices belonging to the narrated world: Discourse Actors will be called in as characters in the Story–and their voices will be part of the story itself - or as Expert witnesses, producing an interpretation of the story itself. The autonomous plane, however, is not so autonomous after all, at least not as far as the Writer's voice is concerned. Voices on this plane will still be subject to the writer's point of view, evaluated by the Writer and used to construct his or her position and persona. Textual dialogue will cut across discourse planes.

6. Conclusion

Our study of textual voices has focused on how evaluation (of Value and Status, as in Hunston 2000) can contribute to the construction of the authority and persona of the Writer in historical article openings. Attributions of Value and Status were noticed to highlight the Writer's position, often including both his or her main claim and a self-promotional element of authority. Value-words often signal the importance or significance of the Writer's interpretation and may contrast it with other interpretations. Status qualifications, while clearly oriented to constructing the world of the text, may also contribute to constructing the Writer's authority: reference to Future in the Past was analysed as a case in point, where careful control of changes in time settings may help writers display knowledge about future events, thus showing their expertise and distancing themselves from other voices, including those of their own sources.

The results of the analysis can be related to the role played by time setting and time shifts in narrative and to the role played by sources in historical discourse.

Time setting is a key element in the narrative structure of historical discourse. Time setting (Martin 2003) is often changed in history, not just to take us through the past, but also to construct the Writer's authority through interaction with different textual voices. Time setting shifts allow the Writer to interact with all the other textual voices (characters, sources, discourse community, readers): the tendency to associate future statements attributed to characters/ and experts with counter-factuality can be set against the aura of factuality which is attached to Writer's averral. Juxtaposition of the two is highlighted in openings that otherwise tend to show a preference for focusing on events rather than starting from placing the topic within a disciplinary debate. Future projection helps Writers interpret causes and circumstance of the story *ex post*, from a privileged point of view in time; access to later knowledge up to the present of discourse can also be used as a marker of Writer's authority, sometimes justifying the Writer's argumentative position. By allowing themselves a double perspective or time axis, Writers can present events–whether directly or through Expert voices–and at the same time add future knowledge, thus emphasizing their own expertise and the different possibilities of access to knowledge along the time line.

The role of sources was also shown to contribute widely to the co-construction of the Writer's argument. History is largely the study of documents and language is its principal tool, but the Writer's voice makes distinctive use of interaction with the voices of discourse actors, and Expert voices in particular. When extending the study of evaluative directions to the sources of the historian, we noticed that the presentation of their textual voices always produces evaluation along two lines: Writer's evaluation of the textual voice of the Expert and of Expert's evaluation of the attributed proposition. Patterns of conflict and convergence proved particularly interesting: by moving from conflict to convergence with their sources or vice-versa, Writers do not only gain access to the time of the story and to Expert's interpretation, but they can also build their position vis à vis the discourse community or the reader. When building their own argument on the basis of the interpretation of Expert voices, or calling them in as object of debate within the discourse community, Writers use sources to co-construct their own position in the text and textual dialogue cuts across the interactive and the autonomous plane of discourse.

7. References

Bakhtin, Michail. *The Dialogic Imagination.* M.Honquist ed. Austin, Texas: University of Texas Press, 1981.

Breivega, Kjersti, Trine Dahl and Kjersti Fløttum 2002. "Traces of Self and others in Research Articles. A Comparative Pilot Study of English, French and Norwegian research Articles in Medicine, Economics and Linguistics." *International Journal of Applied Linguistics,* 12/2 (2002): 218-39.

Bondi, Marina. "Metaargumentative Expressions across Genres: Representing Academic Discourse". In *Dialogue within Discourse communities. Metadiscursive Perspectives on Academic Genres*, edited by Julia Bamford & Marina Bondi, 3-28. Tübingen: Niemeyer, 2005.

—. "Polyphony in Academic Discourse: A Cross-cultural Perspective on Historical Discourse". In *Cross-cultural and Cross-linguistic Perspectives on Academic Discourse,* edited by Eija Suomela-Salmi. University of Turku, forthcoming

Bondi, Marina and Marc S. Silver. "Textual voices. A Cross-disciplinary Study of Attribution in Academic Discourse". In: Anderson, L. & J.Bamford (eds.) *Evaluation in Spoken and Written Academic Discourse,* 121-141. Roma: Officina, 2004

Charles, Maggie. "Phraseological Patterns in Reporting Clauses used in Citation: A Corpus-based Study of Theses in two Disciplines", *English for Specific Purposes,* 25(3), (2006): 310-331.

Chatman, Seymour. *Story and Discourse: Narrative Structure in Fiction and Film.* New York: Cornell University press, 1978.

Coffin, Caroline. "Constructing and giving value to the past: an investigation into secondary school history". In *Genre and Institutions: social processes in the workplace and school*, edited by Frances Christie & James R. Martin, 196-230. London: Cassell,1997.

—. Reconstruals of the past: settlement or invasion? The role of judgement analysis. In *Re/reading the past,* edited by James R. Martin & Ruth Wodak, 219-246. Amsterdam: Benjamins, 2003.
Dahl, Trine. "Textual metadiscours ein research articles: a marker of national culture or of academic discipline?". *Journal of Pragmatics* 36(2004): 1807-1825.
Eggins, Sue, Peter Wignell and James R. Martin. "The discourse of history: distancing the recoverable past". In: Ghadessy, M. (ed.) *Register Analysis: theory and practice,* edited by Mohsen Ghadessy, 75-109. London: Pinter, 1993.
Fløttum, Kjersti. "Bibliographical references and polyphony in research articles". In *Academic Discourse: multidisciplinary approaches,* edited by Kjersti Fløttum & François Rastier, 97-119. Oslo, Novus Press,2003.
—. "The self and the others: polyphonic visibility in research articles". *IJAL,* 15/1(2005): 29-44.
Fløttum, Kjersti, Trine Dahl and Torodd Kinn. *Academic Voices.* Amsterdam/ Philadelphia: John Benjamins, 2006.
Fløttum, Kjersti and François Rastier, eds. *Academic Discourse: multidisciplinary*
Groom, Nick. "Attribution and Averral Revisited". In: *Patterns and Perspectives: Insights into EAP Writing Practice,* edited by Paul Thompson, 15-26. University of Reading: CALS, 2000.
—. "Pattern and Meaning across genres and disciplines: an exploratory study". *Journal of English for Academic Purposes,* 4(2005): 257-277.
Hunston, Susan. "Professional Conflict. Disagreement in Academic Discourse". In, *Text and Technology. In Honour of John Sinclair,* edited by Mona Baker, Gill Francis & Elena Tognini-Bonelli, 115-134.Amsterdam: Benjamins, 1993.
—. "A Corpus Study of some English Verbs of Attribution". *Functions of Language* 2/2 (1995): 133-158.
—. "Evaluation and the planes of discourse: Status and value in persuasive texts". In *Evaluation in Text: Authorial Stance and the Construction of Discourse,* edited by Susan Hunston & Geaoffrey Thompson, 176-207. Oxford: Oxford University Press, 2000.
—. "'It has rightly been pointed out …': Attribution, Consensus and Conflict in Academic Discourse". In *Academic Discourse, Genre and Small Corpora,* edited by Marina Bondi, Laura Gavioli & Marc S. Silver eds., 185-201. Roma: Officina, 2004
Hunston, Susan and Geoffrey Thompson eds. *Evaluation in Text: Authorial Stance and the Construction of Discourse* Oxford: Oxford University Press, 2000.

Hunston, Susan and John Sinclair. "A Local grammar of Evaluation". In *Evaluation in Text: Authorial Stance and the Construction of Discourse*, edited by Susan Hunston & Geaoffrey Thompson, 74-101. Oxford: Oxford University Press, 2000.
Hyland, Ken. "Academic Attribution: Citation and the Construction of Disciplinary Knowledge". *Applied Linguistics* 20/3 (1999): 341-367.
—. *Disciplinary discourses: Social interactions in academic writing*. Harlow: Longman, 2000.
—. "Humble Servants of the Discipline? Self-mention in research articles". *English For Specific Purposes* 20 (2001): 207-226.
—. "Authority and Invisibility: authorial identity in academic writing". *Journal of Pragmatics* 14 (2002a): 1091-1112.
—. *Metadiscourse*. London: Continuum, 2005
Hyland, Ken and Marina Bondi eds.. *Academic Discourse across Disciplines*. Bern: Peter Lang, 2006.
Ivanič, Roz. *Writing and Identity. The discoursal construction of identity in academic writing*. John Benjamins: Amsterdam, 1998.
Martin, James R. "Life as a noun: arresting the universe in science and humanities". In *Writing Science: Literacy and Discursive Power*, edited by Michael A.K. Halliday & James R. Martin, 221-267. Pittsburgh: University of Pittsburgh Press, 1993a.
—. "Technology, Bureaucracy and Schooling: Discoursive Resources and Control". *Cultural Dynamics* 6/1 (1993b): 84-130.
—. "Making history: Grammar for interpretation". In *Re/reading the past*, edited by James R. Martin and Ruth Wodak, 19-57 Amsterdam: Benjamins, 2003.
Martin, James R. and Ruth Wodak eds. *Re/reading the past*. Amsterdam: Benjamins, 2003.
Parry, Sharon. "Disciplinary discourse in doctoral theses". *Higher Education* 36 (1998): 273-299.
Samraj, Betty. "Introductions in Research Articles: variations across disciplines". *English for Specific Purposes* 21/1 (2002): 1-17.
Scott, Michael. *Wordsmith Tools*. Oxford: Oxford University Press, 1998.
Scott, Michael and Christopher Tribble. *Textual Patterns. Key words and corpus analysis in language education*. Amsterdam: Benjamins, 2006.
Silver, Marc S. and Marina Bondi. "Weaving voices: A study of article openings in historical discourse". In *Academic Discourse: Linguistic Insights into Evaluation*, edited by Gabriella Del Lungo Camiciotti & Elena Tognini Bonelli, 141-159. Bern 2004: Peter Lang, 2004.
Sinclair, John. „planes of Discourse". In *The Two-fold Voice: essays in honour of Ramesh Mohan*, 70-89. Salzburg: Salzburg University Press, 1981.

—. "Mirror for a Text". Manuscript, 1987. (Published 1988, *Journal of English and Foreign Languages*, Hyderabad, India, 15-44).
Swales, John. *Aspects of Article Introductions*. Language Studies Unit: University of Aston in Birmingham, 1981.
—. *Genre Analysis*. Cambridge: Cambridge University Press, 1990.
—. *Research Genres*. Cambridge: Cambridge University Press, 2004.
Tadros, Angele. "The Pragmatics of Text Averral and Text Attribution in Academic Texts". In *Data, Description, Discourse,* edited by Michael Hoey, 98-114. London: Collins, 1993.
Thompson, Geoffrey. "Voices in the Text: Discourse Perspectives on Language Reports". *Applied Linguistics* 17/4 (1996): 501-530.
—. "Interaction in academic writing: learning to argue with the reader". Applied Linguistics 22/1 (2001): 58-78.
Thompson, Geoffrey and Yeyun Ye. "Evaluation in the Reporting Verbs Used in Academic Papers". *Applied Linguistics* 12/4 (1991): 365-382.
Thompson, Geoffrey and Susan Hunston. "Introduction". In *Evaluation in Text: Authorial Stance and the Construction of Discourse,* edited by Susan Hunston & Geaoffrey Thompson, 1-26. Oxford: Oxford University Press, 2000.
Thompson, Paul. "Citation practices in PhD theses". In *Rethinking Language Pedagogy from a Corpus Perspective,* edited by Lou Burnard & Tony McEnery eds., 91-102. Hamburg: Peter Lang, 2000
—. "Aspects of identification and position in intertextual reference in PhD theses". In *Strategies in Academic Discourse,* edited by Elena Tognini-Bonelli & Gabriella Del Lungo Camiciotti, 31-50. Amsterdam: Benjamins, 2005
Veel, Robert and Caroline Coffin. "Learning to think like an historian: the language of secondary school history". In *Literacy in Society,* edited by Ruquaya Hasan & Geoff Williams, 191-231. London: Longman, 1996.
Weinrich, Heinrich. *Tempus: Besprochene un Erzhälte Welt*. 1964, 6th ed. 2001. Italian translation *Tempus: Le funzioni dei tempi nel testo*. Bologna: Il Mulino, 2004.

CHAPTER FIVE

DIFFERENT STROKES FOR DIFFERENT FOLKS: DISCIPLINARY VARIATION IN ACADEMIC WRITING

KEN HYLAND

In this paper I address the complex notion of discipline and offer a discoursal way of exploring variations in the activities of different communities. I argue that academic writing is a community situated activity and that the writer's observation of appropriate interactional relationships is a crucial element of this. The paper therefore discusses one line of inquiry in the emerging field of disciplinary studies, reporting a series of investigations conducted over the last decade to understand the ways that academic persuasion is accomplished through the interactions between writer and readers. This view sees academics as not only producing texts that plausibly represent an external reality, but using language to acknowledge, construct and negotiate social relations so that controlling the level of personality in a text not only becomes central to building a socially-situated convincing discourse, but also helps define broad areas of disciplinary endeavour.

Writers always seek to offer a credible representation of themselves and their work and they do this by claiming solidarity with readers, evaluating their material and acknowledging alternative views in ways which seem appropriate and persuasive to their target audience. In other words, through their rhetorical choices writers create a recognisable social world as their discourses both reflect and construct their communities. Following this social constructionist perspective, I investigate ways in which language use varies in the argumentative practices of diverse sections of academia, as revealed in broad disciplinary domains. I begin by looking briefly at the concept of discipline and go on to sketch out an interactional model based on the ideas of stance, or how writers convey their attitudes and credibility, and *engagement*, or the ways they bring their readers into the discourse. I then show how the choices writers make from these systems work to reflect and construct disciplinary communities.

1. Disciplines and communities

Under the challenge of post modernism, which sees intellectual fragmentation and the collapse of disciplinary identity at every turn, and institutional changes such as the emergence of practice-based and mix-and-match modular degrees, the idea of discipline is increasingly questioned (e.g. Gergen & Thatchenkery, 1996; Gilbert, 1995). New disciplines spring up at the intersections of existing ones while others decline and local struggles and institutional convenience ensure that boundaries are never stable or objects of study immutable. Driven by personal, institutional, commercial and intellectual imperatives, this search for knowledge in different fields is underpinned by different interests, values and epistemologies. The differences between practitioners in the various fields are therefore pervasive and can rightly be described as cultural ones (Becher, 1989; Hyland, 2000). Interdisciplinary work is often valorized but seldom practiced effectively precisely because it requires transcending unconscious habits of thought and ways of constructing knowledge and consequently collaborations across fields is often multidisciplinary rather than interdisciplinary.

It is indisputable that particular disciplines established in different cultural and institutional contexts have taken different forms and I agree that there is no natural necessity for a particular discipline of geography, history, chemistry and so on. The notion of discipline has, however, a remarkable persistence and the distinctive existence of different disciplines is an issue which can be empirically informed by study of their rhetorical practices. Successful academic writing does not occur in an institutional vacuum and largely depends on the individual writer's projection of a shared professional context. That is, writers seek to embed their writing in a particular social world which they reflect and conjure up through approved discourses; and a great deal of research has confirmed the distinctiveness of discourses cohering around the concept of *community*. Following work in the sociology of science (Knorr-Cerina, 1981; Latour, 1987) and Bazerman's (1988) pioneering study of a single text from biology, sociology and literary studies, this work has been taken up by rhetoricians (Dillon, 1991; Gross, 1990) and applied linguists (Hyland, 2000; MacDonald, 1994) to suggest how writers seek to typically position themselves and their work in relation to other members of their communities.

Research into differences in academic practices and the texts that these produce is relatively new, partly because the notion of discipline, and its underlying reliance on the idea of community, has been difficult to pin down in discourse studies, and partly because of our fixation with genre in recent years. While genre has provided a significant way of understanding situated language use, it's power of harnessing generalisations about text has led us to overemphasize resemblances between texts at the expense of variation. But as Swales made clear in 1990, we need to see community and genre *together* to offer a framework of how meanings are socially constructed by forces outside the individual. As we enter the 21st century, I think it might be fair to say that research on language variation across the disciplines is rapidly becoming one of the dominant paradigms in EAP (e.g. Hyland, 2000; Fløttum et al, 2006; Hyland & Bondi, 2006).

The study of is not simply motivated by idle curiosity or a perverse antagonism to the fragmentation seen by post modern theorists. On the contrary, the more the unconscious habits of academic practice are explicated and the more we understand how the disparate characteristics of the various intellectual cultures are related to the necessarily different interests, values, and epistemologies, the more feasible becomes the goal of describing the construction of knowledge, of teaching academic writing, and of transcending the thought habits which imprison us.

2. Interactions in academic writing

The notion of interaction, and especially the linguistic mechanisms used by speakers and writers to convey their personal feelings and assessments, has become a heavily populated area of research in recent years. This research has been conducted under various labels, including 'evaluation' (Hunston 1994, Hunston and Thompson 2000), 'intensity' (Labov 1984), 'affect' (Ochs 1989), 'evidentiality' (Chafe and Nichols 1986), 'hedging' (Hyland 1998), and 'stance' (Biber and Finegan, 1989; Conrad and Biber 2000). The expression of evaluation and stance in academic research writing has been especially productive (e.g., Bondi, 1999; Hunston 1994; Hyland, 2001a) and much of this work focuses on features such as the use of hedging devices to express tentativeness and possibility (Hyland (1998), authorial self mention (Hyland, 2001b) and reporting verbs (Thompson & Ye, 1991; Hyland, 2000). This line of research has been extended by looking at how authors actively try to involve the reader in the communication process. Specific studies in this line of research have investigated the use of addressee features (Hyland, 2001) and directives (Hyland 2002a).

Interaction in academic writing essentially involves 'positioning', or adopting a point of view in relation to both the issues discussed in the text and to others who hold points of view on those issues. In persuading readers of their claims writers must display a competence as disciplinary insiders which is, at least in part, achieved through a writer-reader dialogue which situates both their research and themselves, establishing relationships between people, and between people and ideas. Writers therefore seek to project a shared professional context which only partly depends on domain knowledge, as meanings are ultimately produced in the interaction between writers and readers in specific social circumstances. In other words, claims for the significance and originality of research have to be balanced against the convictions and expectations of readers, taking into account their likely objections, background knowledge, rhetorical expectations and processing needs. All this is done within the broad constraints of disciplinary discourses.

This view aligns itself with perspectives which challenge the idea that academic writing is based on the non-contingent pillars of impartial observation, replication and falsifiability. Quite simply, this argues that because observations and experiments are necessarily filtered through selection and highlighting, they are as fallible as the theories they presuppose. They cannot, therefore, provide a solid foundation for the acceptance of scientific claims, and this moves our attention to the ways that academics argue their claims. Influenced by thinkers such as Geertz (1983) and Kuhn (1970), who argued that knowledge depends on individuals acting as members of communities, a substantial body of research has emerged which explores how disciplines mediate reality in different ways through their preferred modes of argument.

3. Stance and engagement

Interactions are accomplished in academic writing through the systems of stance and engagement. *Stance* refers to the writer's textual 'voice' or community recognised personality, an attitudinal, writer-oriented function which concerns the ways writers present themselves and convey their judgements, opinions, and commitments. *Engagement*, on the other hand, is more of an alignment function, concerning the ways that writers rhetorically recognise the presence of their readers to actively pull them along with the argument, include them as discourse participants, and guide them to interpretations (Hyland, 2001a). Together they recognise that statements need to both present the writer and his or her ideas as well as anticipate readers' possible objections and alternative positions, incorporating an appropriate awareness of self and audience.

Stance and engagement are two sides of the same coin and, because they both contribute to the interpersonal dimension of discourse, there are overlaps between them. Discrete categories inevitably conceal the fact that forms often perform more than one function at once because, in developing their arguments, writers are simultaneously trying to set out a claim, comment on its truth, establish solidarity and represent their credibility. In addition, the marking of stance and engagement is a highly contextual matter as writers can employ evaluations through a shared attitude towards particular methods or theoretical orientations which may be opaque to the analyst. Nor is it always marked by words at all: a writer's decision not to draw an obvious conclusion from an argument, for example, may be read by peers as a significant absence (Swales, 2004). It should also be recognised that many lexico-grammatical features can be used to indicate the personal stance of a writer in English, including value-laden word choice and paralinguistic devices (such as punctuation and typographical like underlining, capitalisation, scare quotes and exclamation marks in writing (Hyland, 2005). Nearly any word can be analyzed as reflecting an evaluation, making it hard to identify a closed set of words used to convey specific attitudes and evaluations.

For these reasons, the present study is restricted to grammatical devices that express stance and engagement, identifying predominant meanings to compare the rhetorical patterns in different discourse communities. The key resources by which these interactional macro-functions are realised are summarised in Figure 1.

Figure 1. Key resources of academic interaction

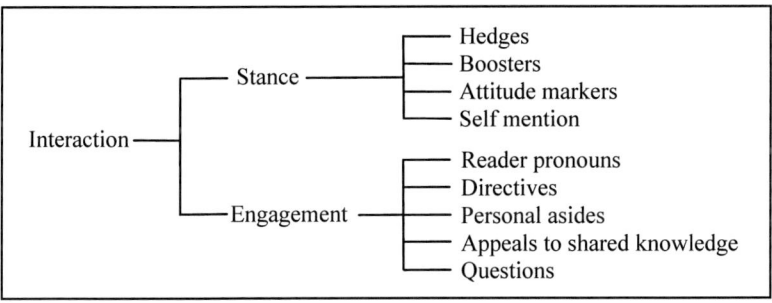

Together these resources have a dialogic purpose in that they refer to, anticipate, or otherwise take up the actual or anticipated voices and positions of potential readers (Bakhtin, 1986). Distinguishing between these two dimensions is a useful starting point from which to explore how interaction and persuasion is achieved in academic discourse and what these can tell us of the assumptions and practices of different disciplines.

The description has emerged through studies I have conducted over the last few years into a corpus of 240 research articles of 1.4 million words. This corpus was selected to represent a broad cross-section of academic practice and comprises three papers from each of ten leading journals in eight disciplines. The fields are mechanical engineering (ME), electrical engineering (EE), marketing (Mk), philosophy (Phil), sociology (Soc), applied linguistics (AL), physics (Phy) and microbiology (Bio). These sub corpora were searched for 320 potentially productive items based on previous research, grammars and the most frequently occurring items in the texts themselves. The analyses were supplemented with interviews with experienced researcher/writers from the target disciplines to discover respondents attitudes about writing and their own discoursal preferences and practices. The next sections briefly sketch out the key resources of stance and engagement. Then I go on to discuss what differences in their use tell us about the epistemological and social beliefs of disciplinary cultures.

4. Stance and writer-oriented interaction

Stance concerns *writer-oriented features* of interaction and conveys different kinds of personal feelings and assessments, including attitudes that a writer has about particular information, how certain they are about its veracity, how they obtained access to it, and what perspective they are taking to it and to the reader. I take it to have three main components: *evidentiality, affect* and *presence*. Evidentiality refers to the writer's expressed commitment to the reliability of the propositions he or she presents and their potential impact on the reader; affect involves a broad range of personal and professional attitudes towards what is said; and presence simply concerns the extent to which the writer chooses to project him or herself into the text. It is comprised of four elements: hedges, boosters, attitude markers and self mention, which I will briefly mention below.

Hedges are devices which withhold complete commitment to a proposition, allowing information to be presented as an opinion rather than fact (Hyland,1998). They imply that a claim is based on plausible reasoning rather than certain knowledge and so both indicate the degree of confidence it might be wise to attribute to a claim while allowing writers to open a discursive space for readers to dispute interpretations. This is an example from biology:

> (1) We propose several *possible* reasons for this: (1) pressures increase upon freezing and thus *may* force bubbles back into solution at the time of thaw; (2) since xylem water is degassed by freezing there is *a strong tendency* for bubbles to redissolve at the time of thaw; and (3) xylem water *may* flow in advance of ice formation and *could* refill some of the previously embolized vessels. (Bio)

Boosters, on the other hand allow writers to express their certainty in what they say and to mark involvement with the topic and solidarity with their audience (Hyland, 2005). While they restrict opportunities for alternative voices, they also often stress shared information and group membership as we tend to get behind those ideas which have a good chance of being accepted. Like hedges, they often occur in clusters, underlining the writer's conviction in an argument:

> (2) *Of course*, I do not contend that there are no historical contingencies. On the contrary, the role of contingencies *should be* stressed. If there were no contingencies, there would be no innovations, whether scientific or moral. On this point, we must *definitely* stop following Hegel's intuitions. *Nobody* can foretell that tomorrow totalitarian regimes will not reappear and eventually spread over the planet. (Soc)

Both boosters and hedges represent a writer's response to the potential viewpoints of readers and an acknowledgement of disciplinary norms of appropriate argument. Both strategies emphasise that statements don't just communicate ideas, but also the writer's attitude to them and to readers.

Attitude markers indicate the writer's affective, rather than epistemic, attitude to propositions, conveying surprise, agreement, importance, frustration, and so on, rather than commitment. Attitude can be expressed in a wide range of ways, as Martin (2000) and White (2002) have attempted to show by mapping the options available to speakers in conveying *affect* in their model of *appraisal*. Attitude is most explicitly signalled by attitude verbs, sentence adverbs, and adjectives, and this marking of attitude in academic writing allows writers both take a stand and align themselves with disciplinary-oriented value positions.

> (3) No doubt there are a number of criticisms that adherents to the justice-based paradigm might make of the moral model Dworkin proposes. Still, *I believe that* Dworkin's investment model has *remarkable* resonance and *extraordinary* potential power. *The worry I have* about Dworkin's proposal arises from inside his model. It is *interesting* right off the bat to notice that ... (Phil)

Self mention refers to the use of first person pronouns and possessive adjectives to present information (Hyland, 2001b). Presenting a discoursal self is central to the writing process (Ivanic, 1998), and we cannot avoid projecting an impression of ourselves and how we stand in relation to our arguments, discipline, and readers. The presence or absence of explicit author reference is a conscious choice by writers to adopt a particular stance and disciplinary-situated authorial identity.

> (4) *Our* investigation of writing at the local government office comprised an analysis of the norms and attitudes of each individual. *We* asked the different employees about their norms concerning a good text and a good writer. *We* also asked them about their attitudes toward writing at work. What *we* found interesting about this context, however, is the degree of uniformity of their norms and attitudes. (Soc)

5. Engagement and reader-oriented interaction

Unlike stance, the ways writers bring readers into the discourse has been relatively neglected in the literature. Engagement seeks to build a connection with readers to both stress solidarity and position them by anticipating possible objections and guiding their thinking. Based on their previous experiences with texts, writers make predictions about how readers are likely to react to their arguments and craft their texts to explicitly address them at certain points (Hyland, 2001a). Engagement markers include reader pronouns, personal asides, references to sharedness, directives and questions.

Reader pronouns offer the most explicit ways of bringing readers into a discourse but y*ou* and *your* are rare in research articles, perhaps because they imply a separation between participants, rather than seeking connections, and this helps to account for the high use of inclusive *we*. There are several motivations for using this form, but most centrally it identifies the reader as someone who shares similar understandings to the writer as a member of the same discipline. At the same time as expressing peer solidarity, however, it also anticipates reader objections, presuming mutual understandings while weaving the potential point of view of the reader into the argument.

Directives are mainly expressed through *imperatives* and *obligation modals* and they direct readers to engage in three main kinds of activity:
- **textual acts:** direct readers to another part of the text or to another text (*see Smith 1999, refer to table 2*, etc.)
- **physical acts** direct readers how to carry out some action in the real-world (e.g. *open the valve, heat the mixture*).
- **cognitive acts** instruct readers how to interpret an argument, explicitly positioning readers by encouraging them to *note, concede* or *consider* some argument or claim in the text.

Personal asides allow writers to address readers directly by briefly interrupting the argument to offer a comment on what has been said. By turning to the reader in mid-flow, the writer acknowledges and responds to an active audience, often to initiate a brief dialogue that is largely interpersonal, adding more to the writer-reader relationship than to propositional development:

(5) And - as I believe many TESOL professionals will readily acknowledge - critical thinking has now begun to make its mark, particularly in the area of L2 composition. (AL)

He above all provoked the mistrust of academics, both because of his trenchant opinions (often, it is true, insufficiently thought out) and his political opinions. (Soc)

Appeals to shared knowledge are marked by explicit signals asking readers to recognise something as familiar or accepted. These constructions of solidarity ask readers to identify with particular views and in so doing construct readers by assigning to them a role in creating the argument, acknowledging their contribution while moving the focus of the discourse away from the writer to shape the role of the reader:

(6) It is, *of course*, possible to realise capacitors using the inter-metal, linearmetal-poly, metal-diffusion, or poly diffusion (with an SiO2 dielectric) capacitances. (EE)

This tendency *obviously* reflects the preponderance of brand-image advertising in fashion merchandising. (Mkt)

Questions are the strategy of dialogic involvement par excellence, inviting engagement, encouraging curiosity and bringing interlocutors into an arena where they can be led to the writer's viewpoint (Hyland, 2002b). Over 80% of questions in the corpus, however, were rhetorical, presenting an opinion as an interrogative so the reader appears to be the judge, but actually expecting no response. This is most apparent when writers answer their question immediately:

(7) Is it, in fact, necessary to choose between nurture and nature? My contention is that it is not. (Soc)

What do these two have in common, one might ask? The answer is that they share the same politics. (AL)

The process of audience evaluation involved in making choices from the options of stance and engagement clearly assists writers to construct an effective argument, but in addition, it reveals something of how language is related to specific institutional contexts. In the remainder of this paper I explore what these choices tell us about disciplinary communities.

6. Stance and engagement: disciplinary practices

Overall, it appears that the expression of stance and engagement is an important feature of academic writing, with about one occurrence every 28 words. Table 1 shows that stance markers were about five times more common than engagement features and that hedges were by far the most frequent feature of writer perspective in the corpus, reflecting the critical importance of distinguishing fact from opinion and the need for writers to present their claims with appropriate caution and regard to colleagues' views.

Table 1. Stance and Engagement features in the research articles

Stance	Items per 1000 words	% of total	Engagement	Items per 1000 words	% of total
Hedges	14.5	46.6	Reader pron.	2	49.1
Attitude m.	6.4	20.5	Directives	1.9	32.3
Boosters	5.8	19.2	Questions	0.5	8.5
Self mention	4.2	13.7	Shared knowl.	0.5	8.2
			Pers. asides	0.1	1.9
Totals	30.9	100		5.9	100

When we compare these frequencies with other common features of published academic writing we find that overt interaction markers are an important element of academic prose. Biber et al. (1999), for instance, records 18.5 cases per thousand words for passive voice constructions and 20 per thousand words for past tense verbs in a large corpus of academic writing. More interesting however are the disciplinary distributions. Table 2 shows the density of features in each discipline normalised to a text length of 1,000 words. As can be seen, the more discursive 'soft' fields of philosophy, marketing, sociology and applied linguistics contained the highest proportion of interactional markers with some 75% more items than the engineering and science papers.

I do not want to dwell on these frequencies, but it is clear that writers in different disciplines represent themselves, their work and their readers in different ways, with those in the humanities and social sciences taking far more explicitly involved and personal positions than those in the science and engineering fields. We do not have to search far for an explanation for this. As I noted at the beginning of this paper, the resources of language mediate their contexts, working to construe the characteristic structures of knowledge domains and argument forms of the disciplines that create them. Most centrally, these discourse conventions embody the particular sets of values, practices and beliefs which are held by, and help define, academic disciplines.

Table 2. Stance and engagement features by discipline (per 1,000 words)

Feature	Phil	Soc	AL	Mk	Phy	Bio	ME	EE	Total
Stance	**42.8**	**31.1**	**37.2**	**39.5**	**25.0**	**23.8**	**19.8**	**21.6**	**30.9**
Hedges	18.5	14.7	18.0	20.0	9.6	13.6	8.2	9.6	14.5
Attitude	8.9	7.0	8.6	6.9	3.9	2.9	5.6	5.5	6.4
Boosters	9.7	5.1	6.2	7.1	6.0	3.9	5.0	3.2	5.8
Self ref.	5.7	4.3	4.4	5.5	5.5	3.4	1.0	3.3	4.2
Engagement	16.3	5.1	5.0	3.2	4.9	1.6	2.8	4.3	5.9
Reader ref	11.0	2.3	1.9	1.1	2.1	0.1	0.5	1.0	2.9
Directives	2.6	1.6	2.0	1.3	2.1	1.3	2.0	2.9	1.9
Questions	1.4	0.7	0.5	0.3	0.1	0.1	0.1	0.0	0.5
Shared	1.0	0.4	0.6	0.4	0.5	0.1	0.3	0.4	0.5
Asides	0.2	0.2	0.1	0.1	0.0	0.0	0.0	0.0	0.1
Totals	**59.1**	**36.2**	**42.2**	**42.7**	**29.9**	**25.4**	**22.6**	**25.9**	**36.8**

In broad terms, rhetorical practices are inextricably related to the purposes of the disciplines. Natural scientists tend to see their goal as producing public knowledge able to withstand the rigours of falsifiability and developed through relatively steady cumulative growth (Becher, 1989). The fact that this research often occupies considerable investments in money, training, equipment, and expertise means it is frequently concentrated at a few sites and commits scientists to involvement in specific research areas for many years. Problems therefore emerge in an established context so that readers are often familiar with prior texts and research, and that the novelty and significance of contributions can be easily recognised. The soft-knowledge domains, in contrast, produce discourses which often recast knowledge as sympathetic understanding, promoting tolerance in readers through an ethical rather than cognitive progression (Dillon, 1991; Hyland, 2000).

7. Authorial involvement in knowledge construction

While there are clear dangers in reifying the ideologies of practitioners, these broad ontological representations have real rhetorical effects which are clear in the use of stance markers and particularly apparent in the use of hedges and self mention.

Both hedges and boosters tended to be more common in the humanities and social science papers with about 2½ times as many devices overall and hedges particularly strongly represented. This is mainly because the soft-knowledge fields are typically more interpretative and less abstract than the hard sciences and their forms of argument rely more on a dialogic engagement and more explicit recognition of alternative voices. Research is influenced far more by contextual factors, there is less control of variables, more diversity of research outcomes, and generally fewer unequivocal bases for accepting claims. Writers in the soft fields cannot therefore report their research with the same confidence of shared assumptions. They must rely far more on focusing readers on the claim-making negotiations of the discourse community, the arguments themselves, rather than relatively unmediated real-world phenomena.

This tends to mean that arguments have to be expressed more cautiously in the soft disciplines, remaining open to heteroglossic diversity in the community by using more hedges:

(8) Wilson leaves us disappointed, *it seems to me*, in the sense that his theory is far from being general. (Soc)

We tentatively suggest that The Sun's minimalist style creates an impression of working-class language, or restricted code, while the very wordy Times themes remind one of academic, formal discourse. (AL)

The fact that methodologies and results are more open to question also means that writers in the soft fields need to work harder to establish the significance of their work against alternative interpretations. This means they also have to restrict, or fend off, possible alternative voices, closing them down using boosters to emphasise the strength of the writer's commitment and thereby convince the reader through the force of the argument. Two comments from informants typify this view:

You have to be seen to believe what you say. That they are your arguments. It's what gives you credibility. It's the whole point. (Phil interview)

I'm very much aware that I'm building a façade of authority when I write, I really like to get behind my work and get it out there. Strong. Committed. That's the voice I'm trying to promote, even when I'm uncertain I want to be behind what I say. (Soc interview)

This kind of commitment is evident in these extracts:

(9) *It is certainly true* that many arguments involve multiple premises. (Phil)

This particular result is *undoubtedly* attributable to the impending incorporation of Hong Kong into the People's Republic of China. (Mk)

In the hard sciences argument is very different as an important aspect of a positivist-empirical epistemology is that the authority of the individual is subordinated to the authority of the text and facts should be allowed to 'speak for themselves' (Hyland, 1998). Writers generally seek to disguise both their interpretative responsibilities and rhetorical identities behind linguistic objectivity. The less frequent use of hedges and boosters is one way of minimising the researcher's role in this process as is the preference for modal verbs over cognitive verbs such as *think, believe* and *suspect*, which downplay the person making the evaluation and can more easily combine with inanimate subjects:

> (10) The theory given above simply provided some insight into the various mechanisms and configurations that *might or might not* yield a polarimetric effect. (Phy)
>
> There was a good correlation between the four values. For V. trifidum, ANOVA showed a significant increase from L to L' and FI, which *could be interpreted* as reflecting the dynamics of fungal colonization. (Bio)

Two scientist informants commented on this kind of use:

> Of course, I make decisions about the findings I have, but it is more convincing to tie them closely to the results. (Phy interview)
>
> You have to relate what you say to your colleagues and we don't encourage people to go out and nail their colours to the mast as maybe they don't get it published. (Bio interview)

For similar reasons we also find different uses of self mention across these domains. The reason for this is that strategic use of self-mention allows writers to claim authority by expressing their convictions, emphasizing their contribution to the field, and seeking recognition for their work (Hyland, 2001b; Kuo, 1999). It sends a clear indication to the reader of the perspective from which statements should be interpreted, distinguishing the writer's own work from that of others. It is not surprising therefore that some 69% of all cases of self-mention were in the humanities and social science papers, with an average of 38 per article, compared with only 17 per paper in science and engineering. Successful communication in the soft fields depends far more on the author's ability to invoke a real writer in the text. Personal reference is thus a clear indication of the perspective from which a statement should be interpreted, enabling writers to emphasize their own contribution to the field and to seek agreement for it.

> (11) I argue that their treatment is superficial because, despite appearances, it relies solely on a sociological, as opposed to an ethical, orientation to develop a response. (Soc)

I bring to bear on the problem my own experience. This experience contains ideas derived from reading I have done which might be relevant to my puzzlement as well as my personal contacts with teaching contexts. *(AL)*

So in the humanities and social sciences, self-mention can help construct an intelligent, credible, and engaging colleague by presenting an authorial self reflecting an appropriate degree of confidence and authority:

Using 'I' emphasizes what you have done. What is yours in any piece of research.. I notice it in papers and use it a lot myself. *(Soc interview)*

The personal pronoun 'I' is very important in philosophy. It not only tells people that it is your own unique point of view, but that you believe what you are saying. It shows your colleagues where you stand in relation to the issues and in relation to where they stand on them. It marks out the differences. *(Phil interview)*

While the first person assists soft discipline authors to make a personal standing in their texts and to demarcate their own work from that of others, hard science writers are generally seeking to downplay their personal role in the research to highlight the phenomena under study, the replicability of research activities, and the generality of the findings. Research usually consists of conducting experiments to propose solutions to specific disciplinary problems and typically involves familiar procedures, broadly predictable outcomes, and relatively clear criteria of acceptability (eg. Becher, 1989). By electing to adopt a less intrusive or personal style, they suggest that research outcomes are unaffected by individuals, strengthening the objectivity of their interpretations and subordinating their own voice to that of nature. One of my respondents expressed this view clearly:

I feel a paper is stronger if we are allowed to see what was done without 'we did this' and 'we think that'. Of course we know there are researchers there, making interpretations and so on, but this is just assumed. It's part of the background. I'm looking for something interesting in the study and it shouldn't really matter who did what in any case.... In theory anyone should be able follow the same procedures and get the same results. Of course reputation is important and I often look at the writer before I look at a paper, but the important thing is whether the results seem right. *(Bio interview)*

8. Participant relationships and interpersonal engagement

In addition to creating an impression of authority, integrity and credibility through choices from the stance options, writers are able to either highlight or downplay the presence of their readers in the text. Engagement devices refer to the various ways writers bring readers into the discourse to relate to them and anticipate their possible objections. As shown in Table 2, these devices were far less frequent than stance items, but exhibited similar variation across disciplines.

Reader pronouns were the most frequent engagement items in the corpus and over 80% of these occurred in the soft discipline papers where they functioned to appeal to scholarly solidarity, presupposing a set of mutual, discipline-identifying understandings linking writer and reader.

> (12) Adopting a reflexive and continuously critical approach towards *ourselves* and *our* sociological practices is especially necessary because *our* profession is an all-embracing calling that penetrates *our* self and collective identities, and serves for many of *us* as a functional equivalent of ideology or civil-religion. (Soc)
>
> We would expect that over time, plant genotypes that maximize mycorrhizal benefits would be at a selective advantage. (Bio)

In addition, however, reader pronouns also claim authority as well as communality, addressing the reader from a position of confidence as several of my informants noted:

> I suppose we helps to finesse a positive response—we are all in this together kind of thing. I use it to signal that I am on the same wavelength, drawing on the same assumptions and asking the same questions. *(Mkt Interview)*
>
> It helps to locate you in a network. It shows that you are just doing and thinking what they might do and think. Or what you would like them to, anyway. *(Soc interview)*

By weaving the potential point of view of readers into the discourse, writers are able to claim collegiality and authority as they anticipate reader objections, stepping in to voice their concerns and views. Thus *we* helps guide readers through an argument and towards a preferred interpretation, as can be seen here:

> (13) Now that *we* have a plausible theory of depiction, *we* should be able to answer the question of what static images depict. But this turns out to be not at all a straightforward matter. *We* seem, in fact, to be faced with a dilemma. Suppose *we* say that static images can depict movement. This brings *us* into conflict with Currie's account ... (Phil)
>
> Although *we* lack knowledge about a definitive biological function for the transcripts from the 93D locus, their sequences provide *us* with an ideal system to identify a specific transcriptionally active site in embryonic nuclei. (Bio)

Several of my informants were well aware of this more Machiavellian purpose:

> Part of what you are doing in writing a paper is getting your readers onside, not just getting down a list of facts, but showing that you have similar interests and concerns. That you are looking at issues in much the same way they would, not spelling everything out, but following the same procedures and asking the questions they might have. *(Bio intw)*
>
> I often use 'we' to include readers. I suppose it brings out something of the collective endeavour, what we all know and want to accomplish. I've never thought of it as a strategy, but I suppose I am trying to lead readers along with me. *(ME interview)*

There was an even greater disciplinary imbalance with the use of questions, which were almost exclusively confined to the soft fields. Here they served to structure the text and rhetorically position of readers by responding to a question immediately, simultaneously initiating a dialogue to engage readers and closing it to present a claim:

> (14) Does the Brain-in-a-vat thereby succeed in including the relation in which it stands to its environment in the extension of its term 'the delusive relation'? There are, I think, compelling reasons to say that it does not. (Phil)
>
> What do these two have in common, one might ask? The answer is that they share the same politics. (AL)

The fact they reach out to readers was seen as a distraction by my science informants:

> Questions are quite rare in my field I think. You might find them in textbooks I suppose, but generally we don't use them. They seem rather intrusive, don't they? Too personal. We generally prefer not to be too intrusive. *(ME interview)*
>
> I am looking for the results in a paper, and to see if the method was sound. I am looking for relevance and that kind of dressing is irrelevant. People don't ask questions as it would be seen as irrelevant. And condescending probably. *(EE interview)*

In contrast the soft knowledge writers saw them as an important way of relating to readers:

> In my field that's all there are, questions. Putting the main issues in the form of questions is a way of presenting my argument clearly and showing them I am on the same wavelength as them. *(Phil interview)*

Often I structure the argument by putting the problems that they might ask. *(Mkt interview)*

Finally, directives were the only interactive feature which occurred more frequently in the science and engineering papers than those in the humanities and social sciences. Generally, explicit engagement is a feature of the soft disciplines, where writers are less able to rely on the explanatory value of accepted procedures, but directives are a potentially risky tactic as they instruct readers to act or see things in a certain way. As a result, most directives in the soft fields were textual, directing readers to a reference rather than informing them how they should interpret an argument. Two of my respondents noted this in their interviews:

> I am very conscious of using words like 'must' and 'consider' and so on and use them for a purpose. I want to say 'Right, stop here. This is important and I want you to take notice of it'. So I suppose I am trying to take control of the reader and getting them to see things my way. *(Soc interview)*

> I am aware of the effect that an imperative can have so I tend to use the more gentle ones. I don't want to bang them over the head with an argument I want them to reflect on what I'm saying. I use 'consider' and 'let's look at this' rather than something stronger. *(AL interview)*

The more linear and problem-oriented approach to knowledge construction in the hard knowledge fields, on the other hand, allows arguments to be formulated in a highly standardised code. This helps explain why cognitive directives, potentially the most threatening type, were overwhelmingly predominant in the natural science corpus. These explicitly position readers by leading them through an argument to the writer's claims (15) or emphasising what they should attend to in the argument (16):

> (15) *Consider* a sequence of batches in an optimal schedule. (EE)

> ... a distinction *must be* made between cytogenetic and molecular resolution. (Bio)

> (16) What *has to be recognised* is that these issues ... (ME)

> *It is important* to remember that primary electrons induce x rays. (Phy)

This facilitates succinctness and an economy of expression highly valued by space-conscious editors and information-saturated scientists as several informants noted:

I rarely give a lot of attention to the dressing, I look for the meat–the findings - and if the argument is sound. If someone wants to save me time in getting there then that is fine. No, I'm not worried about imperatives leading me through it. *(EE interview)*

I'm very conscious of how I write and I am happy to use an imperative if it puts my idea over clearly. Often we are trying to work to word limits anyway, squeezing fairly complex arguments into a tight space. *(ME interview)*

9. Conclusions

These different features, taken together, are important ways of situating academic arguments in the interactions of members of disciplinary communities. They represent relatively conventional ways of making meaning and so elucidate a context for interpretation, showing how writers and readers make connections, through texts, to their disciplinary cultures. My claim has been that effective academic writing depends on rhetorical decisions about interpersonal intrusion and I have suggested a model which attempts to show how writers select and deploy community-sensitive linguistic resources to represent themselves, their positions and their readers. My picture of these interactions, however, has been painted with a very broad brush, focusing on general categories of interaction and broad domains of academic endeavour. There are certainly more fine-grained distinctions to be made, both among these resources and disciplines, which are likely to offer further insights into the rhetorical options available to writers and the patterns of effective persuasion employed by different communities.

10. References

Bakhtin, M. *The dialogic imagination: four Essays*. Edited by M. Holquist. Austin: University of Texas Press, 1986.
Bazerman, C. *Shaping written knowledge* . Madison: University of Wisconsin Press, 1988.
Becher, T. Academic tribes and territories: Intellectual inquiry and the cultures of disciplines. Milton Keynes: SRHE/OUP, 1989.
Biber, D. & Finegan, E.. Styles of stance in English: lexical and grammatical marking of evidentiality and affect. *Text*. 9 (1), 1989: 93–124.
Biber, D., Johansson, S., Leech, G., Conrad, S., & Finegan, E. *Longman grammar of spoken and written English*. Harlow: Longman, 1999.
Bondi, M. English across genres: language variation in the discourse of economics. Modena: Edizioni Il Fiorino, 1999.

Chafe, W. L., and Nichols, J. (eds.). *Evidentiality: The linguistic coding of epistemology.* Norwood, N.J.: Ablex, 1986.
Conrad, S., and Biber, D.. Adverbial marking of stance in speech and writing. In Hunston and Thompson (eds.), (2000): 56–73.
Dillon, G. *Contending rhetorics: writing in academic disciplines.* Bloomington: Indiana University Press, 1991.
Fløttum, K., T. Dahl and T. Kinn. *Academic Voices - Across languages and disciplines.* Amsterdam/Philadelphia: John Benjamins, 2006.
Geertz, C. *Local knowledge: Further essays in interpretive anthropology.* New York: Basic Books, 1983.
Gergen, K. J. & Thatchenkery, T. J. Organisational science as social construction: postmodern potentials. *The Journal of Applied Behavioral Science*, 32. 4 (1996): 356–377
Gilbert, S.. Introduction: Postmodernism and science. *Science in Context 8* (1995): 559–561.
Gross, A. G. *The rhetoric of science.* Cambridge, Mass: Harvard University Press, 1990.
Hunston, S.. Evaluation and organisation in a sample of written academic discourse. In *Advances in written text analysis*, edited by M. Coulthard, 191–218. London: Routledge, 1990.
Hunston, S, & Thompson, G. (Eds.). *Evaluation in text* . Oxford: OUP, 2000.
Hyland, K. *Hedging in scientific research articles.* Amsterdam: John Benjamins, 1998.
Hyland, K. Disciplinary discourses: Social interactions in academic writing. London: Longman, 2000.
—. Bringing in the reader: addressee features in academic writing. *Written Communication*. 18 (4) (2001a): 549–574.
—. Humble servants of the discipline? Self-mention in research articles. *English for Specific Purposes*. 20 (2001b): 207–226.
—. Directives: power and engagement in academic writing. *Applied Linguistics*. 23 (2) (2002a): 215–239
—. What do they mean? Questions in academic writing. *TEXT*. 22 (4) (2002b): 529-557.
—. *Metadiscourse.* London: Continuum, 2005.
Hyland, K. & Bondi, M. (Eds). *Academic discourse across disciplines.* Frankfort: Peter Lang, 2006.
Ivanic, R. Writing and Identity: The discoursal construction of identity in academic writing. Amsterdam: John Benjamins, 1998.
Knorr-Cetina, K. *The manufacture of knowledge.* Oxford: Pergamon Press, 1981.

Kuhn, T. *The structure of scientific revolutions.* 2nd ed. Chicago: University of Chicago Press, 1970.
Kuo, C-H. The use of personal pronouns: Role relationships in scientific journal articles. *English for Specific Purposes,* 18 (2) (1999): 121–138.
Labov, W. Intensity. In *Meaning, form, and use in context: Linguistic applications,* edited by D. Schiffrin, 43–70). Washington, D.C.: Georgetown University Press, 1984.
Latour, B. *Science in Action.* Cambridge, MA: Harvard University Press, 1987.
MacDonald, S. *Professional academic writing in the humanities and social sciences.* Carbondale: Southern Illinois University Press, 1994.
Martin, J. Beyond exchange: APPRAISAL systems in English. In Hunston & Thompson (Eds.), 2000.
Ochs, E. (Ed.). *The pragmatics of affect.* Special issue of *Text,* Vol 9, 1989.
Swales, J. *Research genres.* Cambridge: CUP, 2004.
Thompson, G. & Ye, Y. Evaluation of the reporting verbs used in academic papers. *Applied Linguistics, 12* (1991): 365–82.
White, P. Beyond modality and hedging: a dialogic view of the language of intersubjective stance. *TEXT* 23 (2) (2003): 2594–8.

CHAPTER SIX

THE PROSECUTOR AND THE DEFENDANT: CONTRASTING CRITICAL VOICES IN FRENCH- AND ENGLISH-WRITTEN ACADEMIC BOOK REVIEWS[*]

FRANÇOISE SALAGER-MEYER, MARÍA ÁNGELES ALCARAZ ARIZA AND MARYELIS PABÓN

1. Introduction

Within the academic context, the independent genre of the book review (BR) presents a particular interest, considering, on the one hand, its frequency and importance as a discussion forum in which new contributions to a particular discipline are evaluated by experts and professional writers, and, on the other hand, its essentially evaluative and communicative nature. Indeed, the BR reflects, in an exceptionally clear manner, the functioning of the interaction between its participants: the reviewer and the reviewee who are supposed to be members of the same academic or scientific community[1]. Most academic journals today publish BRs in addition to their articles. What is more, some specialist journals publish nothing but BRs which, contrary to the sacrosanct research paper, are, in the main, solicited by journal editors and are not subjected to the normal refereeing process.

---

[*] This research was conducted thanks to Grant CDCHT-M-792-04-06 and Grant CONICIT S1-98003578. We would also like to thank Dr. Abdel Fuenmayor for his advice as a specialist informant.
[1] In fact, today's BRs generally conclude with a brief reference to the reviewer's professional status, the main objective of this appendix being to establish the reviewer's scientific authority which should guarantee the validity of the critical evaluation carried out. The readers of the BRs thus assume that the reviewer is an expert on the subject of the book under review. i.e., a renowned member of the relevant academic community.

Academic BRs thus accomplish an important informative and evaluative role[2] that consists in the "time saving sorting out that the disciplines, with their ever increasing influx of new publications, always require." (Belcher 1995: 140). But such attempts to respond to the needs of busy people for relevant research information are not new at all. As a matter of fact, they already existed more than three centuries ago when the output of books, and thus new knowledge, increased dramatically[3]. Two English-language journals–*Weekly Memorials* (mostly non medical) and *Medicina Curiosa*, both launched in 1684– already contained abstracts of articles and books published in non-English speaking countries (Colman 1999). Two other journals, entirely devoted to chronicling and summarizing the explosion of learning in the sciences, also made their appearance at that time on the scene of scholarship: *Analytical Review* and *The Monthly Epitome* (cf. Hyland 2000).

Later, in the mid-18th century, the German periodical *Commentarii de Rebus in Scientia Naturali et Medicina Gestis* was published in Leipzig (Tröhler 2000). It contained abstracts of scientific and medical books and was to serve as a model for the first English-language journal of abstracts of books relevant to busy clinicians, *Medical and Philosophical Commentaries* which was launched in Edinburgh in 1773[4]. The journal became sufficiently well regarded to justify translation into languages other than English (Chalmers 2000).

Book reviews, then, have contributed to the improvement of medical and/or scientific research in general and have played an earlier role in the construction of scientific knowledge than the research article itself, a scholarly genre which emerged in the closing years of the 19th century and to which so much attention has been dedicated within the English for Specific Purposes (ESP) movement in the past three decades or so (Swales 1990 and 2004, among many others).

In spite of the fact that the disincentives to write book reviews are many (see Felber 2002) and that BRs have a marginal status[5], we cannot deny that this

---

[2] As Hyland (2000) points out, all academic genres are evaluative to a certain extent, but the book review is the most evaluative of all.
[3] In a wide-ranging and informative paper, Orteza y Miranda (1996) traces the history of book reviewing from 140 BC on.
[4] In 1796, *Medical Commentaries* became the *Annals of Medicine*, and in 1805, the new periodical was renamed *The Edinburgh Medical and Surgical Journal*. In 1855, the words "and surgical" were dropped and the journal lasted for another 100 years (Colman 1999). But most medical journals started carrying book reviews in the 1930's. *Annals of Internal Medicine*, for example, published book reviews since its first issue in 1927. Book reviews were also a feature in the journal's predecessor *Annals of Clinical Medicine* which was first published in 1924.
[5] Felber (2002) notes that the marginal status of reviews is most apparent in the annual faculty performance report where it is evident that they are considered as "service" or "professional service", akin to sitting on a committee. Felber further remarks that the

"intermediate genre" (Felber 2002: 169) serves a useful function for book reviewers (they can boost a fledging researcher's profile), book authors, publishers and universities. The BR section indeed provides a space where academics can participate to the ongoing conversation in their disciplines by arguing to what extent others' research contribute to the process of knowledge construction and discussion. Moreover, by offering a discussion forum in which new contributions to a particular discipline are assessed for their quality, integrity and value to a given field, BRs reflect, as we said before, the functioning of the social interaction between their communicative participants: the reviewer and the reviewee. We then believe that BRs provide a particularly fertile ground for research, although, their limited significance as reference texts–especially when compared to that of the research article–might in part explain why this "unsung genre" (Hyland 2000: 43) has been largely neglected in the LSP literature. As Hyland (2000: 43) remarks: "Neither strictly a 'research-process genre' nor one of Swales' 'occluded genres' (1996) of academic life, the BR seems to have largely escaped applied linguistic scrutiny."

2. Review of literature on book reviews

To our knowledge, North (1992) was the first to draw attention to the fact that the study of scholarly BRs was an urgent concern, and that it was thus necessary to develop a model in order to account for the discursive practices involved in the writing of a BR because its specifics are a matter of unarticulated conventions.[6] In that same year, Johnson (1992) stated that BRs constitute an important and frequent communicative act in academic life, involving a high degree of social interaction between their participants, but Johnson's study was mainly concerned with the use of complimenting strategies in peer-review texts written by graduate students. In general terms, Johnson argued that these strategies are employed in order to redress specific and global face-threatening acts which characterize the genre of the critical review. As a matter of fact, criticisms and suggestions for improvement are at the core of the reviewer's evaluative task.

Taking another stance on BR writing, Belcher's (1995) study primarily aimed at establishing a rationale for the teaching of critical writing to ESL graduate students, and pointed out the important role played by critical writing

---

placement of BRs in the back of journal issues makes it clear that they take second place to original scholarship.

[6] Today some journals provide electronic templates for reviewers to follow when writing their reviews (see Hartley 2006a and 2006b).

in graduate student education. At this level, indeed, students generally feel reluctant to carry out critical writing assignments, since they do not consider themselves sufficiently prepared to challenge authority, i.e., to critically assess the work of expert writers and professionals.

A few years later, Motta-Roth (1998) published the first rhetorical analysis on the macrostructure of English-written BRs. She could identify four recurrent moves in her corpus of 180 BRs evenly distributed between the disciplines of linguistics, chemistry and economics. Then followed other more sociologically-oriented studies, such as that of Burgess (2000) who examined the role of the book reviewer in two contexts of publications, viz., on-line (unsolicited) BRs vs. solicited BRs; that of Gea Valor (2000) who analyzed politeness markers and modalized statements in a corpus of BRs from the field of linguistics. Giannoni (2002), for his part, explored the pragmatic features of software reviews, while De Carvalho (2001) and Suárez (2005) studied academic BRs from a contrastive rhetorical perspective: the former compared Portuguese- and English-written BRs, and the latter Spanish and English-written ones. Both studies revealed interesting rhetorical differences in the structure of English-written BRs, on the one hand, and Spanish- and Portuguese-written BRs, on the other. Perhaps the most comprehensive study of BRs is Hyland's (2000) analysis of speech acts encoding praise and criticism in BRs from 8 different hard and soft disciplines. We should finally refer to two diachronic studies that have lately been conducted on BRs, one in economics (Shaw 2002) and the other in medicine (Salager-Meyer 2001).

All in all, these studies–which, it is important to point out, all examined BRs written in English --, have underlined that, from a pragmatic standpoint, BRs must be regarded as a highly face-threatening act (FTA) since they basically involve the assessment of a colleague's work. They have also underscored that BRs stand out as an important rhetorical means to challenge textual authority for the general benefit of the discipline, and to establish relations and solidarity with the members of the academic community.

Moreover, drawing on Halliday's functional view of language, these studies have also shown that the BR fulfils two primary functions: an ideational one where book reviewers express cognitive judgments and perceptions, and an interpersonal one which refers to the effort book reviewers make to strike a balance between compliments and praise, between critique and collegiality. These studies have also evinced that outright criticism (which is generally avoided in today's Anglo-American research papers) is an integral feature of BRs, and that conflict, as Giannoni so nicely expresses (2002: 356) "is the common thread that holds this genre together." It is precisely that "common evaluative thread" that interests us here, evaluation certainly being a topic worthy of study. As Thompson and Hunston (2000: 5) put is: "The expression of the writers' or speaker's opinion is an important feature of language ... it needs to be accounted for in a full description of the meaning of texts."

3. Purpose

With the present study, which forms part of a wider research project on the linguistic and rhetorical evolution of scholarly BRs over a two-century period, we intend to build on, complement and enrich the results of the previously mentioned research by examining the pragmatico-rhetorical issue of criticism or critical remark (CR) in BRs published in French- and English-written medical journals in the closing years of the 20th century. By "CR" we mean any disagreement, criticism or conflict, whether it be a sentence, a minor sentence (a sentence with no verb), a clause (dependent or independent), an elliptical syntactic pattern or a fragment sentence so characteristic of journalistic style, such as "All in all, uninteresting".

In this paper we are particularly interested in examining:
1) the overall characteristics of the books reviewed in each linguistic sample. We recorded the language in which the books reviewed were written (i.e., whether they were originally written in English or French or whether they were translations; if so, from which language). We were also interested in knowing the type of the books being reviewed, i.e., whether it is a single- or multi-authored book, an edited collection of papers, etc.;

2) the percentage of BRs containing critical remarks in each linguistic sample;

3) the frequency of epistemic modality devices used when encoding a CR. We indeed agree with Hyland (2000) who remarks that the way conflict is framed is an important consideration since that framing carries a socio-pragmatic force beyond the propositional meaning of the utterance. Because epistemic modality has been found to be "the most common realisation of negative politeness strategy" (Gea Valor 2000: 64) resorted to by book reviewers to mitigate their critical evaluation acts, special emphasis will then be made upon its use in the criticism formulation in the two languages concerned[7];

---

[7] We are aware of the fact that there are other ways of mitigating negative evaluative acts in BRs. Apart from epistemic modals, Hyland (2000), mentions 5 other rhetorical hedging strategies that aim at assuaging the full illocutionary force of specific criticisms: 1) juxtaposition of polar comments in praise-criticism pairs (or "good news/bad news" strategy), 2) labelling of a criticism as a personal opinion, 3) attribution of critical comments to an abstract reader or a general audience, 4) metadiscourse to announce the presence of criticism in the text and 5) limited praise. In Hyland's study, hedges account for 61% of all the mitigating strategies used, thus corroborating Gea Valor's findings.

4) the linguistico-rhetorical choices made by the book reviewer to refer to him/herself in each linguistic sample, i.e., the way the book reviewer's voice is linguistically expressed when formulating a criticism;

5) the degree of subjectivization/objectivization of the CR, i.e., who or what is held responsible for the flaws put forward by the book reviewer: is it the book itself? a chapter of the book? the reviewee(s)?, and, finally,

6) any other CR-related peculiarities which could be ascribed to the language in which BRs are written.

4. Corpus and methods

Towards that end, we analyzed a corpus of 100 randomly selected BRs, 50 written in French (totalling 16.251 running words) and 50 in English, totalling 21.282 running words (see Table 2). These BRS were drawn from top-ranking medical journals (see Appendix 1).

Each BR was read and scanned manually to locate critical remarks. The percentage of BRs containing criticisms was then calculated in each linguistic sample. The recorded CRs were in turn examined as to their rhetorical framing (see "purpose section" above, points 3, 4 and 5).

With respect to epistemic modality, the following epistemic modal elements were underlined whenever we encountered them in the framing of a CR:

a) modal auxiliary verbs expressing possibility, i.e., used epistemically (*would, may, might, could*, etc)
b) semi-auxiliary verbs, such as *to appear* and *to seem;*
c) non-verbal modality which includes nouns, adjectives and adverbs related to the modals (e.g., *perhaps, possibly, probably, presumably)*[8]

Chi-square tests were applied to the quantitative data thus obtained in order to determine whether the intra- and interlinguistic comparisons were statistically significant or not. The analysis was performed by the three authors in a sample of 10 BRs in each language and results were compared for reliability. In general, the level of agreement between the co-authors of this paper was quite high (86%). Discrepancies were discussed with a specialist informant, a medical doctor fluent reader of the two languages.

---

[8] The French equivalents of these epistemic elements were obviously recorded in the French sample.

5. Results and discussion

5.1 Linguistic origin and type of books

Table 1. Overall characteristics of the books reviewed

Linguistic origin of books (original language)		
	FRENCH	**ENGLISH**
English	28 (56 %)	50 (100%)
French	18 (36%)	-
Spanish	1 (2%)	-
Italian	1 (2%)	-
Translations	2 (4%)	-
Authored-vs (co)-edited books		
Authored books	21 (42%)	21 (42%)
(Co)-edited works	29 (58%)	29 (58%)

Almost 60% of the books reviewed in the French BR sample were books originally written in English (Table 1), whereas only 36% were written in French. In the French sample, only 2 books were originally written in languages other than English and French: 1 in Italian and 1 in Spanish. Finally, as far as the French sample of BRs is concerned, translations only account for 4% of the total number of books making up the sample. By contrast, not a single book written in a language other than English formed part of our English-written BR sample.

Another quite interesting finding is that both in the French and the English samples, the number of co-edited books (i.e., books whose chapters are written by several contributors) outnumber, though not in a statistically significant fashion, the number of books written by "authors": 58% for co-edited works vs. 42% for authored-books. (For a diachronic analysis of these issues in French-written BRs, see Salager-Meyer et al. 2006). These quantitative findings certainly stand in sharp contrast with books written up to the mid-20th century, which were mostly single-authored works (Salager-Meyer 2001).

We do not think that the above observations are due to the random sampling procedure adopted here. We rather contend that these are general trends in today's academic world (Western and probably Non-Western as well) that have great significance in socio-constructivist terms, i.e., in terms of the construction of today's scientific knowledge. Analyzing these trends in detail would be very interesting indeed, but it is beyond the scope of the present paper.

5.2 Percentage of book reviews containing critical remarks

Table 2. Percentage of book reviews (BRs) containing critical remarks (CRs), and percentage of hedged CRs

	French BRs (50)	English BRs (50)
Total number of running words	16.251	21.282
Percentage of BRs with CRs	76%	70%
Percentage of hedged CRs (only epistemic modality)	42%	12%

p = .0001

As Table 2 shows, 76% in the French sample and 70% in the English sample contained CRs. Almost a quarter, then, of the French- and English-written BRs are more neutral summaries of the book objectives, descriptions and content than critical analyses *per se*. These essentially a-critical BRs thus resemble late 18th and 19th century medical BRs that avoided applauding and condemning any author. As Duncan (cited in Chalmers 2000) stated in one of the editorial prefaces published during the first decade of *Medical and Philosophical Commentaries* (between 1773 and 1783): "We shall, on every occasion avoid, as much as possible, either applauding or condemning any author. Our chief aim will be, to give such a view of books as may enable every reader to judge by himself."

This finding then leads us to argue that conflict is perhaps not so much, even today, the "common thread" that holds the genre together: not all BRs indeed necessarily contain critical remarks[9]. It is however a more frequent rhetorical feature of the BR cognitive structure than it is of the *letters to the editor* cognitive structure. Indeed, in a recent study, Bloch (2003) found that only 58% of the letters to the editors published in *Science* were criticizing other researchers' claims.

5.3 Framing of critical remarks: use of epistemic modality

The rhetorical feature of CRs which most differentiates between French CRs on the one hand, and English CRs, on the other, lies in the use of epistemic modality. Indeed, as Table 2 shows, hedges were recorded in 42% of the French

---

[9] It is our contention that BRs published in prestigious journals all include some sort of critical remark. This does not mean that the higher the impact of the journal, the more critical the BR. It simply means that it seems that the BRs published in leading scientific journals have to make some kind of negative evaluation (see point 5.3.5. below).

BRs which carried CRs, whereas only 12% of the English-written BRs which contained CRs were hedged (p= .0001). Before discussing these somewhat surprising findings[10], let us first present a few examples.

By far, the favourite hedging mitigating device in the French sample is the use of the conditional, almost always with the verbs "regretter", "aimer", "souhaiter","mériter" or "pouvoir" (see examples 1 to 6 below). The semi-auxiliary "paraître" ('to seem', ex. 7 below) is rarely used.

> 1. Le livre *aurait* (certainement) *mérité* [11]...
> 2. L'auteur *aurait pu* ...
> 3. Il *aurait été utile* que l'éditeur ...
> 4. Il est *un peu* dommage/regrettable que l'auteur ...
> 5. On *aurait aimé/souhaité* que l'auteur ...
> 6. On *peut / pourrait* (toutefois/cependant) *regretter* que les auteurs n'aient pas consacré un chapitre aux syndromes myasthéniques.
> 7. Il nous *paraît* important ...

Emotionally-charged expressions such as "à mon grand regret", "un petit regret', "Il est (un peu) dommage", the adjectives "surprenant", "regrettable", the adverbs "un peu", "malheureusement"–which all soften the CR and underline the book reviewer's emotional involvement and solidarity with the reviewee–sometimes accompany the CRs recorded in our French sample.

With respect to the English-written BR sample, the preferred hedging elements encountered are those already noted by Hyland (2000) and Gea Valor (2000), i.e., the modals *could* and the semi-auxiliary *to seem* (ex. 8 and 9 below), but, we repeat, these were very infrequent:

> 8. Coverage of basic topics does not *seem* to be sufficient.
> 9. The text is not without flaws, but they *seem* minor.

The following example illustrates what we elsewhere called "compound hedges" (Salager-Meyer 1994: 152), i.e. the combination of a modal verb and a probability adverb:

> 10. Editorial summaries of various parts of the book *would be helpful*.... *Perhaps* the main consumer-relevant parts *could be pulled together* into one section.

---

[10] Surprising indeed because one of our previous study on medical *research articles* (Salager-Meyer et al 2003) showed that critical speech acts in today's scientific research papers written in English are more heavily hedged than those written in French and/ or Spanish.

[11] In all the examples, CRs are written in italics, and hedged CRs are underlined.

As example 10 above and examples 11 and 12 below illustrate, another way of softening the force of CRs is to resort to the use of the passive voice (examples 11 and 12 below), but this is rather infrequent. In fact, we only found 2 such examples in the whole English-written sample. What is more, these 2 examples were found in one and the same BR:

> 11. *The chapter* on oncogenes <u>*should have been placed*</u> *earlier in the book.*
> 12. *These reference guides* <u>*might have been combined*</u> and *moved* to the front of the book.

The very low frequency of hedged CRs contradicts Hyland's and Gea Valor's findings according to which epistemic modality occurred in all but a handful of the book reviews they examined in their research. This discrepancy could be attributed to the fact that Gea Valor analyzed BRs in the field of linguistics only, and Hyland examined a wide sample of BRs from the soft and the hard disciplines, but not from the medical field. Medicine, understood as medical praxis, is neither a soft nor a hard discipline. It indeed draws its knowledge from both the hard sciences (e.g., histology, anatomy, physiology) and the soft ones (e.g., psychology, sociology). This peculiarity of the medical field could perhaps account for the interdisciplinary differences observed in the use of hedged CRs in BRs.

The low frequency of hedged CRs in English BRs then indicates that criticism in medical BRs written in English is expressed more bluntly than it is in medical research articles (Salager-Meyer *et al.* 2003), i.e., in formal academic writing, thus resembling the strong and direct fashion of expressing negative evaluation in *letters to the editors* (Bloch 2003) and in private conversations among scientists (Gilbert and Mulkay 1984). The specific communicative purpose (or "privileged criterion" Askehave and Swales 2001) of the two genres of scholarly writing (BR, on the one hand, and research articles, on the other) very likely accounts for the difference observed in the linguistic realization of critical comments in each genre. It could also be argued that the prestige and face of a book reviewer is not so much at stake as those of the author of a scientific research paper.

At any rate, as Hyland (2000) and Gea Valor (2000) argue, in BRs epistemic modality expressions are not so much used to convey the reviewer's degree of commitment to the truth of the proposition uttered (as would be the case in knowledge making genres such as the research paper), but to express affective meaning and therefore politeness. In other words, the purpose of hedging in BRs is not only to make the CRs more palatable, but also to help maintain social harmony and solidarity with the reviewee(s).

5.4 The prosecutor's voice
(or how the book reviewer's voice is linguistically expressed)

Table 3. The prosecutor's (book reviewer's) voice in French- and English-written book reviews

Book reviewer's voice	French	English
"*On*"/ "*One*"	42 (65.6%)	-
Impersonal/neutral "*Il* "/ "*It*"	17 (26.5%) $\Big]$ p=.0001	-
"*Nous*" / "*We*"	5 (7.8%)	-
"*Je*" / "*I*"	-	25 (100%)
TOTAL	**64**	**25**

As Table 3 indicates, a total of 64 instances of the book reviewer's voice was recorded in the French sample. Of those, the pronoun "on" is by far the most frequent rhetorical choice used (65.6% of the total number of personal pronouns recorded in the whole sample), followed by the neutral "il" (26.5 %) and the first person plural "nous" (7.8%). Not a single instance of the first person singular "je" was recorded. Statistically significant differences were observed between the frequency of "on" and "it" (p= .0001), on the one hand, and between that of "il" and" nous", on the other (for more information on the use of "on" in scientific articles, see Flottum 2003 and Flottum and Rastier 2003).

As examples 5 and 6 above and 13 to 19 below show, the "expert-sounding" pronoun "on" is quite frequently accompanied by the modal verb "pouvoir" and the verb "regretter". In fact, of the 42 examples recorded with the "*on*" pronoun, about 60% are hedged by means of the modal verb "pouvoir".

13. *On regrette simplement* que ne soit pas évoqué le problème des lymphomes du MALT et de leur fréquence.
14. *On peut regretter* que la bibliographie qui accompagne chaque chapitre ne soit pas très complète.
15. *On peut regretter* que les auteurs n'aient pas consacré un chapitre aux syndromes myasthéniques.
16. *On peut simplement regretter* les délais de parution et que l'abondance des communications impose une trop grande brièveté de certains articles qu'on aimerait plus développés.
17. *On peut cependant regretter* l'absence de chapitre sur la méniscectomie, les fractures de l'extrémité inférieure du fémur, les ostéotomies (tibiales ou fémorale).
18. *On peut aussi déplorer* quelques a priori sur la sémiologie des crises.

19. *On peut regretter* que des sujets sans rapport avec l'arthroplastie soient abordés dans un livre dont le titre est *Arthroplastie du Genou*.

The "on" pronoun is also frequently hedged by means of the conditional, mostly with the verb "aimer" (example 20 below):

20. *On aurait aimé* savoir si la fréquence de l'HLA B-35 était identique ou non dans ces deux groupes.

Here are some examples of criticism expressed by the impersonal "il", much less frequent than "on":

21. *Il est surprenant* de constater que l'auteur considère les infarctus lacunaires comme un groupe homogène.
22. *Il est un peu regrettable* que ce ne soit pas également le cas pour les épilepsies partielles.

With respect to the English BR sample, only 25 instances of the book reviewer's voice were recorded, and all these corresponded to the use of the first person pronoun "I" (examples 23 and 27 below). In a few cases, the personalized CR is hedged by means of adverbs (ex. 25 below) or through the use of the conditional, as it is in French (ex. 26 below).

23. *I disagree* with several of the author's statements. *I also dispute* their figure of 50% mortality.
24. Although the discussions are balanced and critical, *in my opinion*, they are not critical enough.
25. *I was rather surprised* that the extensive work from St. Jude Children Research Hospital did not figure prominently in this chapter.
26. *I would have preferred* to see more detailed discussion.
27. *I was surprised* by some omissions.

One example only of a very harsh and devastating CR was recorded in the whole corpus of 100 BRs. It was drawn from a BR on bioethics which condemns the whole book.

28. *I was not only disappointed but offended. My reaction to Singer's book is akin to discovering that a friend has served me her pet for dinner.*

The book reviewer thus tends to identify him/herself more conspicuously in English BRs than in their French counterparts. Indeed, in English, the book reviewer generally identifies himself/herself by means of expressions such as "in my opinion", and the first person singular "I" sometimes followed by emotionally charged adjectives such as "surprised" or "disappointed" (ex. 25, 27 and 28 above). By labelling the CR as a personal opinion, the book reviewer then softens the illocutionary force of his/her criticism, and does not have to use so many hedges. As Hyland expresses (2000: 57):

> By foregrounding their commentary as a personal response, reviewers adopt a less threatening authorial voice, repositioning themselves and their authority by reacting as an ordinary reader rather than as an expert.

By contrast, as the French examples clearly show, the French book reviewer rather refers to him/herself by means of the impersonal, "expert-sounding" pronoun "on" (rarely "nous") as representing the whole scientific community. This rhetorical strategy makes the CR more authoritative, because it allows reviewers to consider themselves as experts qualified to speak for the discipline. It is perhaps one of the reasons why these "expert sounding" opinions are so frequently mitigated/hedged by the use of the conditional and/or modal verbs.

5.5 The defendant (or who is responsible for the flaws mentioned)

5.5.1 Animate/concrete/personal defendant (French-written book reviews)

Table 4. The defendant: flaws responsibility in French- and English-written book reviews

	French	English	p level
Book chapter	29 (29.8%)	57 (75%)	p=.0001
Whole book	----	1 (1.3%)	p=.0001
Authors/editors	68 (70.1%)	18 (23.6%)	p=.0001
Total	97	76	

We will now examine and contrast the rhetorical choices used in the two languages to refer to the entity which is held responsible of the flaws mentioned in the BR: is it the book author(s)/editor(s), the book itself, a book chapter?

As Table 4 indicates, book authors/editors are most frequently held responsible for the flaws mentioned in the French-written BRs (70.1% of all the cases recorded) and these are generally mentioned by their surnames, even at times by both their names and surnames (see examples 29 to 32 below). The difference between the frequency of animate/inanimate defendants in the French sample is statistically significant (p= .0001).

> 29. La démarche de *Mr. Gagey* échappe à la logique ayant habituellement cours dans les facultés de médecine.
> 30. Le chapitre de *Cerril Waters* n'est qu'une liste descriptive des nouveaux aspects pharmacologiques.

31. Bien que *les auteurs* définissent leurs objectifs comme "très limités", le domaine couvert est immense et çà et là se glissent des erreurs.
32. On peut regretter le choix de *Bayer et Altman* pour le chapitre d'embryologie.

The above examples thus underline the more personal character of French academic writing already noted in our earlier research on academic criticism (Salager-Meyer *et al*. 2003).

5.5.2 Inanimate/abstract/impersonal defendant (English-written book reviews)

The highly personal, *ad hominem* "subjectivized" reference to the book author(s) characteristic of French BRs is extremely rare in the English sample. As a matter of fact, the proportion of animate/inanimate defendants is exactly the reverse of that observed in the French sample. Indeed, book authors/editors appear as defendants in only 23.6 % of the cases (examples 32 to 5 below). Here too, the difference between animate and inanimate culprits is statistically significant.

33. *Tapper provides only sketchy details* ... and *omits discussion* about the disastrous misinformation provided about the disease during the Black Panther campaigns.
34. *I am disappointed at Kuhse and Singer's edited collection* of philosophical papers on bioethics.
35. Sadly, *Summers discusses little of the role* of bacteriphages in these developments.

In English-written BRs, it is mostly the book itself and/or a book chapter that are the villains (76.3% of all the CRs recorded). The book indeed "fails", "lacks", "suffers from", "succeeds partially in meeting its goal" (examples 36 to 40) and/or chapters are "poorly focused" and "lack depth and details".

36. *The chapter* on neurosurgical approaches *concentrates too much* on pathophysiology and *does not clearly explain* the indication for surgery... *The book also lacks* any comment on the occurrence of Parkinson's disease ... *and fails to* mention the genomic impact of levodopa.
37. *The book reads like a report to funding bodies and it is insufficiently distilled to the editors' target audience.*
38. *The selection is deeply conservative.*
39. *The book certainly does not encompass* the whole range of gastroenterology and hepatology.
40. *The chapter on lung cancer is especially unsophisticated,* given what we know about the disease.

Lastly, regarding the frequency of animate/concrete/personal vs. inanimate/abstract/impersonal defendants in both linguistic samples, it is worthwhile mentioning that the difference observed between the two linguistic samples is statistically significant (p= .0001 in both cases).

Let us now present a few pragmatico-rhetorical features that could be considered characteristic of either French or English BRs.

5.6 A few national/linguistic discursive peculiarities

5.6.1 Anglo-American/French competition (French book reviews)

A criticism encountered in our French sample only reflects the competition between the French and the Anglo-Saxon scientific worlds. Here are 2 examples (41 and 42 below) of such criticism drawn from 2 different reviews of books written by North American researchers but published in French medical journals. Both book reviewers denounce the lack of reference to French scientists and/or the lack of opportunity French scientists are given to publish the results of their research in books published in the United States of America.

> 41. La bibliographie est assez détaillée, mais, à mon grand regret, *elle ne fait appel presque exclusivement qu'à la littérature Nord Américaine*, "scotomisant" presque totalement l'Europe qui, en matière d'anatomie, a pourtant beaucoup fait.
> 42. *Il n'y a aucun français* ayant participé à la dernière édition de neuropathologie de Greenfield.

5.6.2 Structured book reviews (English book reviews)

A few years ago, medical journals such as *Annals of Internal Medicine* started publishing "structured book reviews" (in opposition to "narrative book reviews") which remind us, on the one hand, of the so-called structured abstract imposed upon medical researchers by the editors of the most prestigious medical journals and, on the other, of the plea from medical editors themselves for a "structured discussion" for research papers (Smith 1999, Clarke *et al.* 2002). Such BRs, called "Book Notes", are "structured abstracts of information on newly published books". They contain 9 obligatory moves, among them a "limitation" move which precisely indicates the conceptual and textual flaws of the book under review.

Each one of these 9 moves is preceded by the following heading: 1) Field of medicine, 2) Format (e.g., softcover book), 3) Audience (e.g., primary care physicians), 4) Purpose, 5) Content, 6) Highlights (i.e., positive aspects of the book), 7) Limitations (i.e., CRs) 8) Related readings, and 9) Reviewer, the final move that mentions the book reviewer 's name, his/her medical specialty and the institution s/he works at (see Appendix 2 for an example).

Thus, at least in some English-written medical journals, the progressive standardization and structure of BRs oblige book reviewers to follow the formal constraints of the genre and to necessarily make critical remarks to the book reviewed.

6. Conclusions

The present research on the analysis of critical remarks in French- and English-written book reviews disclosed some interesting quantitative and qualitative features of this genre of academic writing which only recently became the object of linguistic enquiry. To start with some general features of the books reviewed, it was found that the majority of those reviewed in the French sample were originally written in English, whereas not a single book written in a language other than English was recorded in our sample of English-written BRs. It was also found that in both linguistic samples, edited works and multi-authored books by far outnumber single-authored books.

Our findings also revealed that outright criticism is perhaps not so much an integral feature of BRs as is generally thought since we found that almost a quarter of the BRs analyzed were criticism-free.

Regarding prosecutors, i.e., book reviewers, our study indicates that native-English speakers insert themselves more directly and openly into the semi-formal academic conversation of BRs by identifying themselves more personally (through the use of the "I" pronoun) when taking a critical stand than French native speakers do. In fact, French book reviewers tend to adopt a more authoritative, expert voice by using the impersonal pronoun "on" as if they were representing the whole scientific community. We thus speculate that this is one of the reasons why CRs are more frequently hedged or modulated in the French-written BRs than in their English counterparts. Our findings thus corroborate the fact that French scientists tend to consider themselves as the "détenteurs du savoir" (knowledge "holders"), whereas Anglo-American writers rather act as humble servants of the discipline (Myers 1989).

As for the defendant identification, book authors in French BRs are frequently personally referred to and held responsible for the flaws put forward by the reviewee (criticisms are then *ad hominem*), whereas in English BRs, it is book chapters that are the thematic accusees of the flaws denounced in the BR. The more personal character of French academic writing is thus also confirmed by the findings of the present research.

In academic BRs, then, each language uses its own linguistico-rhetorical strategies to establish a solidarity framework with the reviewee and to minimize the interpersonal damage of critical comments/remarks, i.e., to deal with interpersonal issues (such as concord seeking, rapport, collegial respect and peer antagonism), and to negotiate the delicate and sensitive social interactions inherent to the genre.

7. References

Askehave, Inger and John Swales. "Genre identification and communicative purpose: a problem and a possible solution." *Applied Linguistics* 22/2 (2001): 195-212.

Belcher, Diane. "Writing across the curriculum." In *Academic Writing in a Second Language: Essays on Research and Pedagogy*, edited by Diane Belcher and George Braine, 135-154. Norwood (NJ): Ablex Publishing Corporation, 1995.

Bloch, Joel. "Creating materials for teaching evaluation in academic writing: using letters to the editor in L2 composition courses." *English for Specific Purposes* 22 (2003): 347-364.

Burgess, Sally. "Books for review and reviewers for books: A genre analysis of print and electronic book reviews in Linguistics." Paper presented at the Research & Practice in Professional Discourse, Hong Kong, November 15/17th, 2000.

Chalmers, Iain. "Helping physicians to keep abreast of the medical literature: Medical and Philosophical Commentaries, 1773-1795." *Annals of Internal Medicine* 133/3 (2000): 238-243.

Clarke, Mike, Alderson, Phil and Ian Chalmers. "Discussion sections in reports of controlled trials published in general medical journals." *JAMA* (Journal of the American Medical Association) 287/21 (2002): 2799-2800.

Colman, Eric. "The first English medical journal: Medicina Curiosa." *Lancet* 354 (1999): 324-326.

De Carvalho, Gisèle. Rhetorical patterns of academic book reviews written in Portuguese and in English. In *Studies in Contrastive Linguistics*. Edited by Luis Iglesias Rábade and María Susana Doval Suárez. 261-268. Proceedings of the Second International Contrastive Linguistics Conference. Santiago de Compostela. October 2001.

Duncan, Andrew. *Medical and Philosophical Commentaries*. Introduction, Vol. First, part I/8. London: Murray, 1773.

Felber, Lynnette. "The book review: scholarly and editorial responsibility." *Journal of Scholarly Publishing* 33/3 (2002): 166-172.

Fløttum, Kjersti. "Personal English, indefinite French and Plural Norwegian scientific authors? Pronominal author manifestation in research articles". *Nordsk Lingvistik Tidsskrift* 21/1 (2003): 21-55.
Fløttum, Kjersti and François Rastier, eds. *Academic Discourse: Multidisciplinary Approaches.* Oslo: Novus, 2003.
Gea Valor, Lluïsa. *A Pragmatic Approach to Politeness and Modality in Book Reviews.* SELL Monograph. Valencia: Universitat de València, 2000.
Giannoni, Davide Simone. "Hard words, soft technology. Criticism and endorsement in the software review genre." In *Conflict and Negotiation in Specialized Texts*, edited by Maurizio Gotti, Dorothee Heller and Marina Dossena, 335-363. Bern: Peter Lang, 2002.
Gilbert, Nigel and Michael Mulkay. *Opening Pandora's Box.* Cambridge: Cambridge University Press, 1984.
Hartley, James. "Writing and editing book reviews." *Science Editors' Handbook* (European Association of Science Editors) (2006a): 1-4.
—. "Reading and writing book reviews across the disciplines." *Journal of the American Society for Information Science and Technology*, 2006b (in press).
Hyland, Ken. *Disciplinary Discourses. Social Interactions in Academic Writing.* London: Longman, 2000.
Johnson, D.M. "Complimenting and politeness in peer-review texts." *Applied Linguistics* 13/1 (1992): 51-71.
Motta-Roth, Désirée. "Discourse Analysis and academic book reviews: a study of text and disciplinary cultures." In *Genre Studies in English for Academic Purposes*, edited by Inmaculada Fortanet, Santiago Posteguillo, Juan Carlos Palmer and Juan Francisco Coll, 29-59. Castellón de la Plana: Universitat Jaume I, 1998.
Myers, Greg. The pragmatics of politeness in scientific articles. *Applied Linguistics* 10 (1989): 1-35.
North, Stephen. "On book reviews in rhetoric and composition." *Rhetoric Review* 10 (1992): 348-363.
Orteza y Miranda, Evelina. "On book reviewing". *Journal of Educational Thought* 30/2 (1996): 191-202.
Salager-Meyer, Françoise. "Hedges and textual communicative function in medical English written discourse." *English for Specific Purposes* 13 (1994): 149-170.
—. "This book portrays the worst form of mental terrorism: critical speech acts in medical English book reviews (1940-2000)." In *Approaches to the Pragmatics of Scientific Discourse*, edited by András Kertész, 47-72. Bern: Peter Lang, 2001.
Salager-Meyer, Françoise, Françoise, Alcaraz Ariza, María Ángeles and Nahirana Zambrano. "The scimitar, the dagger and the glove: Intercultural

differences in the rhetoric of criticism in Spanish, French and English Medical Discourse (1930-1999)." *English for Specific Purposes* 22/3 (2003): 223-247.

Salager-Meyer, Françoise, María Ángeles Alcaraz Ariza and Maryelis Pabón. "Big science, internationalisation, professionnalisation et fonction sociale de la science à travers l'analyse de recensions d'ouvrages." *LSP and Professional Communication* 16/1 (2006): 8-25.

Shaw, Philip. "How do we recognise implicit evaluation in academic book reviews?" In *Proceedings of the conference on 'Evaluation in Academic Discourse'* Certosa di Pontignano (Siena), 14-16 June 2003, edited by Gabriella Del Lungo Camiciotti and Elena Tognini Bonelli.

Smith, Richard. "The case for structuring the discussion of scientific papers." *British Medical Journal* 318 (1999): 1224-1225.

Suárez, Liliana. "Is evaluation structure bound? An English-Spanish contrastive study of book reviews." In *Strategies in Academic Discourse*, edited by Elena Tognini Bonelli and Gabriella Del Lungo Camiciotti, 117-132. Amsterdam/Philadelphia: John Benjamins, 2005

Swales, John. *Genre Analysis: English in Academic Research Settings*. Cambridge: Cambridge University Press, 1990.

—."Occluded genres in the academy: the case of the submission letter." In *Academic Writing: Intercultural and Textual Issues*, edited by Eija Ventola and Anna Mauranen, 45-58. Amsterdam: John Benjamins, 1996.

—. *Research Genres: Exploration and Applications*. Cambridge University Press. 2004

Thompson, G. and Susan Hunston. "Evaluation: an introduction" In *Evaluation in Text*, edited by Susan Hunston and G. Thompson, 1-27. Oxford: Oxford University Press, 2000.

Tröhler, Ulrich. *To improve the evidence of medicine: the 18th century British Origins of an Approach*. Edinburgh: Royal College of Physicians, 2000.

Appendix 1

French medical journals consulted:
Revue Neurologique
La Presse Médicale
Journal Français d'Ophtalmologie
Revue de Chirurgie Orthopédique

Anglo-American journals consulted:
JAMA (Journal of the American Medical Association)
The New England Journal of Medicine
The Lancet
Annals of Internal Medicine

Appendix 2

The "book note" or the "structured book review"

The book note has a 9 move-structure with explicit headings. Book review of the book entitled *Medical Quality Management Sourcebook*, 2000 Edition.

- **Field of medicine:** Quality improvement and patient safety.
- **Format:** Softcover book.
- **Audience:** Quality improvement leaders, physicians, hospital executives, managers, and purchasers of health care.
- **Purpose:** To provide an overview of …
- **Content:** Eight chapter cover… Each chapter includes.. Some also include… Detailed information about .. is also provided.
- **Highlights:** The book offers a useful update on .. The material on … may be especially useful …
- **Limitations:** This collection lacks a unifying introduction… Many of the articles are self-promoting … Many recent initiatives on quality management are never mentioned… Much of the information is available from any medical library or on the Internet.
- **Related readings:** Several websites provide information about … including http://www……
- **Reviewer:** Patrick S. Romano, MD. MPH, University of …

CHAPTER SEVEN

COOPERATION AND CONFLICT BETWEEN
AUTHORIAL VOICES AND MODEL READERS
THROUGH RHETORICAL TOPOI
IN HISTORICAL DISCOURSE

JOHAN L. TØNNESSON

1. Introduction

> Everything was black or white: Good Norwegians or traitors. This is not entirely unjustified. Can we dismiss the disgust and the denunciation of NS (National Unity, Quisling's party. JLT) when we think of the atrocities which were committed, also in this district? (Olstad 1997:183)

This quote is taken from Norwegian historian Finn Olstad's local history of Sandefjord, a city and a district in Eastern Norway. What we read about is the atmosphere during the first days and weeks after the German capitulation in May 45. We have just been stimulated to feel a certain sympathy with girls who had had relationships with German soldiers and who were now exposed to brutal revenge from the local mob. For a long time these events were something of a taboo in Norwegian historiography. Sixty years after, most of the children of these girls, the so-called "German's children" still have to hide themselves: The history of World War II was to a high degree written as the history of the victors until a few revisionists entered the historians' arena two decades ago. However, in the late 90s, at the time when the second volume of History of Sandefjord was written, de-tabooing and slight revisionism was more *comme il faut*.

In my dissertation *Text as a score* (2004), I have analyzed several chapters from Olstad's two volume history of Sandefjord in some detail. World War II was one of a few central topics. After having finished my analysis, I had an interview with the author, professor Olstad, about his ideas on the history of the German occupation of Norway. He said that his intention had been to bring a «critic of the critique, and a revision of revisionism». (Tønnesson 2004:565) This seems sound, both with regard to the quote above and its co-text. In this paper, I will present this larger analysis and interpretation through a discussion of the "black or white"-quote. The main question will be: *How does the actual text–be it close to Olstad's conscious intention or not–realize such a double or even multiple critical revision?* I shall propose three answers.

2. First answer: Three implied authorial voices in parallel

It is not very risky to state that the realization of the revision, and also of the intentionality of the text altogether, [1] takes place through *multi-vocalism*. This, however, is not the same phenomenon as *polyphony*, neither in the linguistic (Nølke 1989) nor in the bakhtinian sense (Bakhtin 1973). Following Bakhtin, we should, in accordance with musical terminology, draw a dividing line between three types of textual composition: 1) polyphony, with full equality between the voices, 2) homophony, where one voice may be compared with the *cantus firmus*, the main voice which we shall name *tenor*, and 3) monophony– with only one voice. In academic texts–possibly with the exception of some branches of philosophy–full-fledged polyphony will not be acceptable, as the scientific author has to give some clear-cut arguments. But this does not mean that monophony–often named "monologism" or "homoglossia" when Bakhtin is translated into English–should be either an ideal or a normal feature in academic prose. More than this: Polyphony in *parts of* the academic's texts should not be restricted by the ethos of science.

As a result of a combination of contextual information and close reading of Olstad's work, I have concluded that there are three authorial voices present simultaneously in his chapters on World War II in Sandefjord. It may be argued that two of them can be heard as one, or, on the contrary, that more voices are to be found in the text. This is not a matter of final proof, but I still believe that the division into the following three voices is reasonable:

Voice I: The neutrally balancing historian
Voice II: The classical WWII occupation historian
Voice III: The revisionist WWII occupation historian

None of the voices seem to express sympathy with the NS in the text. Neither did I find any "popular" fanatic, patriotic voice, like those commonly found in popular histories from the post-war period.

---

[1] The distinction between *intention* and *intentionality* is inspired from phenomenology (Husserl 1985).

It should be mentioned at this point that the division of the utterance into three *authors in multi-vocal interplay* was not the first, but rather the last stage in my analytical procedure. It was a result of a rather detailed scrutiny of possibly embedded *topoi* and *model readers* in the text, to which we will soon return. These again were based upon interviews with empirical readers as well as discussions on text-related questions concerning the situational and cultural contexts which at the same time surrounds and inhabits the text. To do such an analysis, I believe–in accordance with) both historic-scientific ethos and the methodological guidelines from John Swales' genre school–the researcher has to know something about the involved discourse communities and the text cultures they take part in. In this case the most relevant discourse communities are: a) people engaged in local history and b) professional historians in Norway. In a broader text culture, Norwegian official debate on the relevant controversies, is important. Such contextual knowledge is, of course, necessary if you want to qualify your statements and suggestions about voices and related phenomena in texts.

The implied authorial voices of a text may partly be identified by paraphrasing or even "translating" the text. To do so, the analyst/interpreter has to rely upon his contextual knowledge as well as his ability to do close reading of various meaning potentials in the text. I will now present my translation of a few of Olstad's written formulations. We will call them "Supra"–i.e. the upper voice, the voice at the surface, so to say, and we shall translate them into the three authorial voices. Beside these voices, one line in the "score" is reserved for the *privileged authorial voice,* which I will call the *tenor,* from Latin: *tenere,* to keep or hold. (My use of this word is related to–but not identical with–the hallidayan "tenor" in the triad tenor-field-mode). In European renaissance music the tenor, not the supra or *soprano,* most often kept the melody.

Table 1. "Bar" 759 from the "score" of History of Sandefjord.

SUPERIUS	(759) Everything was black or white:
AUTHOR I	To many people in Sandefjord the world seemed to be just black or white, as we have already seen during the first time after 8 May 1945.
AUTHOR II	The fact that the population was divided in such a way into two categories,
AUTHOR III	In the emotionally loaded atmosphere of the May-days of 1945, of which we have described certain results, it was almost *comme il faut* to paint everything in black or white
TENOR	— (none)

Superius: Olstad's written formulation. Authors I-III: "translations" in parallel. Tenor: Privileged voice

In "bar" 759 of the score (table 1) there is no privileged authorial voice. This means that this isolated utterance is polyphonic: Each voice is equal, here in an ethical sense. All three voices include a reference to the preceding co-text dealing with the popular actions of revenge («as we already have seen», «in such a way» and «which we have described»). We notice that voices I and II objectivise the historical actors by the notions «many people» and «the population», and that III says with detachment that it was «almost *comme il faut*» to express black or white-thinking, thus implying that this is no longer so. Author II includes, more than the other two, the *vox populi anno 1945*, but through the passive «was divided». Author II makes a generalization which creates some distance even here. The topos analysis below will give a final argument for the conclusion that this is a polyphonic utterance in which the potential meaning is vibrating, so to say.

Now, let us take a look at the next bar from the score (table 2; see Table 1 for explanations).

Table 2: "Bar" 760 from the "score" of History of Sandefjord.

SUPERIUS	(760) Good Norwegians or traitors.
AUTHOR I	People were divided into two distinct categories which, in the terms of the time, were called "good Norwegians" or "traitors".
AUTHOR II	«good Norwegians or traitors»,
AUTHOR III	You were either a so-called "good Norwegian" or you were, and that's a pretty strong word indeed if you listen to it: a "traitor".
TENOR	*People were divided into two distinct categories which, in the terms of the time, were called "good Norwegians" or "traitors". (I)*

The heavily value-loaded words in the *supra* of bar 760 are repeated by author II. In spite of this, I would argue that the subject-oriented distance prevents the utterance from being dominated by clear ideology. On the other hand, through the lack of inverted commas this utterance is not a clear revisionist statement. Conclusion: Author I sings the tenor voice in utterance 760. But even here all three voices are audible in parallel. If we try to read the text aloud, only minor phonological changes will put the focus on revisionism or patriotism.

In this paper there is no room for further samples from this stage in the procedure, but let me show the results not only from the three sentences of the quote, but from the whole paragraph which follows.

Table 3. Distribution of tenor (privileged voice) in bars 759-786 in the "score" of History of Sandefjord.
The symbols from card-playing have some correspondence with the tendency in the authorial voices: Diamond for balanced reasoning, spades for ideological engagement against the evil-doers. Hearts stand for rationality-based sympathy with the loser. Club stands for neutrality, i.e. absence of privileged voice.

Auth. I ♦	♦		♦	♦			♦		
Auth. II ♠				♠	♠	♠		♠	♠
Auth. III ♥									
Neutral ♣	---								
Utterance	759	760	761	762	763	764	765	766	767

Auth. I ♦			♦	♦	♦		♦		
Auth. II ♠	♠					♠			
Auth. III. ♥		♥							♥
Neutral ♣								---	
Utterance	768	769	770	771	772	773	774	775	776

Auth. I ♦									♠	
Auth. II ♠										
Auth. III. ♥	♥	♥	♥	♥	♥	♥	♥	♥		♥
Neutral ♣										
Utterance	777	778	779	780	781	782	783	784	785	786

As we see from Table 3, there is a shift in the beginning of the text, from which our three sentences are taken, from domination by a scientific towards a more patriotic position, while the revisionist enters the chair at utterance no. 776, to keep it for the rest of the paragraph.

3. Second answer: Topoi–the link between Authorial voices, Model Readers and context

A topos does not have to be a fixed expression, a proverb, a slogan or a familiar quotation, it is–as the etymology tells us–a commonplace, cf. Latin *loci communes* for topoi, but often only a mental place. It may simply be seen as "a place in the landscape of consciousness" (Togeby 1986), but this consciousness is, of course, embedded in social life. Thus topoi and groups of topoi are the presuppositions necessary for communication, they are mental and social tools that prevent us from having to start at A in the alphabet each time we make an utterance. The intertextual or interdiscursive interplay of such commonplaces build up the common ground for various discourse communities and text cultures. One single text can certainly communicate with more than one discourse community, and thus topos analysis can help us to understand to whom the text is directed. We shall shortly return to this point.

My procedure for finding the topoi in the text–often parallel, as they are related to various implied readers or Model Readers or Authorial voices–is that of paraphrase and condensation. Here is one simple sample out of a few hundreds:

Table 4: Paraphrasing of utterances 762–763 into topoi. Categorization in topos groups derived from larger parts of Olstad's text (column 4)

Utterance	Paraphrase	Topos	Topos group
762. Can we dismiss the disgust and the denunciation of NS?	We cannot dismiss the disgust and the denunciation of NS	We cannot dismiss the disgust and the denunciation of NS when we know what actions the party is guilty of.	Pathos 4: Many NS people committed harsh atrocities! (P4 ATROCITIES!)
			Logos, Classic historiography 12: The one-sidedness and the denunciation among the majority after May 8,1945, are fully understandable (LC12 UNDER-STANDABLE BLACK/WHITE – 45)

763. when we think of the atrocities which were committed,	In the appraisal of the majority's attitudes and its actions in the wake of the war, med must take the atrocities of NS into consideration	"	" (both)
		From time to time the historian must be able to take clear-cut stands and call an outrage an outrage.	

The number of topos groups derived from the chapters in Olstad's Volume II is 73 altogether. I have divided them into the following main categories, following the rhetorical *pisti* or means of evidence:

Examples of ethos-topos-groups:
- «I do science through solid examining of sources.»[2]
- «The reader is welcome to control for himself.» This second topos represents recipient oriented ethos or *engagement*. This topos is derived from the reference itself and I would suggest this as a new category in Ken Hyland's taxonomy of interpersonal markers.[3]

Logos-topos-groups:
- Topos groups from classical Norwegian historiography on WWII. *Example:* «NS were the obedient helpers of the occupants, i.e. followers»
- Topos groups from a more revisionist Norwegian historiography on WWII. *Example:* «Occupant and occupied had certain basic common interests »
- Historical-methodological topos groups. *Example:* «Historians and history interested should both be familiar with the meaning of the concepts of the past»
- Historical-theoretical topos groups. *Example:* «Chance may decide apparently free human choices»

---

[2] This exemplifies sender oriented ethos or *stance* in Ken Hyland's terms. See Hyland's contribution to this volume.
[3] Cf. once more Hyland's contribution to this volume.

- Topos groups dealing with local history. *Example:* «In a local history it is part of the job to emphasize contributions which have had successful effects also beyond the local environment»

Examples of pathos-topos-groups:
- «What happened then? We shall let the drama go on!» Many pathos-topoi deal with enthusiasm related to dissemination.
- «Many NS people committed harsh atrocities!» (patriotic), cf. P4 ATROCITIES in table 4.
- «The Norwegians who joined the German army and died at the East Front also deserve our compassion!» (revisionist).

We promised above to give a topos-related argument to support the statement that at least one of the utterances–no. 759 (Table 1)–was polyphonic, i.e. free from any privileged tenor-voice. The argument is simply that in this utterance the topoi (or topos-groups) «The historian should have the possibility to express changing and contrasting viewpoints» (LHM8) sounds side by side with «The one-sided picture seen by the majority after May 8 1945, is understandable, but quite misleading » (LR 17). It seems difficult to argue that any of these two should be on top.

The topoi and topos groups–various and standardized arguments (not necessarily connected with argumentation)–may also be seen as additional or contrasting voices in "autocommunicative" systems (Lotman 1990). By identifying them we can more easily speculate on which authorial voices exist in the text, and not least, which model readings, or Model Readers can be found in the text.

4. Model Readers: Definition

What then is a Model Reader? Briefly we may say that he or she is a model for adequate reading of a text. Among scholars engaged in literature within the institution of art ("Literature") it is not very popular, and perhaps not even useful, to talk about adequacy. But indeed there is a Model Reader in Literature, namely the reader who accepts the institutional demands and read the text as Literature. This single Model Reader, however, can be split into an endless number of sub-model-readers. That is why the Model Reader perhaps is not a useful tool in interpretation of Literature (von der Fehr 1999). But in subject oriented prose like history it certainly is. This *model* shows us the way through the text, so to say. The main reason why–along with a large number of reception theorists–I choose to call this model a *reader*, not just a reading, is that the whole idea of readers-in-the-texts permits us to examine more of the potential dialogue in the text: Like the empirical reader of flesh and blood, the Model Reader has to develop himself and his competence throughout the reading process.

The term *model reader* or *lettore modello* is Eco's (Eco 1979a and b), but it is, despite a good start, poorly developed. Here is my proposal for a more precise definition than Eco and others have offered (cf. Tønnesson 2003). It is based on Eco, but it goes a little further:

1. The construction of Model Readers is an intentional (not necessarily conscious) textual strategy which creates felicity conditions for a text to be actualised in its potentialities of meaning. The Model Reader, who is never entirely identical with any empirical reader, possesses a linguistic and cultural competence that is, in principle, identifiable. But the Model Reader also builds up new competence in the course of the reading process.

2. For the empirical reader it is a respectable project to approach the Model Reader, which in the first clause of the definition was described as actualising the text in its full content. Particularly in the creation of meaning around blanks/Leerstellen, an acquaintance with empirical readers will facilitate the identification of Model Readers.

3. Intertextually a Model Reader is primarily constituted through an interplay of norms. In practice this means that, when the empirical reader is to approach the Model Reader, lack of normative confidence is a stronger barrier for the empirical reader than lack of textual familiarity.

4. A text may include more than one, but not an unlimited number of Model Readers.

5. The basis for identifying different Model Readers can especially be found by establishing the communicative purposes of the various situational contexts, by studying relevant rhetorical strategies, by interpreting explicit manifestations in the course of the text, and by (re)constructing norm-based response to concrete utterances. Such analysis presupposes a thorough, preferably congenial knowledge of norms and behaviour in the social field in question.

One source to knowledge about norms and behaviour was my intensive interviews with four Empirical Readers with connection to Sandefjord–one old, female patriot with membership in the conservative party, one middle-aged female history professor with SV (Socialist Left Party) membership, one idealistic, young female student, one mid-aged male left-oriented chief librarian and even one mid-aged man, a right-wing-oriented son of an industrial worker, now director of industry in the municipality of Sandefjord, a man with heavy international experience. One of these readers' tasks was to respond to each utterance in the paragraph beginning with "Everything was black or white". But the main purpose of the interviews was to learn about various readers' attitudes towards the text and the topics in question. Based on this knowledge I made an imaginative "Gallup test", asking "what appeal has each topos group to each of the empirical readers?" And I answered by giving points from 0 to 3. Perhaps someone would find this to be too speculative. But what I do is to articulate my interpretations and presumptions in a concrete manner instead of just formulating some general and rather abstract reasoning. This produced a more solid ground for further discussion on "who are the model readers"?

Trying to follow the rest of the procedure recommended in point 5 of the definition, I proposed a number of potential model readers–ten altogether. One of the means to exclude some and combine others, was to test the appeal of the topos groups to them as well. The test protocol is far to big to be commented in detail here. Just to give an idea about the technique, I present an extract from it (table 5; "Model Reader" abbreviations are explained in table 6).

Table 5: Extract from the test protocol "measuring" the appeal of various topoi to possible Model Readers (Tønnesson 2004, appendix 28).

"Model Reader" / Topos group	PLH	EVA	÷PA	+PA	JØS	REV	PAT	CRI	FAC	UND
Ethos										
E1 Sources	3	3	1	1	1	3	1	2	2	2
E2 Original	3	3	1	1	1	2	1	2	1	2
E3 Solid footnote	3	3	1	1	1	3	1	3	1	3
E4 Solid background	3	3	2	2	2	3	1	3	2	3
E5 Kind	3	3	2	2	2	2	2	2	3	3
SUM ETHOS	*15*	*15*	*7*	*7*	*7*	*13*	*6*	*12*	*9*	*13*
Logos, Classic occupation History										
LK1 The follower	1	1	2	2	3	1	2	1	2	2
LK2 Isolated and small NS	2	1	1	2	3	2	2	1	2	2
LK3 Important NS	2	1	1	2	3	2	2	1	2	2
LK4 Moral struggle	1	1	2	3	3	1	3	2	1	1
LK5 NS atrocities	1	1	2	2	3	1	3	1	3	2

LK6 Anti-democratic NS	1	1	2	1	3	1	2	1	2	2
LK7 Führer-governed community	1	1	2	1	3	1	1	1	3	2

In Table 6 one will find the results. The sums are based on all the topoi in a larger extract from volume 2 of History of Sandefjord.

Table 6. The results of the test illustrated in table 5.

POSSIBLE MODEL READERS	*POINTS*
1. SEARCHER OF UNDERSTANDING (UND)	320
2. REVISIONIST (REV)	297
3. CRITIC OF IDENTITY POLITICS (CRI)	289
4. PROFESSIONAL LOCAL HISTORIAN (PLH)	285
5. LOCAL ANTI-PATERNALIST (÷PA)	271
6. PROFESSOR EVALUATOR (EVA)	258
7. "JØSSING" (WWII PATRIOT) (JOSS)	248
8. CONTEMPORARY LOCAL PATRIOTS (PAT)	243
9. SEARCHERS OF FACTS (FAC)	239
10. LOCAL PRO-PATERNALIST (+PA)	229

Following the whole procedure of point 5 in the definition above, I ended up with four Model Readers altogether:

Model Reader A (the patriotic inhabitant of Sandefjord)
Model Reader B (the critical, new-thinking inhabitant of Sandefjord)
Model Reader C (the appraising, professional historian free from prejudice with regard to the time of German occupation)
Model Reader D (the comprehension-searching historian interested in local history, with a vivid, though not fanatic anti-NS (Quislings party. JLT) attitude)

The Model Reader analysis gave a lot of insight with regard to the meaning potential of the text. In particular I find the "(re)construction of norm-based response to concrete utterances" productive, although I must admit that it is a product of some fantasy. We will return to this part of the procedure.

5. Third answer: The orchestration of authorial voices, topoi and Model Readers

The third answer to the main question–*how does the text realize a multidimensioned critical and historiographic revision*–is more of a synthesis of the first two than an additional answer. The synthesis, however, is not a Hegelian, dualistic one, but rather an orchestration of various resources or potentials in the text. In accordance with the "orchestra" metaphor the answer will be presented as a *score*. The authorial voices–identical or not with the *supra*– are already known, including the privileged *tenor* voice. Also the *topoi* are explained above. But the score also includes my (re)construction of the presumed responses of the Model Readers. In addition, the responses to the two first utterances from five empirical readers–people of various age, class background and education with a close connection to Sandefjord–are included. Their responses certainly do not have an equal status with the more text-inherent voices of the text, but as competent commentators they can illuminate the text and illustrate what five "performances" of the score may look like.

Three paragraphs from History of Sandefjord:
Score for Ten Voices
including comments from five empirical readers

The Voices

SUPERIUS (utterances)
AUTHOR I (Author's voice I–the neutrally balancing historian)
AUTHOR II (Author's voice II–the classical WWII occupation historian)
AUTHOR III (Author's voice III–the revisionist WWII occupation historian)
TENOR (privileged author's voice)

TOPOI
MODEL READER A (the patriotic inhabitant of Sandefjord)
MODEL READER B (the critical, new-thinking inhabitant of Sandefjord)
MODEL READER C (the appraising, professional historian free from prejudice with regard to the time of the German occupation)

Cooperation and Conflict Between Authorial Voices and Model Readers 141

MODEL READER D (the comprehension-searching historian interested in local history, with a vivid, though not fanatic anti-NS (Quisling's party. JLT) attitude)

The empirical readers
AN (Reidunn Asphaug Never, 90 years old, former bookseller)
MD (Marianne Dahl, MA student)
JB (Jorunn Bjørgum, history professor)
HG (Hans Gjerløw, director of the public Sandefjord Library)
EM (Ernst Midttun, industrial director of the municipality of Sandefjord)

SUPERIUS AUTHOR I	(759) Everything was black or white: To many people in Sandefjord the world seemed to be just black or white, as we have already seen during the first time after May 8 1945.
AUTHOR II	The fact that the population were divided in such a way into two categories,
AUTHOR III	In the emotionally loaded atmosphere of the May-days of 1945, of which we have described certain results, it was almost *comme il faut* to paint everything in black or white
TENOR	— (none)
TOPOI	The historian should have the possibility to express changing and contrasting viewpoints (LHM8)/ The one-sided picture seen by the majority after May 8 1945, is understandable, but quite misleading (LR 17)
MODEL READER A	Black or white? Yes, that's exactly how it was
MODEL READER B	Well, that's the picture you get in the midst of all the excitement.
MODEL READER C	Very well. Now I'm a bit excited about the discussion of this topic.
MODEL READER D	Of course it was a situation of sharp conflict, most people had been dreaming of this for five years!

AN : Yes, yes, that is how it was. I actually kept watch of some "German's girls" who were taken into custody, taken, teken care of [clears her throat], and I actually knew some of them girls beforehand, been to school with some oft them. And .... I was indeed extremely surprised that "Jesus Christ, have you kind of been involved in this?" But et .... I was indeed most surprised [clears her throat] that certain, certain ladies, I would say, could really do such a thing.

MD .. Mm, Well, I believe I think that either, that either, well I believe you thought that if you were a German's girl, you had gone over to the enemy on your own free will and so on, and if you were not a German's girl, then you would automatically have fought against, been a good Norwegian, this was what people thought. /Interviewer (T:) Yes. D: you kind of didn't look at other factors.

JB Yes. Yes. "Everything was black or white". .. Do you ask me, I nearly said, eh, about the validity of such a statement as a description of the situation and the attitudes there and then, or what are you asking me about? /Interviewer: Yes, I do./ B: Yes/ Interviewer (T): Or just interpret it that way. /B: Yes. / [The old lady, then] B: [Yes]/ T: there I asked/ B: [Certainly] /[in a way about] her view upon /B: Yes/ T: what was legitimate, then/ B: Yes/ T: But eh/ B: Yes, but, it is valid that it *looked like* everything was black or white, precisely in the days of the liberation, that is valid enough, isn't it? If it *was* like that, that's another matter. Or if it was not, and that was problematic when much later we evaluate their black-white thinking as problematic, that is, that is something else. But that Finn's description of everything being black and white there and then, or looked like that for most people, I think that is a *valid* description.

HG I guess I believe, as I sort of have heard and experienced this, I certainly think this is very correct

EM [My association] immediately goes to the Germans' girls./ T: Yes. /M: And eh, and eh I quite agree with his point, that there was a tendency, just in the libera, the moment of the liberation, when they become very much heroes, those who are heroes, and you get a little of that show off and muscles which was not there before and which suddenly turns up enormously, and and then it is something of an *un-nuanced* acting, and I have been against this in many other of those social connections, I, I can sometimes be aggressive as a person and things like that, but that thing, to let things, do harm to an individual without understanding that you have things like love, you have things like necessity, you have things like survival, I think that is silly and we certainly saw much of that just at the end of the war, and this *especially* hit the girls, I believe.

SUPERIUS	(760) Good Norwegians or traitors.
AUTHOR I	People were divided into two distinct categories which, in the terms of the time, were called "good Norwegians" or "traitors".
AUTHOR II	«good Norwegians or traitors»,

Cooperation and Conflict Between Authorial Voices and Model Readers   143

AUTHOR III	you were either a so-called "good Norwegian" or you were, and that's a pretty strong word indeed if you listen to it: a "traitor".
TENOR	*People were divided into two distinct categories which, in the terms of the time, were called "good Norwegians" or "traitors".* (I)
TOPOI	The historian should be able to express changing and contrasting viewpoints (LHM8)/ The one-sided picture drawn by the majority after May 8, 1945, is understandable, but entirely misleading (LR 17)
MODEL READER A	I quite agree, there *were* in fact two sorts of people.
MODEL READER B	Well, at least it seemed so to those who considered themselves as "good".
MODEL READER C	No inverted commas? I suppose that's all right. Those were the terms of the time.
MODEL READER D	Yes, and then there were of course the "striped". [Norwegian missing a clear-cut pro or contra Nazi standpoint. JLT].

AN	..yes, that is you know there were a good deal of those who both had a job and worked for the Germans. T: Yes/AN: Yes there certainly was. /T: Exactly. /AN: And there were, there were many who, especially also here in Sandefjord, where they had a shop or a business, which had success before the war, and then the Germans came and claimed both their products, and [with a sigh] you know they had to, they had to accept a good deal to be able to keep the firm and the employment to all their people, and thus it was also here, that lots of people worked for the Germans, even at Framnes [shipyard JLT], very much so at Framnes, who worked for the Germans. But what did you expect them to do? T: Yes. /AN: They were certainly not, they were certainly no Nazis, on the contrary, they tried as much as they could to avoid their work./ T: Yes. AN: You know?
MD	Yes.
JB	. Eh, it was, I guess, my impression is that *this* was a type eh an attitude which was very common, it *was* either or. We certainly know that, it *was* not like that.
HG	Yes, I I believe that this also is a fair description of the attitudes at that time.
EM	Yes, there there we see the same thing, really, because I eh came from Selmer [large Norw. Contractor. JLT] who built like hell during the war, they made *big* money, right, and ☺ [laughing] were they good Norwegians ☺ or were they traitors, they certainly built for the Germans, they were in service of the Germans, they made money like hell, so, eh here it is something of the same thing, that it

does not exist any eh either or here, it was a situation where there is something you *have to do* if you want to survive, and and then we know that, at least psychologically to survive is extremely important.

SUPERIUS	**(761) This is not entirely unjustified.**
AUTHOR I	To a certain degree there was a basis for such a simplified picture..
AUTHOR II	Well, this could not be wondered at.
AUTHOR III	Many people could indeed have a reason to experience the world as quite simple.
TENOR	*To a certain degree there is a basis for such a simplified picture.. (I)*
TOPOI	The historian should have the possibility to express changing and contrasting viewpoints (LHM8)/ The one-sided picture drawn by the majority after May 8, 1945 is understandable, but entirely misleading (LR 17)/ Many NS members committed atrocities (LK5)
MODEL READER A	Unjustified, oh no! Won't people remember what went on during the war?
MODEL READER B	A feeling is seldom unjustified. Here it is a question of feelings, and nothing is ever entirely black or white.
MODEL READER C	Typically Olstad, a balanced discussion.
MODEL READER D	Exaggerated, yes, but not unjustified.

AN   Well, to see it like that wasn't unjustified. No, no but eh . no, well, everything *was no* black and white, I won't say it was.

MD   Yes I suppose this is the sort of remark from ☺ the author ☺ and/T: Yes/D: who more or less says that it must have been a bit like that as well, so in a way it's said a bit implicitly that if you *were* a good Norwegian, then you would, then you would never have anything to do with a German, perhaps.|

JB   . . Black white, good Norwegians, is this completely unjustified? Yes and no. . Well it is a a normative statement on his part which is perhaps a bit more problematic than that. I don't know.

HG   No, well, the fact that one can *understand* that in such a situation, people are able to think and feel that way, but from there to accept it, that is of course another thing, one one may *understand* it, that is, there I agree.

EM   No, you will find of course, well, inside all this there certainly were some dirty beasts, eh, Rinnan (notorious Norwegian informer JLT)is an OK example, and it is quite clear that they, that you will find the worst of them among people who are power-hungry or those who

Cooperation and Conflict Between Authorial Voices and Model Readers   145

> were attracted by big profit, I mean you can almost classify them on the basis of power and profit, one thing or the other, or a combination of both. And then, then I think you will find, you will find those who really *were,* well who wanted to profit from this, but there were certainly *political* as well, that is youngsters who ended up at the Eastern Front, I remember I read that, that there were eight or eleven, eleven of them from Sandefjord I think, and ☺ ☺ if you have got the wrong lot then ☺ then you've got he who was shot, I remember that as well when you say so, the one who was fired at by a machine gun on his way to Sweden or England or wherever it was, and then returns to end up as a German, that's the play of coincidence.

SUPERIUS	**(762) Can we dismiss the disgust and the denunciation of National Unity [Nasjonal samling, NS. Quisling's party. JLT]**
AUTHOR I	You cannot just dismiss the disgust and the denunciation of NS.
AUTHOR II	«The disgust against and the denunciation of NS» was inevitable
AUTHOR III	The aggression which was now directed towards NS is understandable.
TENOR	*The disgust and the denunciation of NS » were inevitable (II)*
TOPOI	Many NS people committed harsh atrocities (P4)/ The one-sidedness and the denunciation among the majority after May 8, 1945, are fully understandable (LC12)
MODEL READER A	Dismiss? No, I do both: I still disgust and denunciate, and I certainly do not feel ashamed about it.
MODEL READER B	It cannot be dismissed, but one should leave it behind after a time.
MODEL READER C	No, but has anyone been likely to dismiss this?
MODEL READER D	No, it should not be dismissed, but it should be contextualized.
AN	(commentary in text "bar")
MD	→
JB	→
HG	→
EM	→

SUPERIUS	**(763) when you think of the atrocities which were committed,**
AUTHOR I	When you think of the harsh actions that NS people were guilty of
AUTHOR II	«when we think of the atrocities which were committed »,

146 Chapter Seven

AUTHOR III	in the light of the actions which were committed
TENOR	*when we think of the atrocities which were committed (II)*
TOPOI	Many NS people committed harsh atrocities (P4)/ The one-sidedness and the denunciation among the majority after May 8 1945, is quite understandable (LC12)
MODEL READER A	Yes, exactly, these were essentially unforgivable *atrocities*.
MODEL READER B	Yes, but try to think for a while of the atrocities which. today's South Africans are beginning to cope with..
MODEL READER C	"Outrage" is quite a strong word. Now we should see what he is thinking about.
MODEL READER D	I agree that we should not forget this. The years of occupation were not a Sunday School.

AN	→
MD	.. Yes, that goes to some extent in the same direction that he, that there is a question about, wasn't there still, there must have been some, some ill will beneath this, I was about to say, if one joined the NS, then one must have been, it can't *only* have been coincidences or something like that, you must have had certain weak attitudes, perhaps.
JB	→
HG	→
EM	. This, no I guess this can't be *dismissed,* but it should certainly be moderated, but it has, that is actually what he does in this book /T: Yes. /M: He moderates the , sort of, violent *Nazi* and *the nationalist or the patriot,* so here he has been successful, I feel.

SUPERIUS	**(764)also in this district?**
AUTHOR I	not only at the national level and in other regions and districts, but also locally in Sandefjord and Sandar.
AUTHOR II	«» by our own folks «here in this district ».
AUTHOR III	in Sandefjord as in other places.
TENOR	*also by our own folks here in this district. (II)*
TOPOI	Many NS people committed harsh atrocities (P4)/ The one-sidedness and the denunciation among the majority after May 8 1945, are fully understandable (LC12)
MODEL READER A	Yes, here too. I remember several harsh cases which it seems extremely difficult to forgive.
MODEL READER B	I suppose it was not worse here than in other districts, but it was bad, of course it was.

MODEL READER C	He is quite good at filling his writing with credibility.
MODEL READER D	Now, let us have a look at the examples he emphasizes here.

AN	No. Absolutely not.
MD	Yes ☺ ☺ it is a bit like, that it should be something special then, with Sandefjord? Or, or perhaps perhaps more like, it must have been that way in Sandefjord as well as all other places, sort of.
JB	. . Oh!. . . But here he implicitly says that there are a good deal of people who dismiss it, and that is not correct, it is not true. He hints that, something that is not correct. Yes, that is my reflection.
HG	No, I don't think one can just . . push it aside. °No°
EM	Yes, yes. [he means that the former answer is relevant also here]

6. Conclusion

As a field of research, the study of voices in academic texts is rather heterogeneous, although corpus linguistics has been much of a methodological core. As will be seen from the present book, there has recently been a move from micro-level studies to more macro-oriented discussions. Context–intertextual, situational and cultural–plays a more crucial role than before. But as linguists and textologists we must still primarily focus on the text and its linguistic resources.

How can we combine this focus with the insight that text and context are always woven together, as the very etymology of the word *textus* points to? My suggestion is to combine the concept of topoi from classical rhetoric with Eco-inspired reception theory as well as the radical, dialogical and polylogical perspectives of the bakhtinian tradition (Bakhtin 1973, 1986). To reconstruct a score based on various interpretations of smaller and larger components of the texts and their contexts may seem somewhat speculative to a scientific mind. But as we all know: No description is free from interpretation.

The success or failure of linguistic and textual description and interpretation will always depend on its reasonability. In our case this is mainly a question of the relation between the supra and the proposed topoi, voices and potential responses. I leave it to my critical readers to judge.

7. References

Bakhtin, Mikhail M. *Problems of Dostoevsky's poetics.* Michigan: Ardis, 1973 (1963/1929).
—. *Speech genres and other late essays.* Austin: University of Texas Press, 1986.
Eco, Umberto. *Lector in fabula. La cooperazione interpretativa nei testi narrativi.* Milano: Bompiano, 1979a.
—. *The Role of the Reader. Explorations in the semiotics of texts.* London, 1979b.
Fehr, Drudge von der. *Violenza e interpretazione. La Storia di Elsa Morante,* Pisa/Roma: Instituti Editoriali e Poligrafici Internazionali, 1999.
Husserl, Edmund. "*Encyclopedia Britannica*-Artikel" in ——. *Die phänomenologische Methode. Ausgewählte Texte I,* Stuttgart: Universal-Bibliothek, Reklam, 1985 (1927).
Lotman, Jurij M. *Universe of the Mind. A Semiotic Theory of Culture,* London: Tauris, 1990.
Nølke, Henning. *Polyfoni. En sprogteoretisk indføring.* Copenhagen: Copenhagen Business School, ARK 48, 1989.
Olstad, Finn. *Sandefjords historie. Bind 2. En vanlig småby?* ("History of Sandefjord. Vol. 2. A common, small town?"). Sandefjord: Sandefjord kommune, 1997.
Togeby, Ole. *STEDER i bevidsthedens landskab – grene på ideernes træ. Om at finde stof til belysning af en sag.* ("Places in the Landscape of Consciousness – Branches on the Tree of Ideas.") Copenhagen: Gyldendal,1986.
Tønnesson, Johan L. 2003: "Model readers and other textual strategies in Norwegian historian Professor Finn Olstad's paper "New perspectives on the rise and fall of the working class" (2000)". In Kjersti Fløttum and François Rastier (eds.). *Academic discourse. Multidisciplinary approaches.* Oslo: Novus Press, 2003:158-180.
—. *Tekst som partitur eller Historievitenskap som kommunikasjon. Nærlesning av fire historietekster skrevet for ulike lesergrupper,* ("Text as a Score or Historical Research as Communication. A Close Reading of Four History Texts Written for Various Groups of Readers."). Oslo: Unipub. Acta humaniora; nr 207, 2004.

PART III

LANGUAGE FOCUS

CHAPTER EIGHT

THE 'IFFINESS' OF MEDICAL RESEARCH ARTICLES: A COMPARISON OF ENGLISH *IF* AND FRENCH *SI*

SHIRLEY CARTER-THOMAS

1. Introduction

This chapter will focus on the use of English *if* and French *si*, in the medical research article (RA) in oncology. Although it is always challenging to find connectives that correspond across languages, *if* and *si* are considered as the typical lexical exponents of conditionality in both languages with a wide degree of overlap in their prototypical functions. One of my main aims will therefore be to determine whether they are used in the same way in English and French medical research articles.

Studying the role of these two items in the research world would seem profitable for several reasons. Firstly, the 'iffiness' afforded by conditional clauses, with their characteristic non-assertiveness, provides a highly valuable resource in the attainment of various objectives of medical research communication, such as hedging, hypothesising and promoting research claims. In medical research, and particularly in clinical investigations of the type analysed here, where the reasoning is inductive rather than deductive (being observation based), the need to weigh evidence carefully in order to make space for claims is of paramount importance. The hypotheses proposed must often therefore be necessarily tentative, due to a great number of factors or variables and results are usually given in probabilistic form (Horsella & Sindermann 1992). At the same time results obtained in medical research are established under strictly controlled conditions (randomization and large-scale trials, for example). The researchers need to delimit the research space and specify the conditions under which the research was carried out; conditional clauses can also play an extremely important role here too, in specifying for example the eligibility criteria for patients involved in trials.

The importance of conditional constructions in RAs is also linked to their role as potential polyphonic operators, often enabling implicit (and sometimes explicit) polyphonic interaction. The RA is both a competitive and cooperative text (Fløttum 2005). Researchers need to be competitive, creating a new space for their own claims and promoting their research, whilst remaining at the same time cooperative towards peers: recognizing the contribution of others, in order to delimit the import of their specific research within the community research effort. By building, for example, on shared knowledge and on mutually acceptable assumptions (*If X is admitted*), or on reference to others' research (*If as these studies indicate*), medical researchers can summon different voices into the text–negotiating their own research claims whilst still respectfully acknowledging the sum of mutual research already accomplished. It has been suggested that medical researchers are rather remote writers who do not let themselves or others be heard directly in their texts (cf. the provocative title of Dahl 2004: "Absent doctors, shy economists, polemic linguists?"). Although the polyphonic potential of conditional constructions is perhaps more apparent in some of the other medical genres (cf. Rowley-Jolivet, this volume), it would seem that even in the RA, medical writers are more visible and polemic than originally thought–albeit with some slight language-related differences.

The article is organised as follows: after a presentation of the data, I will outline the general descriptive framework and methodology adopted for this study, focusing on certain quantitative and formal features of the constructions in order to build up a general picture of baseline usage of *if* and *si* in the medical RA. This will be followed by the cross-linguistic analysis which is divided into two main sections, the first focusing on the distribution of the various occurrences in the different RA sections and the second on a qualitative comparison of the functions fulfilled by the *si*- and *if*-constructions collected in the different author groups.

2. Data sample

This study is based on an analysis of **90 RAs**, taken from four different refereed journals (two English, two French[1]), all dealing with clinical oncology. The articles were roughly of the same length, followed very strictly an IMRD (Introduction-Methods-Results-Discussion) structure and could be considered as standard data-based medical RAs[2]. Three author groups were distinguished:

---

[1] The articles published in 2002-2003 are from the following journals: International Journal of Radiation Oncology (30), Journal of Clinical Oncology (30), Bulletin du Cancer (15) and Cancer-Radiothérapie (15).
[2] The main difference, between the French and English journals, is essentially in terms of the likely audience reached–with the readership of the French journals restricted to oncology specialists in Francophone North Africa and France (see Burgess (2002) and Swales (2004) for a discussion of the restricted readership issue).

French (Fr) authors of articles in French, English speaking authors of articles in English (En) and French speaking authors (Fse) of articles in English–the latter identified through their names and laboratory affiliations. This third subset was isolated in order to take into consideration the possible influence of national origin, arising from the French/English comparison. As many cross-cultural studies on academic communication have pointed out (for example, Mauranen 1993; Ventola & Mauranen 1996; Sionis 1997; Rowley-Jolivet & Carter-Thomas 2005), different national traditions can be expected to impact on the *lingua franca* of academic communication, English. By also comparing research articles in English by French speaking and native English-speaking authors, it should be possible to gauge whether the recurrent rhetorical functions attributed to *if* by the two speaker groups reflect underlying cross-linguistic differences between *if* and *si* in their respective native languages, leading to different argumentative implications.

3. Descriptive framework

3.1 Inclusions and exclusions

Isolating and comparing 'conditional' constructions cross-linguistically (and indeed interlinguistically) is in itself problematic, firstly because of the variety of forms that can be used to express conditional meaning, and secondly because of the general problem of identifying a core 'conditional' meaning and attributing a well-defined semantic value to the *si* and *if* operators. In order therefore to limit the variables, a narrow range of data has been chosen as described above. I will consider only one discipline, clinical oncology, and one genre, the academic research article. Differences in use amongst the three sub-groups will be limited to this specific epistemic community and text type. Rather than looking at the various ways conditionality is expressed, I will adopt a bottom-up approach focusing on the ways *si* and *if* as the prototypical lexical exponents of conditionality are exploited by the different author groups, within this very precise discourse context.

A formal definition of conditionality will therefore be employed whereby conditional constructions are typically considered as consisting of two clauses; a subordinate clause introduced by *si* or *if* henceforth termed the P clause and an apodosis or Q clause:

(1) Si une telle analyse était réalisée de manière systématique, la valeur prédictive des emboles (…) augmenterait probablement de manière importante (Fr)
(If such an analysis was carried out systematically, the predictive value of emboli (…) would probably increase considerably).

Other subordinators in both languages, such as *on condition that, provided that, unless*, or various types of inversion (*Should you change your mind, let us know*) were discarded. (A preliminary investigation revealed however very few such occurrences in the data.) Uses involving the adverbial function of *si* in French: *des risques si bas (such low risks)* and occurrences with *as if* or *comme si* were also discounted, as were examples in both languages where the subordinate clause was a subject or object clause and the equivalent of whether: *nous avons voulu savoir si ces enzymes jouent un role / We wanted to know whether(if) these enzymes play a role*. It was however decided to include elliptical *si*- and *if*- clauses, such as *if possible* (*si possible*),–a frequent phenomenon in the dataset.

3.2 Global quantitative features

After the above adjustments, 320 occurrences of *if* and *si* were collected (an average of 0.94 occurrences per 1000 words), which indicates that they are not a marginal phenomenon in this specific type of written discourse. Although considerably less frequent than in speech (Ford & Thompson 1986), the figures tally with those of Ferguson (2001), who in a study focusing solely on English medical data found a ratio of 1.1 *if*-conditional constructions per 1000 words in medical journal articles. As table 1 below illustrates, these occurrences were moreover fairly equally distributed amongst the three sub-groups.

Table 1: Frequency of *si*- and *if*-constructions

Author group	Words total	Number of *si/if* constructions	Ratio per 1000 words
All authors (90 RAs)	337,689	320	0.94
Fr authors (30 RAs)	111,391	103	0.92
En authors (30 RAs)	111, 907	119	1.06
Fse authors (30 RAs)	114, 391	98	0.85

From a purely quantitative perspective therefore, the three author groups can be seen to employ the *si*- and *if*-conditional constructions with a similar frequency in their research articles.

A further similarity amongst the three author groups in this dataset is the preference for final positioning of P clauses. Three categories of position were distinguished, initial P clauses, final P clauses and medial P clauses as illustrated below:

(2) If we exclude perineal recurrences (...), this figure increases to 93%
(3) Patients were eligible for participation if they were 18 years of age or older
(4) The last evaluation, even if performed on D30 (day 30), was used as final data

In the three author groups there were overall 41% of initial P clauses, 6% of medial P clauses and 53% of final P clauses. This is contrary to most findings in French and English, where initial positioning has been presented as the default ordering or even as a language universal (Comrie 1986), with any non-initial positioning being regarded as a very marked choice and frequently often even ignored in subsequent analyses. In one of the few data-driven studies focusing on conditional ordering in English by Ford & Thompson (1986), initial P clause represented 77% of written occurrences and 82% of spoken data. The tendency towards final positioning of P-clauses in all three author groups (Fr 52%, En 55% and Fse 52%) would therefore appear to be a pronounced specificity of the medical RA in both English and French.

Ford and Thompson (*op. cit*) have related the fairly rare post-positioning of *if*-clauses found in their written data (a mixed corpus consisting of a technical manual, a personal narrative account and essays) to a number of syntactic and information-structuring considerations: length and complexity of the P clause, its degree of 'newness' and degree of embedding. In this corpus, positioning also appears to be strongly linked to the precise rhetorical functions fulfilled by the various occurrences, as well as to the more general functions or aims of each section in the medical RA. In all three sub-sets there is, for example, a strong preference for final positioning of P-clauses in the Methods sections of the articles: 42 initial P clauses as opposed to 85 final P clauses in this section of the RA.

Another constant in relation to all the occurrences concerns the verbal forms in the P and Q clauses. In traditional and pedagogical grammars in both English and French, three types of conditional are usually identified in which the verb forms index different degrees of hypotheticality: 1) present + future; 2) past + 'conditional', 3) past perfect + 'conditional' perfect. In all three author subsets there were extremely marked deviations from this paradigm, with the three above combinations accounting together for fewer than 6% of occurrences. On the contrary a wide range of combinations are represented. Once again the location of the occurrences within a particular article section seems to be a decisive factor, with almost exclusively past tenses in the Methods section, and simple presents in the Discussion sections, in line with what is already known about tense usage in general in these sections of the RA (Heslot 1985; Swales

1990; Swales & Feak 1994). There was however a striking difference in the overall number of past tense forms in the French and English RAs. The combination of two past tenses in P & Q represented 48% and 42% of the total occurrences in the En and Fse subgroups, but only 15% of occurrences in the French RAs, where on the contrary the present + present combination was far more common (52%)–a difference linked to the distribution of the *si-* and *if-* constructions amongst the RA component parts (cf. *infra*).

4. Distribution of occurrences across article sections

The medical research article adheres to a very standard format for the presentation of information and the 90 RAs examined all contained the following highly structured explicitly marked sections: Introduction, Methods, Results, Discussion/conclusion[3], preceded by a short abstract reflecting the IMRD pattern of the RA itself.

As is well-known there are considerable differences in communicative function from one section to another (Swales 1990, Nwogu 1997, Salager-Meyer 1994). In particular a sharp distinction is maintained between the research data and its interpretation. The Methods and Results sections are essentially informative and descriptive, and are characterised by a lack of argumentation or matters of discussion: presenting the data in "orderly, dispassionate and logical manner" (Adams-Smith 1984). The Introduction and Discussion sections, on the other hand, are where the authors can be expected to adopt a more overt argumentative strategy, justifying the specific research undertaken within the general disciplinary context in the Introduction and promoting the individual research claims and their wider implications in the case of the Discussion section. With these broad distinctions in mind, it is thus interesting to see how all the *si-* and *if-*constructions collected are distributed over these sections in the three author groups.

Quantitatively we have already observed that *if* and *si-*clauses occur with a similar frequency for all 3 groups in the medical RA. However, as Figure 1 illustrates, the occurrences are not distributed in at all the same way over the RA sections. In the En group's research articles the majority of occurrences are in the descriptive Methods and Results sections (67%). On the other hand, the majority of occurrences in the Fr articles occur within the more argumentative Introduction and Discussion parts of the article (59%), with proportionally far fewer occurrences in the Methods section. (This low percentage in the Methods

---

[3] Three of the journals examined also had, in addition, a short Conclusion section. As this section was absent in the Journal of Clinical Oncology, for the purposes of comparison this section has been amalgamated with the previous Discussion section.

section is undoubtedly linked to the smaller number of past tense forms observed earlier). The results of the third subset examined, those of the Fse writers, fall between these two extremes. Like those of the En group, their articles contain a substantial number of occurrences in the Methodology section (46%), but they show also an almost equally high percentage of occurrences in the Discussion sections (44%), and in this respect they are more in line with the tendency of the Fr authors.

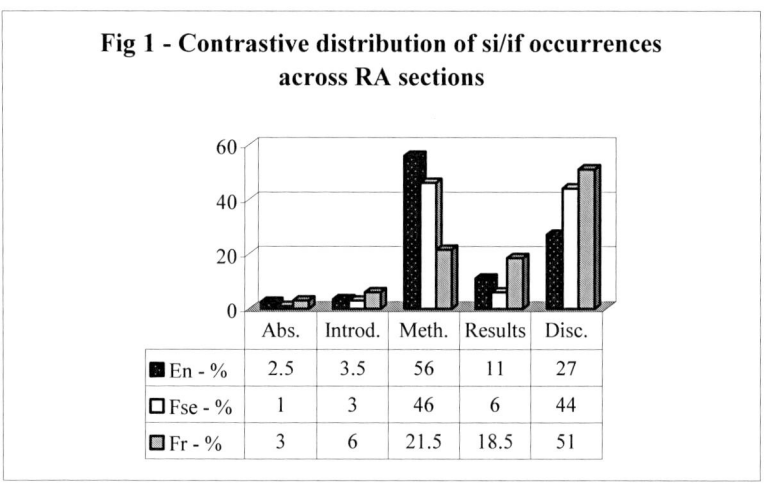

Fig 1 - Contrastive distribution of si/if occurrences across RA sections

	Abs.	Introd.	Meth.	Results	Disc.
En - %	2.5	3.5	56	11	27
Fse - %	1	3	46	6	44
Fr - %	3	6	21.5	18.5	51

These results would tend to suggest a greater recourse to *si*-constructions by the Fr authors in argumentative contexts, a tendency also observed to some extent in the Fse authors' use of *if* in English. In contrast, in the En author group, *if*-constructions are more frequent in descriptive and informative contexts. In order to explore further this potential difference in usage among the three author groups, the following sections will discuss in detail the precise functions fulfilled by all the occurrences collected in the medical RA.

5. Functional classification of *si/if* constructions

Past research has often emphasised the very polysemous nature of the conditional operator. Numerous typologies and classifications have been proposed by philosophers, linguists and grammarians, based for example on logical or truth implications (Lewis 1976), on the conceptual domains or worlds to which the content of the conditional refers (Sweester 1990), on semantic distinctions (Comrie 1986) or simply based on verb forms, as is generally the case in pedagogical grammars. Most past studies, however, have been of an intuitive kind and not based on real data or corpora, with a few notable exceptions such as that of Ferguson (2001), Ford's (1997) study of conditionals in conversation and the panoramic overview of Declerk and Reed (2001) based on the Cobuild and LOB corpora.

In this article a corpus-based genre perspective has been adopted, focusing on the functions served by the English and French conditional clauses in relation to the overall rhetorical aims of the medical RA. No predefined analytical categories were used. Instead, the analytical categories proposed are based on regularities observed in the data within one discipline, that of clinical oncology and within one genre[4], the RA.

As many authors point out (for example, Dancygier 1998; Charolles 2003; Achard-Bayle 2005; Adam 2005), the role of the *if* and *si* operators in a conditional construction can be essentially viewed as an instructional one. The presence of the *si/if* operator acts as a signal to the reader or hearer to consider a situation in which the associated Q clause "is not being asserted in the usual way" (Dancygier 1998: 18). The reader or hearer is invited to provisionally accept a set of circumstances signalled by the P clause against which the Q situation is presented for consideration. Between the P and Q clauses of natural language conditionals there is a particular kind of dependency relation, which the reader is instructed to recreate with the aid of the *si/if* operator. The precise nature of this relation can only be evaluated when considering the roles(s) played by the whole construction in context: No one invariant meaning can be attributed to the operators. It was therefore frequently necessary to examine long stretches of text, in order to determine the nature of the link signalled and its dominant function in relation to the overall rhetorical aims of medical research articles.

The principle functions of the constructions in the medical articles that emerged, following the classification process outlined above, were seen to fall under three main headings: a) Discourse management functions; b) Refocusing functions; c) Factual functions. These categories can then be further broken down into a number of sub-divisions as described below.

---

[4] The functional genre-based classification proposed was developed in collaboration with Elizabeth Rowley-Jolivet. A dual-rating system was adopted throughout the classification process until agreement between the two analysts was reached. See Rowley-Jolivet's article in this same volume for an application of these functional categories to other medical genres.

5.1 Discourse management functions

In the medical RA, the occurrences which have been classified in this category serve to instruct or guide the readers in following the development of the text. Rather than signalling a particular causal or predictive relationship between P and Q, the emphasis is on signalling to the reader the background against which it is pragmatically relevant to interpret the Q clause:

> (5) Si nous étudions plus précisément la nature des 39 discordances, nous notons qu'elles se répartissent en deux types : les sous-évaluations et les problèmes d'échantillonnage. (Results - Fr)
> (If we look more closely at the nature of the 39 false negatives, we note that they can be divided into two categories: under-evaluation and sampling problems)

In this particular example from the Fr sub-set, the *si*-clause allows the author to draw the readers' attention to two new specific sub- topics (*'sous-évaluations' and 'problèmes d'échantillonnage'*) which in turn provide the headings for the two subsequent paragraphs. The presence of the *si* operator, as opposed to another topic-introducing expression such as *Quant à* or *En ce qui concerne* (*En ce qui concerne la nature des 39 discordances*) or on the contrary a balder imperative formulation (*Etudions plus précisément la nature des 39 discordances),* introduces a certain dialogic quality into the text. The reader is politely invited to cooperate in following the subsequent development of the author's argument.

5.2 Factual functions

The category covers many of the features that have been called course of event, generic or habitual conditionals in other approaches (cf. Athanasiadou & Dirven 1997; Ferguson 2001). In medical research it is particularly important to circumscribe the research carried out within a certain set of circumstances, operations or objectives. Over-generalisation needs therefore to be avoided. The *if/si* operator plays an important role here in establishing the boundaries of the research effort, and in thus informing the reader of the conditions under which concepts, facts or cases under observation can be considered valid:

> (6) Fine needle aspiration was performed <u>if</u> involvement of inguinal nodes was clinically suspected (Meth. - Fse)

This definitional work is necessary in order for the methodology to be replicable and for the findings to be comparable to those of other studies (Ferguson 2001). At the same time, the very presence of the *if*-construction, with its characteristic non-asserted quality, enables the author to create a certain textual space, in which the reader participates in the discussion. The reader is invited provisionally (or conditionally) to accept the reality denoted by the fictive P clause, with which the situation in Q is linked. Although the P-Q relation is taking place in the real world, where the *if* or *si* is very close semantically to a *when* (or *quand)*, the non-assertive value of the operator, *if* or *si*, leaves a space open for the reader to question or reject the decision made by the researchers.

Factual functions in the RA sample have been divided into three sub-categories: methodological decisions and definitions, treatment decisions and correlations (cf. section 6.2).

5.3 Refocusing functions

The category comprises those occurrences which have a marked argumentative function. To make claims without overstating, RA authors need constantly to renegotiate–expand or contract–the argumentative space. The *if/si* operator allows a redrawing of the argumentative boundaries and consequently provides more manoeuvring room. The expanding types of refocusing functions are represented by different types of hypothesising and advice-giving or recommendations. Amongst those that, on the contrary, enable the researcher to contract the argumentative space and home in on particular features, we find a number of concessive and contrastive conditionals, restrictions and authorial and metatextual comments. In all these cases, it is argued, the authors' recourse to a conditional construction contributes towards the promotion and negotiation of their research claims. Very often, too, these types of refocusing conditionals enable the expression of other voices: either that of other research teams, as in the hypothesis presented in (7) below, or that of the authors themselves, as the researchers responsible for the research presented, in the recommendation in (8):

(7) If the results of Aoyama et al. [c] are confirmed, HFSR might be the most adequate technique to propose. (Disc. - Fse)

(8) If our Phase II study can demonstrate a 60% 1-year survival rate, the potential efficacy of this regimen is worthy of further study in a randomized clinical trial. (Disc. - En)

Various sub-categories of refocusing functions were identified: recommendations, predictions and hypotheses, restrictions, comments and concessive and contrastive conditionals. Their distribution is contrasted below (section 6.3).

6. Functions in contrast

As already noted, there is a close relationship between the predominant rhetorical functions of the IMRD sections and certain formal features of the *si*- and *if*-clauses, such as the positioning of the P clause and the choice of verb forms used within these sections. The occurrences in each RA section are also highly restricted in terms of the individual functions fulfilled. In the Methods section of the oncology articles, where researchers need to define the eligibility criteria and set out the boundaries of the research presented, the factual functions of the *si/if* operator predominate. Likewise, in the Results sections, where the emphasis is on the presentation of the results observed, we find a number of factual correlations, with the validity of the correlation being circumscribed by the *si*- or *if*-clause. On the contrary, in the Introduction and Discussion sections, where one can expect a more explicit argumentative strategy, refocusing functions prevail. Recourse to the *si/if* operator enables the authors to refocus or reorient their argument by expanding the argumentative space through various predictions, hypotheses or recommendations or alternatively by contracting the space through different types of restrictive, contrastive and concessive conditionals.

There is of course some overspill–criteria-based factual conditionals can occasionally be found in the Discussion sections and the refocusing type conditionals in the Methods sections. Moreover, the categories proposed are not watertight: some occurrences can fulfil several functions. The objective, however, was to attribute a dominant function to all the occurrences collected in order to provide a basis for the contrastive analysis. An examination of the breakdown of these dominant functions in the three author-groups confirms the general tendency noted in relation to IMRD distribution, where we see very different profiles of conditional use emerging depending on linguistic origin.

As Figure 2 shows, while discourse management functions are rare in the three author groups, there are significant differences in the refocusing and factual uses of the *si/if* operator. Factual functions are less represented within the French RAs. The English authors use *if*-clauses far more than their French counterparts for reporting factual correlations and for the various methodological and treatment decisions taken. The refocusing type of *si*-clauses are, however, considerably more prevalent in the French journals analysed, with the French researchers appearing to make greater use of the argumentative possibilities afforded by *si* constructions than their English counterparts do with *if*-clauses. The Fse author group again falls midway between the French articles and those by the native speaker English authors.

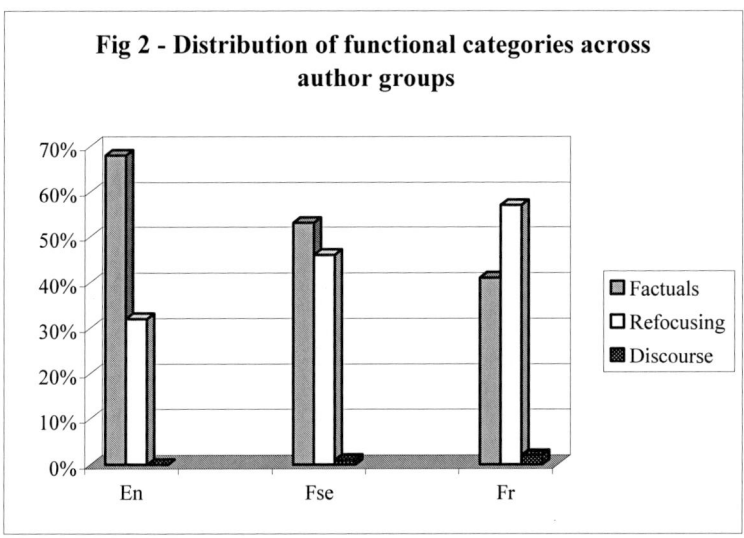

Fig 2 - Distribution of functional categories across author groups

In the same way as the En authors they make considerable use of the factual functions of *if* when writing in English. Their greater exploitation of the refocusing functions of *if* in argumentative contexts, however, would appear to follow that of the Fr group, perhaps indicating a certain impact of the linguistic community here.

6.1 Discourse management functions: En/Fse/Fr

Differences in the recourse to discourse management functions are difficult to assess in this dataset, due to the very small number of these functions noted in all three author groups: En: 0, Fse: 1, Fr: 2. As discussed above (cf. 5.1) this type of construction can be used in the RA to direct the readers' attention from one type of research space to another, from one topic to another, or from one textual space to another (verbal to visual, text to diagram). As all the medical RAs follow a very standardised format (the IMRD structure is rigorously followed with numerous headings) there is little need for these extra meta-discursive signals to guide the reader through the organisation of the article[5].

---

[5] See however Rowley-Jolivet (this volume) for the important use made of these discourse management functions in the conference presentation genre.

6.2 Factual functions: En/Fse/Fr

The first sub-category of factual functions identified, that of **methodological decisions and definitions**, is motivated by the medical researchers' need to define, for example, the eligibility criteria in relation to the patients included in trials, or for various methodological decisions made:

(9) Patients were eligible if there was evidence of spread of tumor to regional lymph nodes (Dukes' C or tumor, lymph node, metastasis stage III tumor). (Meth.- En)

(10) Patients were defined as "downstaged" if the final pathologic stage was less than the preoperative ultrasound stage. (Meth - En).

The validity of the P-Q relation is restricted, or circumscribed to a particular sub-set, as in (9). Similarly the need for precision in the use of terms (i.e what the term does or does not cover) also results in a certain number of defining conditionals, as in (10).

The functions represented in the second sub-category, **treatment decisions,** are motivated by the need to define the criteria for allocating patients to different treatment modalities and likewise need to be carefully defined:

(11) A 7 h 30, elle bénéficiait d'une injection radio-isotopique (Nanocis, 30 MBq) en péritumoral si la tumeur était palpable ou en subaréolaire si la tumeur était très externe ou infraclinique.(Meth. - Fr)
(At 7.30 am the patient was given a peritumoral radio-isotopic injection if the tumor was palpable or a subareolar one if the tumor was very superficial or infraclinical.

The third category of factuals, **correlations,** includes both present and past tense habitual co-occurrences, although in this data they are mostly in the past tense:

(12) An absolute 23% improvement in 5-year survival was achieved if more than 40 lymph nodes were identified. (Results - En)

In medical research, conclusions are usually based on empirical observations rather than theorising. In order to enable valid conclusions to be drawn, this search for regularities and correlations between two or more factors leads to a number of iterative or course of event conditionals, particularly when reporting the results of experiments and studies.

As observed above, factual functions overall are considerably more frequent in both English subsets than in the French journal articles. A detailed examination of the breakdown of factual functions reveals this difference to be particularly striking in the case of the criteria-based methodology and treatment decisions sub-categories. Such functions account for 57% (68 occurrences) and 51% (50 occurrences) of the total occurrences in the En and Fse groups respectively, but for only 26% (27 occurrences) in the Fr group.

How can such differences be accounted for? We might wonder whether the corresponding use of *si* in French, where its value is closer to *quand* (when) or *chaque fois* (whenever) is less frequent overall in the French language. Such usage is however well-documented in French grammar manuals, and there are also a number of factual correlations in the French RAs (16 occurrences) in the Results section, when reporting the results of experiments or observed co-occurrences of two situations:

> (13) Un taux de contrôle tumoral local avec un bon score fonctionnel sphinctérien (grade 0 et 1) a été obtenu dans 56,5 % des cas pour l'ensemble des patients, 72 % des cas en cas de cancer classé T1, 64,5 % *si* T2, 53,5 % *si* T3 et 23,5 % *si* T4 (Results -Fr).
> (A local tumor clinical response rate with a good anal function scoring (score 0 and 1) was obtained in 56.5% of cases for all patients, 72% in the case of cancers classified as T1, 64.5 % if T2, 53.5 % if T3 and 23.5 % if T4.)

In the medical RA data, however, the French researchers do not consistently use the *si*-construction for criteria-based decisions, preferring instead other syntactic means, such as, for example, in the following patient eligibility criteria description:

> (14) Les critères d'exclusion étaient ceux habituels pour la technique du GS : un stade TNM supérieur à T1 ou N1, un cancer multifocal, une chimiothérapie préalable, une allergie, obésité (...)
> (The exclusion criteria were those usually applied for sentinel node surgery: a TNM stage superior to T1 or N1, a multicentric breast cancer, neo-adjuvant chemotherapy, allergy, obesity)

The fact that the eligibility criteria are announced in this way without recourse to a *si*-clause gives a more affirmative feel. This contrasts with the criterial decisions involving the conditional operator *if*, where the non-assertive value of the subordinator leaves a certain space open for the reader to question or reject the decision made by the researchers as in (15):

> (15) Patients were excluded from the study *if* they had evidence of metastases, a documented history of cardiac disease or previous cancer (...) (Meth. - Fse)

The content of the *if*-clause is provisional or less than certain, as the very presence of *if* implicitly acknowledges an alternative (*if* P or *if* ~P). Such features as Ford points out enable speakers or authors to retain a certain distance or to display less than total commitment:

> "These characteristics of if-clauses make them fitting vehicles for encoding information in a hedged way; speakers can say what they want to say and at the same time, in some sense, remain uncommitted to what they are saying" (Ford 1997: 389)

In this respect, the greater recourse to *if* by the En and Fse authors for explaining their methodological and diagnostic decisions contributes to a more tentative and circumspect presentation of the data than that found in the French medical articles.

6.3 Refocusing functions: En/Fse/Fr

The refocusing potential of the *si* and *if* operators is also exploited very differently by the three author groups.

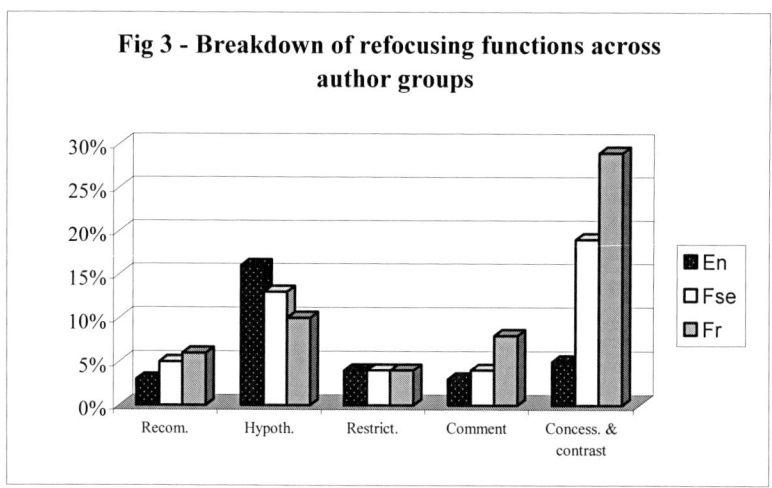

As Figure 3 illustrates, the only category that is equally distributed amongst the three author groups is that of the refocusing sub-function of restrictives. The category of hypothesising is more exploited by the En group. The other sub-functions of refocusing identified (recommendations, comments and concessive and contrastive conditionals) are all more frequent in the Fr author group–with the difference being particularly pronounced in the case of concessive and contrastive functions. The Fse authors' use of the refocusing potential of *if* falls consistently midway between that of the En authors and the corresponding *si* usage by the Fr group; like the Fr authors, however, they have far greater recourse to the concessive and contrastive functions of the conditional operator. In the following sections this rather different exploitation of the various subcategories of the refocusing function will be discussed in more detail.

6.3.1 Restrictive functions

In order to make effective claims, the researcher may need to contract the argumentative space. There are several occurrences in the RAs in the sample where the researchers propose restricting results to a certain category in order to present their research findings in a more favourable light:

(16) ...and *if* only patients <80 years of age were taken into account, the 5- and 10-year overall survival rate was 78% and 52%, respectively, which compares well with surgical results. (Disc. - Fse)

The category of conditional restrictives, though small, is nevertheless equally represented, accounting for 4% of the total occurrences in the 3 author groups. The need to sometimes exclude certain categories of data in order to present one's results in a more favourable light could therefore be seen as a universal in the medical RA. Whatever the speaker origin, no notable difference was noted in this sample.

6.3.2 Predictions and hypotheses

An important way of expanding the argumentative space is through predictions and hypotheses. Such uses of *si* and *if* are indeed often considered as the prototypical conditionals in pedagogical grammars. The P clause presents a potential situation for consideration, and the Q clause outlines the possible consequences that arise from the situation. In the medical RA, the Q clause is invariably heavily modalised, with values ranging from that of the merely probable to doubt and speculation. There is only one occurrence in this dataset of a standard 'prediction' with a future tense Q clause. What is far more frequent in the RA are various degrees of hedged hypotheses, involving modal verbs or other modalising lexis in the Q clause as in:

(17) Also, if preoperative therapy is administered at the time of diagnosis it might be more effective because the metastatic burden may be the smallest at this point. (Disc. - En)

Also common in the RA are examples involving tense backshifting, whereby the author distances himself further from the situation in the P clause as in examples (18) and (19):

> (18) Si une telle analyse était réalisée de manière systématique, la valeur prédictive des emboles pour déterminer l'envahissement ganglionnaire augmenterait probablement de manière importante (Disc. - Fr)
> (If such an analysis was carried out systematically, the predictive value of emboli in determining lymph node invasion would probably increase considerably).
>
> (19) The pN1 designation can have a significant effect on choice of adjuvant chemotherapy. Most medical oncologists would probably be reluctant to simply observe patients with pN1 disease if the patients were good candidates for adjuvant chemotherapy. (Disc. - En)

The category of hypothesising accounts for 10% or more of occurrences in each subset (En: 16%; Fse: 13%; Fr: 10%). It seems to represent a function required by all authors when writing about their research and could therefore be considered as a universal category of the RA. The proportion of hypotheses is, however, slightly higher amongst the En authors than amongst the Fr authors (with the figures for the Fse author group falling once again midway between the two). Although the difference is not statistically significant, we could perhaps speculate that this more frequent recourse to hedged hypothetical projections amongst the English authors is linked to the more circumspect nature of the English medical RAs already hinted at.

There is also some evidence that this difference is perhaps not only a quantitative but also a qualitative one. In example (19) above, the En authors invoke other researchers in support of the assertion made in the Q clause. In the French sample there are also some occurrences where the reference to other researchers' voices is not used to support the particular hypothesis, but serves rather as a stratagem enabling the authors to present a contrary opinion–this time that of the authors themselves–in the subsequent text. In the following example (20), the assertion in Q is attributed to another source. The French authors distance themselves from the assertion, in order to refute it and in fact to propose another approach in the following sentence:

> (20) À la lumière de nombreuses publications sur le sujet, il semblait qu'une approche de préservation laryngée était envisageable si certaines conditions étaient respectées (équipes entraînées, cas sélectionnés, essais randomisés). Toutefois, il apparaissait également souhaitable de savoir (…). Notre étude rétrospective a montré que … (Disc. - Fr)
> (In the light of a number of publications on the subject, it seemed that larynx conservation was feasible if certain conditions were respected (well-trained

teams, selected cases, random trials). However, it would also appear important to know (...) Our retrospective study has shown (...).

In example (21) the same tactic is used:

(21) Si l'on en croit la Société de pneumologie de langue française, le Cyfra 21-1 est actuellement le seul marqueur tumoral dont la valeur pronostique est clairement démontrée dans le cancer broncho-pulmonaire primitif non à petites cellules [4]. Nous avons néanmoins pu constater... (Disc. - Fr)
(If we are to believe the SPLF [the French association for pneumology], Cyfra 21-1 is currently the only tumour marker whose prognostic value has been clearly demonstrated (...). We have however noted (...).

In this case, the reference to another source occurs within the P clause. In both these cases, however, the authors' recourse to another's hypothesis is a purely argumentative ruse. The hypothesis is presented so as to be subsequently refuted with evidence from the authors' own research.

6.3.3 Recommendations

Making recommendations is another way of expanding the argumentative space and promoting research claims. In the research article, however, recommendations require some sort of qualification so as to avoid appearing too dogmatic or overbearing. The P clause does this work for the writer, by specifying the circumstances in which a course of action should or should not be taken:

(22) Il est donc primordial, si l'on veut se dispenser de curage axillaire systématique comme cela est proposé par différentes équipes [23, 24, 37, 48], d'utiliser la technique la plus fiable possible (Disc. - Fr)
(It is thus essential, if we want to dispense with systematic axillary resection as several different teams have proposed, to use the most reliable technique possible.)

The above extract also provides another striking example of the polyphonic interaction afforded by the *si* operator. The desirability of dispensing with 'systematic axillary resection' is attributed to the wide-ranging indefinite pronoun *on*, where the authors are not only including themselves (and perhaps the community at large) but also the four other research teams cited by superscript numbers. In this way the authors provide themselves with ample justification for their rather firm recommendation in the Q clause.

The use of conditional constructions for making recommendations is nevertheless fairly limited in the medical RAs: En 3.3%; Fse 5.1%; Fr 5.8%. Even if the P clause allows the researcher to slightly mitigate the recommendation, we can suppose that advice-giving to peers has a potential face-threatening facet, and for this reason is used sparingly in the medical RA context. There is, nonetheless, a higher proportion of occurrences of this type in the Fr and Fse author groups than in the En author group, perhaps indicating a slightly more forceful attitude on the part of the French researchers.

There are also some rather firm expressions of necessity within the Fr occurrences, such as in (22) above, or other forthright recommendations expressed with a deontic *doit* or *devra* ('must' or 'will have to'):

> (23) L'augmentation des infections du site opératoire après chimiothérapie, récemment mise en évidence, devra, si ces données sont confirmées, être intégrée dans les études coût-efficacité de telles stratégies. (Abs. - Fr)
> (The increase in postoperative infection (…) must, if these data are confirmed, be integrated into the cost effectiveness of such strategies).

Such examples contrast with the more diplomatic and hedged *should* and other more tentative modalised recommendations preferred by the En authors: as in (24) and (25):

> (24) Our results suggest that *if* postoperative diagnostic surveillance is undertaken with a goal of early detection of potentially curable disease relapse, CT for detection of nodal recurrence should be a component of the follow-up program. (Disc. - En)

> (25) This pattern of failure certainly supports the use of adjuvant chemoradiation *if* APR is to be the primary local strategy in this population. (Disc. - En)

Past research has often underlined the more prescriptive and categorical tone of French scientific writing (Régent 1994; Salager-Meyer et al 2003). Although the numbers involved in this sample are too small to enable a full endorsement of such claims, both the greater firmness and higher frequency noted with regard to the 'recommendations' sub-function would indeed tend to suggest that the Fr authors adopt a more authoritative stance than their En counterparts.

6.3.4 Comments

The fourth sub-category of the refocusing function includes the often elliptical inserts by the author to comment on the appropriacy of a textual element or of a particular action:

> (26) La réponse ganglionnaire à la chimiothérapie (si évaluable) a été répartie comme suit entre les groupes 1 et 2. (Results - Fr)
> (The breakdown of the lymph node response to chemotherapy (if it can be evaluated) was as follows in groups 1 and 2)

Through such passing remarks and comments the author can directly make his presence or evaluation apparent. Such comments generally occur in medial position, separated out either by brackets or commas. In the case of comments of a meta-textual type, it is less a question of contracting the augmentative space, than of contracting the textual space, homing in to make a particular comment on a constituent in the Q clause, or to refine its meaning, as in (27):

(27) The prognosis is dramatically poor, with lesions exhibiting diffuse and multicentric local extension rendering surgical resection difficult, and the majority of patients, *if* not all, develop early distant metastases (Disc.- Fse)

Unlike the other categories looked at so far, the scope of such meta-textual inserts usually only extends to a specific word or expression, rather than to the whole of the Q clause or beyond. The P clause often seems to imply some type of scalar implication involving, for example, a downtoning or boosting effect (Declerk and Reed 2001: 342). In the example above, the effect is one of boosting: as the prognosis is dramatically poor it's likely **all** patients will develop metastases. The reader is invited to look higher up the scale than the term *few* indicates, and *all* is therefore deemed a more adequate qualifier than *majority*.

There is a higher proportion of passing insertions and meta-textual comments in the French articles than in the two English sets: En: 3%; Fse: 4%; Fr: 8%. This may suggest a higher degree of author involvement on the part of the Fr author group. Through these rather subtle interjections, the Fr authors are able to make their presence felt, contributing again to the more authoritative toner of their texts.

6.3.5 Concessive and contrastive conditional functions

It is however when we come to compare the frequency and use of the concessive and contrastive functions of *if* and *si* that the differences between the French and English author groups become the most apparent. The proportion of concessive and contrastive conditionals is considerably higher in the Fr authored articles, and also interestingly among the Fse author group: En 5% (6 occurrences); Fse 19% (19 occurrences); Fr 29% (30 occurrences).

A strict comparison between the two languages is however rendered problematic with regard to these particular functions due to the wide range of values that French *si* can assume. French *si* can notably be used instead of other concessive subordinators such as *bien que,* to signal a regular concessive (non conditional) relation:

(28). La limitation de la dissection du curage axillaire au seul étage I, si elle diminue le taux de complications, n'apparaît pas être une alternative satisfaisante ; le taux de faux négatifs observé étant de 10% à 15%. (Disc.–Fr)
(Limiting axillary node dissection to the T1 stage, (if ?) although decreasing the rate of complications, does not provide an satisfactory alternative: the rate of false negatives observed ranges from 10 to 15%.)

Such usage is extremely rare in English. The example above could not have been rendered with an *if*-clause in English. A pure concessive connector such as *although* is usually preferred, when the reality of the P clause is presupposed (Paillard 1989; Ranger 1998). Eight out of the 30 French occurrences in the sample indeed seem to signal a purely concessive relation of the type: *Si (Although?)P, Q.*

However, even discounting several pure concessive uses of this type in the French RAs, the number of real concessive and contrastive conditional clauses remaining with *si* (22), is still three times higher than that of the corresponding use of *if* by the En authors. This would perhaps tend to suggest a more overt argumentative stance by the French authors, rather than just a language difference linked to the wider meaning range of the French *si*. This hypothesis seems to be confirmed when we look at the Fse occurrences. In the Fse sub-corpus, occurrences of concessive and contrastive conditionals (19 occurrences) are almost as frequent as those in the French articles. The great majority of these Fse occurrences would not raise any eyebrows in purist Anglocentric grammar circles. In other words, it is not usually a question of *wrongly* using *if* constructions in English. Rather it would seem to be a question of the linguistic community influencing the writing style in English. There would seem to be some evidence of a national academic style that is more overtly argumentative than that of Anglo-Saxon authors–or that at minimum makes more use of the argumentative potential of conditional constructions.

The greater recourse to contrastive and concessive conditionals provides the Fr and Fse groups with an important manoeuvring potential. **Concessive conditional** constructions with *if* and *si* (invariably preceded by *even* and *même* respectively) are particularly important in the RA context for forestalling objections. Using the form: *even if P, Q* (or Q (,) *even if P*) the researcher asserts Q whatever the status of P. In other words, whether P is the case or not, Q is asserted:

(29) Notre pourcentage est plus élevé que dans l'étude multicentrique, *même si* une comparaison est difficile compte tenu que 13 patientes de notre étude ont été incluses dans cette étude multicentrique. (Disc. - Fr)
(Our percentage is higher than in the multicentric study, even if comparison is difficult as 13 patients from our study were included in this multicentric study)

In this way the authors stave off possible criticism, conceding or appearing to concede in order to clear the way for their own claims:

> (30) Even if noncancer deaths did not differ, the presence of concurrent adverse health conditions, or comorbidity, has been shown to increase cancer mortality. (Disc. - En)

The three language groups avail themselves of this possibility, although the Fr and Fse authors use it to a much greater extent than the En authors.

Contrastive or adversative uses of *if* and *si* are likewise frequently exploited by the Fr and Fse authors. Unlike concessive conditionals where some causal dependency relation is implied between two propositions (one could be a possible obstacle to another), in contrastive conditionals neither proposition runs counter to an expectation created by the other proposition. On the contrary, the comparison created between the two clauses provides the authors with a very effective means for highlighting their research claims. The ideas presented in the initial P-clause are backgrounded, consequently lending more weight to information presented in the main clause (Lewis 2004). In this way the author is also provided with a springboard from which to develop this information in subsequent clauses:

> (31) *If* the results are encouraging for T2 lesions, the rate of local failure with RT (radiotherapy) ... for T3 lesions remains >20%. To improve these results in T3 tumors, various techniques need to be explored. (Disc. - Fse)

In Declerk and Reed's (2001) chapter on "Comparing conditionals", this topic-introducing or transitional function of the construction is firmly underlined. In the comparison between two situations or two participants, the initial P clause containing some already familiar information is seen to function as a starting-point to which the information in the Q-clause is attached:

> (32) Si donc le retard à la première demande de soin tient à une sémiologie ordinaire particulière de la maladie cancéreuse chez nos malades, le retard à la consultation spécialisée dépendrait surtout d'une insuffisance dans la communication soignant-soigné et dans les prestations fournies. (Disc. - Fr)
> (**If the delay in seeking an initial appointment** is linked to a particular representation of cancer illnesses amongst our patients, **the delay in consulting a specialist** would seem to be linked above all to certain communication difficulties between practitioners and patients...)

Such examples as the above are attested in English: Declerk & Reed (*op. cit*) in their corpus-based study provide several examples very similar to the occurrences above, as for example: "If I've had a successful career, I've been a complete failure as far as my private life is concerned". There are, however, no such occurrences in the En-authored articles in this sample. Some contrastive conditionals in English have been found however in the more polemical medical editorial genre (cf. Rowley-Jolivet, this volume).

In this sample of medical RAs, the manoeuvring potential, provided by concessive and contrastive functions of *si* and *if* is thus consistently more exploited by the Fr and Fse authors, contributing to a more overt argumentative stance than that of the En authors.

7. Conclusion and perspectives

The comparison of *if-* and *si*-clauses in medical research articles has revealed some interesting cross-linguistic differences. Although the two conditional operators largely overlap in their prototypical functions and occur with similar frequency, they are not put to the same use. Their distribution across the RA sections is firstly very different. There are a far greater number in the Methodology sections of the En[6] authors' RAs, as opposed to a majority in the Discussion sections in the Fr authors' RAs. Despite some overspill between sections, this translates globally into a greater use of factual functions by the En author group. The criteria-based decisions of the En researchers concerning methodological and treatment options are presented in a diplomatic non-assertive manner, leaving space for possible discussion of the criteria adopted. In the Fr articles, on the other hand, there is greater recourse to the refocusing functions of *si*-clauses. The French authors exploit to a greater degree the argumentative and polyphonic potential of the *si* operator in order to negotiate a path through the body of existing research and to press forward their own research claims.

The broad picture being painted here would tie in with what Francoise Salager-Meyer and her co-authors in their study of academic criticism have called "the dagger and glove" (2003). The respectful and more consensual En authors are the ones wearing the gloves, as opposed to the more argumentative Fr researchers armed with a dagger, who fight more forcefully and directly to promote their research claims.

As regards the Fse author group, we have noticed throughout this study that the Fse uses of *if*-clauses consistently figure midway between those of the En and Fr groups. To some extent the Fse authors follow the En authors in exploiting the factual functions of *if*-clauses. However, in the same way as the Fr authors, they also make greater use of the refocusing and manoeuvring

---

[6] NB : The three author-groups referred to throughout this article (see section 2) were as follows: En = English speaking authors of articles in English; Fse = French speaking authors of articles in English; Fr = French authors of articles in French.

potential of the *if* operator, in particular with a much heavier use of concessive and contrastive *ifs* than amongst the En authors. This leads to a rather different profile of use indicating, as far as the Fse authors in this sample are concerned, that the dominance of English in scientific publications would not seem to have totally erased all traces of linguistic and rhetorical diversity in research writing.

The questions raised here concerning different possible writing styles can only of course remain tentative, due to both the narrow range of structures analysed and the restricted size of the corpus. It would, however, be interesting to examine a range of connectives and other markers cross-linguistically (cf. Vold 2006) to see whether the French indeed exploit to a greater extent the argumentative potential of language in their academic writing. Despite the difficulties involved in using contrastive data–the problem of finding linguistic correspondences across languages (Fløttum 2005) and of using comparable corpora (Swales 2004)–studies examining contrastive rhetorical practices make an essential contribution to our knowledge of the academic discourse world.

8. References

Achard Bayle, Guy. "Si polysémique et Si polyphonique." In *Le sens et ses vois. Dialogisme et polyphonie dans la langue et le discours,* edited by Laurent Perrin, 407-434. Collection Recherches linguistiques n°28, Université de Metz, 2005.
Adam, Jean-Michel. "Variété des usages de SI dans l'argumentation publicitaire." In *Argumentations et communications dans les médias*, edited by M.Burger and G.Martel, 81-109. Québec: Nota Bene, 2005.
Adams-Smith, Diana E. "Medical Discourse: Aspects of Author's Comment." *ESP Journal* 3 (1984): 25-36.
Athanasiadou, Angeliki and René Dirven. "Conditionality, hypotheticality, counterfactuality." In *On Conditionals Again*, edited by A. Athanasiadou and R. Dirven, 61-96. Amsterdam: Benjamins, 1997.
Burgess, Sally. "Packed houses and intimate gatherings: Audience and rhetorical structure." In *Academic Discourse*, edited by John Flowerdew, 196-205. London: Longman, 2002.
Charolles, Michel. "De la topicalité des adverbiaux détachées en tête de phrase." *Travaux de Linguistique*, 47, (2003): 11-51.
Comrie, Bernard. "Conditionals: A Typology." In *On Conditionals*, edited by E. Traugott et al., 77-99. Cambridge: Cambridge University Press, 1986.
Dahl, Trine. "Absent doctors, shy economists and polemic linguists? Writer manifestation in academic texts". *Synaps* 14, 1-4. Instituttserie, Institutt for fagspråk og interkulturell kommuinkasjon, NHH, 2004.

—."Textual metadiscourse in research articles: a marker of national culture or of academic discipline? " *Journal of Pragmatics* 36, (2004):1807–1825.
Dancygier, Barbara. *Conditionals and Predictions: Time, Knowledge and Causation in Conditional Constructions,* Cambridge: Cambridge University Press, 1998.
Declerck, Renaat and Susan Reed. *Conditionals: a comprehensive empirical analysis,* Berlin and New York: Mouton de Gruyter, 2001.
Ferguson, Gibson. "If you pop over there: a corpus-based study of conditionals in medical discourse." *English for Specific Purposes* 20/1 (2001): 61-82.
Fløttum, Kjersti. "The self and others: polyphonic visibility in research articles." *International Journal of Applied Linguistics* 15/1 (2005): 29-44.
Ford, Cecilia E. "Speaking Conditionally: Some Contexts for If-clauses in Conversation." In *On Conditionals Again*, edited by A. Athanasiadou and R. Dirven, 387-413. Amsterdam: Benjamins, 1997.
Ford, Cecilia E. and Sandra A. Thompson. "Conditionals in discourse: A text-based study from English." In *On Conditionals*, edited by E. Traugott et al., 353-372. Cambridge: Cambridge University Press, 1986.
Heslot, Jeanne. "Organisation textuelle de l'article scientifique primaire." In *Discoss: Discours contrastif, sciences et sociétés*, edited by M.M. Jocelyne Fernandez-Vest, 53-62. Paris: Association Discoss, 1985.
Horsella, Maria and Gerda Sindermann. "Aspects of Scientific discourse: Conditional Argumentation." *English for Specific Purposes* 11(1992): 129-139.
Lewis, David. "Probabilities of conditionals and conditional probabilities." *Philosophical Review* 85 (1976): 297-315.
Lewis, Diana M. "Mapping adversative coherence relations in English and French." *Languages in Contrast* 5/1 (2004): 33-48.
Mauranen, Anna. *Cultural differences in academic rhetoric: A textlinguistic study.* Frankfurt: Peter Lang, 1993.
Nwogu, Kevin Ngozi. "The Medical Research Paper: Structure and Functions." *English for Specific Purposes* 16 (1997): 119-138.
Paillard, Michel. "Les chemins de la concession: quelques contrastes entre anglais et français." *Travaux linguistiques du CERLICO* 6, (1989): 207-226.
Ranger, Graham. *Les constructions concessives en anglais: une approche énonciative.* Cahiers de recherché numéro spécial, Paris: Orphys, 1998.
Régent, Odile. "L'article scientifique: un produit culturel." ASp (Anglais de Spécialité) 5-6 (1994): 55–61.
Rowley-Jolivet, Elizabeth. "A genre study of *if* in medical discourse." This volume.
Rowley-Jolivet, Elizabeth and Shirley Carter-Thomas. "Scientific conference Englishes: Epistemic and Language Community Variations." In *Identity,*

Community, Discourse: English in Intercultural Settings, edited by Giuseppina Cortese and Anna Duszak, *295-320*. Bern: Peter Lang, 2005.
Salager-Meyer, Françoise. "Hedges and textual communicative function in medical English written discourse." *English for Specific Purposes* 13/2 (1994): 149-170.
Salager-Meyer, Françoise, Maria Angeles Alcarez Arizia and Nahirana Zambrano. "The scimitar, the dagger and the glove: intercultural differences in the rhetoric of criticism in Spanish, French and English Medical Discourse (1930-1995)." *English for Specific Purposes* 22 (2003): 223-247.
Sionis, Claude. (1997) "Stratégies et styles rédactionnels de l'article de recherche: les ressources de l'utilisateur non-natif devant publier en anglais." *ASp (Anglais de spécialité)* 15–18 (1997): 207–23.
Swales, John. *Genre Analysis: English in Academic and Research Settings*, Cambridge: Cambridge University Press, 1990.
—. *Research Genres: Exploration and Applications*, Cambridge: Cambridge University Press, 2004.
Swales, John and Christine Feak. *Academic writing for graduate students: Essential tasks and skills*. Ann Arbor MI: University of Michigan Press, 1994.
Sweester Eve, 1990, *From Etymology to Pragmatics,* Cambridge University Press.
Ventola Eija and Anna Mauranen, eds. *Academic Writing: Intercultural and Textual Issues.* Amsterdam and Philadelphia: John Benjamins, 1996.
Vold, Eva Thue. "Epistemic modality markers in research articles: a cross-linguistic and cross-disciplinary study." *International Journal of Applied Linguistics* 16 (2006): 61-87.

CHAPTER NINE

A GENRE STUDY OF *IF* IN MEDICAL DISCOURSE

ELIZABETH ROWLEY-JOLIVET

Medical discourse, whether written or spoken, is generally considered to be characterised by a marked degree of hedging. This feature has been studied from various angles: modality, author comment, shields and approximators, politeness strategies, or author stance (Salager-Meyer 1994; Adams-Smith 1984; Prince et al 1982; Hyland 1998). A neglected area in this field, however, is the use of certain syntactic constructions, which by their very nature convey tentativeness or non-assertiveness. Conditional constructions, thanks to their inherent 'iffiness' (Carter-Thomas, this volume), would seem to be an ideal candidate for an exploration of the syntactic dimension of hedging in medical genres.

If, the prototypical operator of conditionality in English, has been selected for this study. Like many other common connectives, *if* appears to be highly polysemous, taking on a variety of values and meanings in different contexts. Underlying this variety, however, there is a set of core functions fulfilled by the operator (Dancygier 1998). In addition to their fundamental non-assertiveness, *if*-clauses are characterised by the fact that they form part of a construction: the *if P, Q* construction. *If* opens up this structure, and has an instructional role, signalling that there is a link between the two clauses, P and Q. The precise semantics of this link however are under-specified by the construction, and will depend on certain formal features such as tense usage or clause order, and also on the discourse context or specific co-text. A third constant value of *if* is its role as a space-builder. This concept, associated with Fauconnier's mental spaces theory (Fauconnier 1994), refers to constructs that are built up in any discourse by certain linguistic expressions. The conjunction *if* sets up a space that is different from the discourse base space in some way–it may create a hypothetical or a counterfactual space, or redefine the framework within which the subsequent discourse is to be interpreted. It is interesting to recall in this connection that the same space metaphor was used by Swales (1990) when analysing the rhetorical structure of research articles (Create A Research Space).

Although the two concepts of mental spaces and rhetorical spaces cannot be conflated, the *if* operator, which enables the text producer to build, contract or expand the space according to his argumentative needs, will be a valuable resource in academic discourse.

Keeping these three constants firmly in our sights, the aim of this study will be to examine to what extent the genre induces variations in how *if* is used in medical discourse, from three angles: variation in the functions fulfilled by *if* in various genres; variations in the basic *if P, Q* constructional pattern; and variations in the types of spaces built by the *if* operator. After presenting the data and methodology, I will address these questions in each of the 4 genres selected for the study.

1. Corpus and method

The corpus collected for this study comprises 4 subsets, all within the medical field of oncology: i) 15 research articles by native English writers from a leading international journal; ii) a comparable set of 15 conference presentations delivered by American speakers at an international conference, recorded on video and transcribed; iii) 58 Case reports from a second major journal; iv) 84 Editorials from two journals. Details of the corpus are given in Table 1.

Table 1. The Corpus

Genre	# texts	# words	Ratio if / 1000w.	Source[1]
Research Articles (RA)	15	54,426	1.1	IJRO
Conference presentations (CP)	15	39,454	3.8	
Case Reports (CR)	58	36,400	0.3	JCO
Editorials (ED)	84	103,014	1.7	LO & JCO

While conditional meaning can be expressed in various ways in English, I have chosen to restrict this study to the *if* operator, leaving aside other subordinators such as *unless, on condition that, provided that,* auxiliary

---

[1] The journals from which the written texts are taken (issues in 2002-3) are: *International Journal of Radiation Oncology* (IJRO), *Journal of Clinical Oncology* (JCO), and *Lancet Oncology* (LO). The conference presentations were delivered at the First Annual European-American Conference on Gastrointestinal Oncology: Cancers of the Lower Gastrointestinal Tract, 22-24 Sept. 1994, Bordeaux.

inversion, etc. as these were found to be either absent or extremely rare in the data. Occurrences where the subordinate clause is a subject or object clause (and where *if* is the equivalent of *whether*) were also excluded, as were occurrences of *as if*. Elliptical *if*-clauses (such as *if necessary*) were included however, as they were common in the data. The subordinate clause introduced by *if* will be referred to as the P clause, and the main clause as the Q clause. The frequency of *if* per 1000 words of running text was calculated for each genre, and P clauses were coded for positioning–initial, medial, or final, as in the following examples:

> Initial: *If* one accepts these treatments as valid, major changes in the management of cancer patients with peritoneal seeding must be considered (ED19)
> Medial: each of these five patients we treated progressively with very little *if* any toxicity (CP 147)
> Final: Patients were excluded *if* there was invasion of the tracheobronchial tree (RA 26)

The dominant functions served by the *If*-clauses were then identified, based on the regularities observed in the data rather than on any predefined analytical categories, as the aim was to investigate the rhetorical functions of *if* in established medical genres. A dual-rating system was used throughout the classification process until agreement between the two analysts was reached (see Carter-Thomas, this volume). Three main functions emerged from this process: Factual, Refocusing, and Discourse functions. These functions and their respective sub-functions are described in the following section.

2. Functional categories

The first main functional category, called **Factuals** in this study, covers features that have been labelled course of event or habitual conditionals in other work (Athanasiadou and Dirven 1997; Ferguson 2001). This category is a cornerstone of scientific investigation, which seeks to establish the 'facticity' (Latour 1987), or status as fact, of its observations of the natural world by observing regularities (*if* [*whenever*] *X, Y*), making correlations, and by a careful definition of the precise import of a term or of the conditions under which the facts hold. In medicine, and oncology in particular, clinical decisions regarding patient treatment have to be made on the basis of statistical data from large randomized trials, or on the acquired expertise of experienced surgeons. For the methodology to be replicable and applicable to other patients, the criteria and conditions of these observational data need to be precisely specified. The *if* operator plays a circumscribing role here in defining the conditions under which the conclusions can be considered to be valid 'facts'. The following examples illustrate this Factual function:

If >50% of the tumor length was proximal to this region, patients were considered to have adenocarcinoma of the rectum and therefore were excluded. (RA 11)
If I think it's full thickness, I will do an operation (CP 34)

Factual functions have been sub-categorised into methodological decisions and definitions, treatment decisions, and correlations.

The **Refocusing** category covers cases where *if* has a marked argumentative function, and where its non-assertive and space-building properties are exploited to redraw the boundaries within which the claim or argument is being made, giving the author room to manoeuvre. This conditional argumentation allows the author to expand or contract the space in order to hypothesise (ranging from near-certainty to speculation), to hedge, or to summon other voices into the discourse:

If the results reported by Mellado et al are observed by other investigators, it is possible that detection of CMC could direct selection of patients.... (ED12)
If the MMSE had been used alone, the authors would have come to the erroneous, and possibly dangerous, conclusion that the agent had no neurotoxic effects (ED98)

The Refocusing function has been broken down into 5 sub-categories: recommendations, hypotheses and predictions, restrictives, comments, and concessive and contrastive conditionals.

The *if* operator can also be used for various **Discourse management** functions, providing readers with guidance about the author's intentions and the structure of the text. In this function, *if*-clauses act as phrasal discourse markers to introduce new topics, or to instruct readers on where to direct their attention. Thanks to the non-assertive value of *if*, these instructions are non-face-threatening, and a form of politeness strategy:

Now if we want to change gears a minute ... (CP65)
If you look at the crossover versus the non-crossover group, there was a doubling of survival (CP93)

3. Comparison of *if* in medical research articles and conference presentations

The RA and CP are close cousins in many ways: both are research genres (Swales 2004), addressed to the same esoteric audience, and often present similar scientific content–many research studies get their first public airing as a CP before being published as an RA. There are, however, major differences in the contextual constraints governing the two communicative events. As Swales, summarising several recent studies of scientific CPs, remarks, these differences explain

> ...why the packaging of information in the oral mode is different from its written counterpart. This is, on one level, partly connected to the discourse management of the information in the stream of visuals and partly connected to the intensive real-time processing required in this genre. From a wider contextual perspective, this intermediate genre presents more preliminary results, often deals with the latest stuff, and may offer only the most provisional of claims and explanations. (Swales 2004:202)

A brief look at some quantitative features will illustrate these dissimilarities.

3.1 Quantitative Features

Table 2. Quantitative comparison of the RAs and CPs

Genre	Frequency		Positioning		
	# occ.	Ratio/1000w.	Initial	Medial	Final
RA	62	1.1	39%	3%	58%
CP	152	3.8	76%	11%	14%

If-clauses are over 3 times more frequent in the presentations than in the articles (see Table 2). This tallies with the findings of several studies comparing *if*-clauses in speech and writing (Ford and Thompson 1986; Biber *et al* 1999; Ferguson 2001).

The two genres also show highly contrasted profiles in relation to the preferred positioning of *if*-clauses. There are more than twice as many initial *if*-clauses in the CP as in the RA[2]. The strong preference for initial position in the

---

[2] Although the default position of *if*-clauses has generally been considered to be initial, this is not borne out by Biber *et al,* who find only a slight preference for initial position in writing, and no preference in conversation (1999:834). Whatever the case may be, the

CPs appears to be related to the processing constraints of the genre (see the next section). Speakers need first to provide the background for the assertion in Q, by specifying under what conditions it holds, in order to avoid misinterpretation or back-processing by the listeners.

The medial position is also more frequent in the CPs than in the RA. Again, the on-line processing of speech may explain this difference, as speakers sometimes make on-the-spot decisions to insert an *if*-clause in mid-sentence to clarify the specific condition under which the Q-assertion holds, as in "This tumor is very amenable *if* it's a carcinoma by biopsy to local excision" (CP40). The medial position is also used in the talks for the Comment function, either downtoning or boosting the value of a particular lexical item in the clause. Such passing comments are extremely rare in the RA (2occ.), but more common in the CP:

...which so far has been fairly predictive in clinical trials *if* not of the exact time at least of the phenomenology (CP 152)

When one examines the functions fulfilled by the *if*-clauses in the 2 genres, further interesting contrasts appear.

3.2 Comparison of *if* Functions in the RA and CP

Figure 1 shows the distribution of the Factual, Refocusing, and Discourse functions in the RAs and CPs.

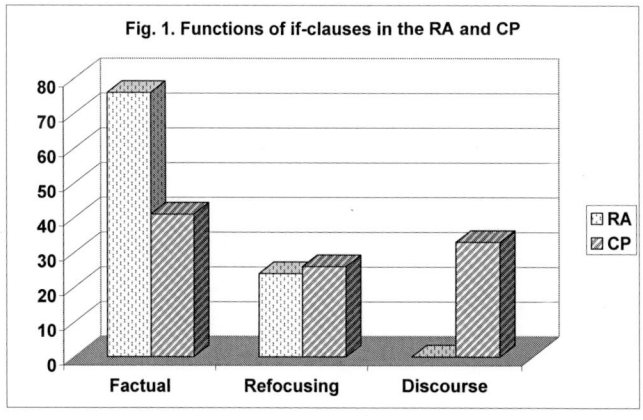

Fig. 1. Functions of if-clauses in the RA and CP

---

weighting towards final position in the RA observed here can nonetheless be considered as marked, compared to general usage.

What is immediately striking is the very high proportion of Factuals (76% of occurrences) in this particular subset of RAs, compared to the much lower proportion (41%) in the CP. In the RAs, 85% of Factuals occur in the Materials and Methods section, where their function is to detail the precise conditions of the study–the eligibility criteria for patients, the protocol or drug regimen, or other methodological and treatment decisions:

> Lesions were deemed T4 *if* there was evidence of invasion of neighbouring organs, and T3 *if* palpation revealed the tumor to be tethered or *if* CT scanning or ultrasonography showed tumor extension into only the perirectal fat. (RA 39, 40 & 41)

As this typical example shows, Factuals are almost exclusively (94% of cases) in the simple past.

In the CP, where time is limited, the methodology is not spelled out in such detail. Speakers gloss quickly over the criteria and methods when these are considered to be part of the audience's shared knowledge:

> And as already mentioned, this is the staging system [i.e. from T1 to T4] that is used (CP)
> Of these 70 patients, these were all followed in the same way, we had a more rigorous protocol which I won't go into detail about (CP)

As one speaker revealingly says, when criticising the methodology of a published study, "Let's look at the study a little closer. This is the section that was included in the Methods section that nobody reads." This highlights the conventional and non-newsworthy character of Materials and Methods sections, and hence the very formulaic nature of many Factual uses of *if* in the RA. Conference talks in contrast focus on breaking news and fresh results (Rowley-Jolivet 2002; Swales 2004). The lower proportion of Factuals in the CP can therefore be related to generic differences in scientific content and rhetorical conventions between RAs and CPs.

In both the RAs and the CPs, about one-quarter of *if*-clauses are used for the Refocusing function. The sub-categories of this function are however somewhat differently distributed, with more comment in the talks, as previously noted, and also more hypothesising, as speakers engage in more speculative interpretation of their results. This can again be related to the different epistemological aims of the two genres. The position of many CPs as 'proto-claims' (Rowley-Jolivet 2002) in the overall genre network of research discourse provides speakers with the freedom to launch into more exploratory, and as yet not-fully-documented, speculation:

I think intuitively you would think these [patients] would do better. I think *if* we had enough numbers maybe that would be the case. (CP 73)

Despite these differences, it is the similarity in the Refocusing function between RAs and CPs that should be underlined. Not only is the global percentage almost identical, but in both genres almost all the sub-categories of refocusing are found, indicating that these functions form a fundamental part of medical research discourse, irrespective of the mode of delivery and generic conventions.

A totally different picture emerges with the third major function of *if*, Discourse Management. No occurrences were found in the RAs, compared to 47 in the CPs, or 33% of all uses. The importance of the discourse category in the talks is related firstly to the different communicative contexts of the two genres. In the CP, delivered to a live audience, speaker presence is considerably more marked than in the RA, entailing the use of interactive syntactic structures (Rowley-Jolivet & Carter-Thomas, 2005). Secondly, the need for discourse management devices stems from the processing constraints specific to speech. Speakers need to focus the listener's attention on the referents needed in the subsequent discourse, leading to prefatory clauses with a topic-introducing role. Initial *if* clauses are one of the preferred syntactic choices in the CP for this role, as in: "Now *if* we look here at the sites of failure, primarily it was the liver in about half..." (CP59). *If* acts as a topic marker (Nattinger & Carrico 1992), enabling the speaker to introduce the new topic (sites of failure) which is then developed over a largish portion of discourse. *If* clauses have a second, closely related, discourse management function of topic shifting, providing the audience with explicit guidance about the speaker's discourse intentions, as he moves from one topic to another:

If we now go on to discuss the other problem, that is the local recurrence problem with rectal cancer, this is a serious problem (CP 66)

Such topic-marking would be to a large extent superfluous in the RA, particularly so in medicine, as the rhetorical structure of the article is highly codified, following the IMRD format in all the articles studied here. In lengthy expository monologues, however, such as conference presentations or lectures, organisational markers play an essential role in chunking the discourse by marking topic boundaries (Rilling 1996; Thompson 2003).

A third discourse function of initial *if* clauses in the scientific CP, which doubtless helps explain the large number of occurrences of this function, concerns the role of *if* as a space-builder. Speakers in scientific talks have constantly to manage two kinds of spaces: the verbal space, or speaker's running commentary, and the visual space, or what is projected onto the screen (Rowley-

Jolivet 2004; Rowley-Jolivet and Carter-Thomas 2005). They therefore need to instruct the audience on when to shift their attention from one to the other. Bald imperatives such as 'Look at this table' would no doubt be inappropriate when addressing a peer audience; the speaker needs to avoid face-threatening acts such as direct commands, which are therefore often attenuated by adverbs such as 'just' or by using an *if*-clause (Thompson 1997; Ford 1997), in order to make a polite directive when asking the audience to focus their attention on the visual space:

> Now *if* we look at just some factors, the disease-free survival was less (CP 72)

This example, like many others in the spoken data, has a rather unusual tense sequence, reflecting the shift from verbal to visual space: there is a move from the present (the ongoing enunciative space) in the *if*-clause, to the past (the research or content space presented on the visual) in the Q clause.

When a concordance is run on *if* in the CPs, it becomes clear that the discourse management function is a pre-packaged phraseological unit, constructed as follows:

Marker (optional)	Operator	Personal pronoun	Verb of perception	
(now)	*if*	you, we	look at…	X
Or:			Speaker's discourse intention	
(now)	*if*	I, we	combine, review, discuss…	X

On occasion, these two operations can be stacked, when the speaker first flags the visual space that he wants the audience to focus on (*look*), then uses a second *if*-clause to flag the discourse operation he will carry out within this space (*total up*):

> Local failures, *if* you just look at some small series, *if* I total them up, T1 lesions by and large very small recurrence (CP 31)

4. Case Reports

The case-report is a genre that has a long-standing history in medicine, and that is specific to this discipline. To a greater extent than many other sciences, medicine draws its conclusions from the detailed observation and narration of individual patient histories. Indeed, medical knowledge has been qualified as fundamentally narrative, based on 'doctors' stories' (Hunter 1991).

Case reports are short (622 words on average in the data used here) and restricted in topic, dealing with a single case which has been selected for analysis because it presents an unusual manifestation of a pathology, as the titles make clear: "Uncommon Presentations of Non-Hodgkin's Lymphoma. Case 3: Primary Renal Lymphoma" (*JCO*, 21:3). In a study comparing various medical genres, Salager-Meyer *et al* showed that case reports are characterised by a tripartite structure: a short Introduction, a more detailed Case Report body, and a brief Comment or Discussion section; in rhetorical aim, they are "essentially descriptive and expository" (1989:155). In conclusion to their analysis of writer-addressee attitudes in 3 medical genres–CR, RA and Editorials–Salager-Meyer *et al* position case reports at the purely descriptive end of a cline, and characterise the writer as an objective informant.

When CRs are examined for their usage of *if*-clauses, a similar positioning at one extreme of the cline is also observed. CRs have by far the lowest frequency of occurrence of *if* in the 4 genres studied here: in the 58 CRs collected, only 11 occurrences of *if* (in 10 CRs) were found, giving an overall frequency of 0.3/1000 words. This very small number obviously precludes any statistical generalisations, but when the 11 occurrences are examined for their functional roles, the dominant function (6 occ.) is found to be Recommendation[3]. As the following typical example shows, however, the recommendations are hedged, generally by using *should*: since the authors are basing their recommendation on a single, often uncommon case, it cannot be 'upgraded' to the more categorical status of *must*, given the very slim data:

> *If* pericardial effusion develops in non-Hodgkin's lymphoma, chylopericardium *should* be considered as one of the differential diagnoses. (CR 3)

From a genre perspective, where it is often as revealing to investigate features that are absent as features that are present, the paucity of *if* in the CR appears to indicate that in a genre where there is no need for discourse management (since the texts are very short), and where there is very little discussion and claim-making (since the aim is primarily descriptive), then authors are unlikely to use, or require, the *if*-operator.

5. Editorials

In Editorials, the fourth genre studied, in contrast, *if*-clauses are a highly valuable resource, and occur with a much greater frequency. There are on

---

[3] Of the remaining 5 occurrences, 3 are Factuals (1 treatment decision, one definition of the pathology, 1 heavily hedged correlation), 1 a concessive, and 1 a comment.

average 1.7 occurrences per 1000 words, though with a perceptible difference between the 2 journals, *Lancet Oncology* (2.6/1000 w.) and *JCO* (1.6/1000 w.)[4]. In terms of positioning of *if*-clauses, Editorials occupy an intermediate position between the highly contrasted RAs (with a majority of final positions) and CPs (where the vast majority of *if*-clauses are initial): in the editorials, 57% of *if*-clauses are initial, 9% medial, and 34% final.

Table 3. Quantitative features and functions in Editorials

Frequency	Positioning			Functions		
Ratio/1000w.	Initial	Medial	Final	Factuals	Refocus	Discourse
1.7	57%	9%	34%	10%	89%	1%

5.1 Functional categories

There is however a striking difference with the other genres examined so far in the distribution of the 3 major functions of *if*-clauses. The Discourse function is practically absent, the proportion of Factuals is very low, and the overwhelming majority of occurrences fall in the Refocusing category.

The explanations for this marked distribution are not hard to find. Editorials, like case reports, are generally short, rarely contain tables or figures, and therefore discourse management devices are seldom required. The only 2 occurrences found are, in one of the longer texts, an intratextual reminder of a previous statement ("*If* one goes back to the anology with …". ED105), and in the second case, the use of an *if*-clause to preface the concluding summary of several pieces of research: "*If* all of these findings are considered, …" (ED 45).

In the Factuals category, a small number of methodological or treatment decisions similar to those in the RA occur, particularly in *JCO* where some editorials, as already mentioned, relate clinical results as a basis or warrant for the opinion put forward. Two-thirds, however, are correlations, whereas in the RA this sub-category represented only a small fraction of Factuals, indicating that editorials are less concerned with reporting specific results than with

---

[4] This difference appears to be due to the rather different objectives and content of editorials in the 2 journals. In *Lancet Oncology* the texts are short (1 page), contain no literature references, and are purely vehicles for the expression of editorial opinion. In *JCO* editorials are sometimes longer, and often contain results of specific trials and references to bolster the opinion expressed. So it is not surprising that the frequency of *if*-clauses in *JCO* inclines more to that of the RAs (1.1/1000 w.) than is the case in *Lancet Oncology*.

surveying established knowledge and making generalisations from several studies, as in the following example:

> Decades of research have proven that *if* an antiemetic drug prevents cisplatin-induced emesis, it will also block emesis causes by other agents as well. (ED115)

The Factual and Discourse functions represent altogether only 11% of *if*-clauses in the Editorials, however. The vast majority have a Refocusing function and occur in argumentative contexts. The breakdown of the various refocusing sub-functions is shown in Table 4, where it can be seen that while hypotheses and its sub-category predictions represent the largest group (45% and 13% respectively), Recommendations (14.5%), and Concessives / Contrastives (10%) are also well-represented, particularly when compared to the other 3 genres studies so far. (No occurrences of restrictives were found in the editorials.)

Table 4. Breakdown of Refocusing functions in the Editorials

Hypothesing		Other Refocusing sub-catgeories		
Hypotheses	Predictions	Recommend.	Concess./Contrast	Comment
45%	13%	14.5%	10%	6.5%

Before examining in detail each of these sub-functions separately, however, I will first point out some constructional specificities of the *if P, Q* construction which occur across several sub-categories in editorials and which are observed only, or markedly, in this genre. These genre-related patterns are: *if P, then Q*; *Q only if P*; and the canonical conditionals.

5.2 Constructional specificities of the *if P, Q* pattern in Editorials

5.2.1. If P, then Q

The addition of the lexical items *then* and *only* to the basic *if P, Q* pattern communicates an additional instruction to the receiver, as each lexeme has its own particular meaning. *Then* is usually an optional element in the conditional construction–it can be used in certain cases, but does not have to be. So why does an author choose to use it?

As Dancygier (1998) and Dancygier and Sweetser (1997) have argued, the presence of *then* in Q implies that P is the unique space in which Q is located or is valid, thereby excluding competing spaces and as a result erasing the tentativeness or 'iffiness' usually associated with the P-clause. Since *then* refers uniquely and anaphorically to the space set up in P, by using *then* the author deliberately constrains the interpretation that the reader can put on the *If* construction, forcing a causal or strong dependency relation between the two clauses. The *if P, then Q* construction is more categorical than the simple *if P, Q* one, and implies a different author stance, one in which the text producer feels authorised to impose his reasoning process on the receiver.

As Hyland, when discussing author stance in research discourse, points out, "choices of rhetorical strategy depend on relations between participants" (Hyland 1999:99). It is interesting to note, therefore, that in the RA, where the adoption of such a position of superiority by the author would be perceived as presumptuous, there are no occurrences of the *if P, then Q* pattern (and only 3 in the CPs), whereas one finds 13 occurrences in the editorials:

> *If* we do not have convincing evidence of antitumor response, *then* we have little to guide our vaccine development. (ED11)

5.2.2. Q only if P

The additional meaning imparted to the construction by this lexeme is rather similar to *if P, then Q*, in that *only* limits the choice of conditions that the hearer might consider relevant to Q to a single one, operating a closure or bounding of the theoretically open space of P, and again imposing a single interpretation on the reader:

> Diagnostic imaging will continue to play a vital part in cancer medicine *only if* sustained long-term investments are made (ED169)

The 'if and only if' interpretation is a pragmatic implicature of many ordinary *if P, Q* utterances, that is when the *only* is not voiced, and is generally referred to as conditional perfection (Horn 2000). The point to be stressed here is that of the 4 genres studied, editorials are the only one in which the *Q only if P* pattern occurs. As with the *if P, then Q* construction, *Q only if P* positions the writer as someone authoritative, licensed to make definitive statements which foreclose all the other possible options that the reader might be tempted to entertain.

5.2.3. Canonical conditionals

A third specificity of the conditional construction in Editorials is the high percentage of the three canonical conditionals compared with the other written genres. These 3 verb forms - 1) present + *will*; 2) past + *would*; 3) past perfect + *would have* - represent 25% of *if*-clauses in editorials, compared to 0% in the 15 RAs and the case-reports studied here (cf. also Carter-Thomas, this volume, who found <6% of canonical conditionals in French and English medical RAs).

In the presentations, where 16% of occurrences are the canonical conditionals, these are restricted to types 1 and 2; conditional 3, or counterfactuals, are encountered only in editorials.

The relevance of these constructional specificities–*if P then Q, Q only if P*, and heavy use of canonical conditionals - for the rhetorical aims of editorials will become apparent when we consider the sub-categories in the Refocusing function.

5.3 Recommendations

Recommendations are extremely rare in the talks (1%) and in the RAs (6%) but more abundant in editorials (14%). Recommending is a recognised feature of editorials. Adams-Smith (1984), for example, comparing author's comment in 3 medical genres, found a much higher percentage of recommendations in Editorials (22.1%) than in RAs and CRs (respectively 13.3% and 7.3%). The editorialist often acts as the spokesperson for the journal or even for the field as a whole, and is empowered by the conventional aims of the genre to adopt a position of authority towards readers and to give them advice, though the non-assertive value of *if* mitigates this. The authoritative author stance pointed out in the previous section is very apparent in recommendations: the enunciator again positions himself as a person warranted in making categorical, and often critical, statements :

> *If* the UK government's targets for health care are to be realised, the leadership needs to be bold, not just in terms of money spent on treatment but also measures focused on prevention. (ED163)

Recommendations in the Editorials concern two domains: firstly, legislative, social and financial aspects of medicine, or its socio-economic environment, where the writer is the spokesman for the medical community in its dealings with governments and institutions:

> Several strategies are needed *if* the shortage of radiologists and the adequate provision of MRI is to be resolved: for example, increased funding for recruitment...; improved hospital networks...; and improved patient prioritisation. (ED168)

Secondly, over half the recommendations concern desirable changes to, or improvements in, current medical practices and procedures. The author here is giving advice not to outside partners, but to his medical peers:

If one accepts these treatments as valid, major changes in the management of cancer patients with peritoneal seeding must be considered. In this new approach,... (ED19)

The deontic modality is of course prevalent in recommendations, with *must* the most frequent modal in Q, and slightly more hedged recommendations using *should*, *could* or *would*. A specific verb form in P, however, found exclusively in recommendations, is '**is to be**':

If the UK government's targets for health care *are to be* realised, the leadership needs to be bold (ED163)

This structure expresses both a projection into the future, and an evaluation of the desirability of the projected action. Declerck & Reed gloss the structure as follows: "it combines the idea of contingency (possible P-actualization in the future) with the idea of purpose and volition..." and "can be used to express the idea that the future fulfilment of the condition is a goal that is striven for" (Declerck & Reed 2001: 209, 225). The syntactic pattern *If X is to be, Q* itself contributes strongly to the interpretation of the sentence, in that there is a preferred form-meaning correlation between this pattern and the function of recommending.

5.4 Hypothesising

Hypotheses and predictions form the largest sub-category of *if*-clauses in the editorials, representing 58% altogether (compared to 10% in the RAs and 16% in the talks). Their frequency can be attributed in part to the reasoning processes of medical research in general, partly to the argumentative aims of the editorial genre.

Reasoning in medicine is generally inductive, rather than deductive, based on the processes of argumentation of informal, rather than formal, logic (Toulmin 1958; Perelman and Olbrechts-Tyteca 1958). Conclusions are probabilistic and made on the basis of a large number of observations. The great number of variables or factors that need to be controlled mean that hypotheses are necessarily tentative. Implicit in hypothesising is the conditional relation– indeed, the use of *if* for making hypotheses is often considered as a core function (see Carter-Thomas, this volume). The role of *if* as a non-assertive space-builder comes out very clearly in this category. As in the RA, the P clause allows the writer to open up a hypothetical space in order to speculate on alternatives or possibilities within this space:

If the results reported by Mellado *et al* are observed by other investigators, it is possible that detection of CMC could direct selection of high-risk patients for high-dose interferon therapy. (ED12)

As the above example illustrates, such hypotheses are characterised by the use of epistemic modality, or, as in the following case, by tense backshifting, heightening the authorial distance towards the hypothesis:

> If this principle were applied to predictive markers in studies where the outcome may require 5 to 10 years of follow-up, few advances would be made (ED35)

Why are hypotheses so prevalent in editorials, however? The aims of editorials are "to raise questions, diagram problems, propose definitions and offer alternatives and/or solutions for future research,... examine, discuss and criticize" (Salager-Meyer *et al.*, 1989:153). Editorials address 'hot' or controversial issues for which there is often no clear-cut solution, or confront results by different research teams which give rise to diverging interpretations. For all these discourse functions, *if*-clauses are an essential instrument in the writer's linguistic toolbox.

An editorialist is also expected, however, to take a stand on the issue–like book reviews (Hyland 2000:41), editorials are an explicitly evaluative genre, and writers of editorials criticise or question in a more direct manner than is customary in the research article. As a result one finds that many hypotheses are attitudinally marked in some way, by a variety of devices which are either rare or absent in the other genres studied here. The following section looks at three ways in which this attitudinal marking is accomplished in *if*-clauses: predictions; interrogative form in the Q clause; and counterfactuals.

5.4.1 Predictions

The centrality of the predictive function to conditional sentences has been firmly asserted by Dancygier - "predictive constructions seem to represent prototypical conditionality" (1998:195)–particularly so in the case of the paradigmatic or canonical conditionals, with their consistent pattern of verb forms. We have already noted that these conditionals are far more common in Editorials than in the other genres. In predictions, the verb form used is overwhelmingly the first conditional (present in P, *will* in Q), and the clause ordering is also the conventional one with initial P in the majority of cases:

> *If* the lack of charity regulation in Scotland is allowed to persist, future scandals such as that involving BCR Scotland will inevitably occur (ED153)

This example also illustrates the topics concerned by predictions: *all* the predictions concern socio-economic issues, such as the provision of medical services and their funding, legislation, developments in trials and drug marketing, and medical education. Unlike the areas of investigation into the causes of disease, or diagnosis and treatment, where certainty is much more difficult, or even impossible to attain–and where pronouncements are therefore often heavily hedged and circumspect–in the economic or legislative domain medical writers feel confident enough of causal relations to use predictive *if P, Q* clauses.

The predictions are frequently made with the evaluative value of a premonitory warning. The author adopts a judgemental approach and writer-reader relations are, as we saw previously with recommendations, unequal:

> *If* the true scale of these issues is not recognised and acted on by the appropriate authorities now, the lack of funding in non-curative healthcare will mean that quality of life will increasingly worsen for future generations of patients living with cancer. (ED174)

5.4.2 Interrogative Q

The use of an interrogative form in Q, rather than the usual declarative, is a strong manifestation of attitudinal marking by the author, and is found almost exclusively in the editorial genre (0 occ. in the RAs, 1 occ. in the CPs, against 15 occ. in EDs).

This is perhaps unsurprising, as questions are much more frequent in editorials in general, either in the titles or in the text itself. Webber (1994), in a study of the function of questions in different medical journal genres, found that editorials and reviews combined contained 9 times more interrogatives than the RAs, and practically none occurred in case-studies. Hyland (2002), in a subsequent comparison of questions in RAs, textbooks, and student reports, found them to be over twice as frequent in textbooks as in RAs, and proposed the following explanations for this difference: questions are dialogic, involving the reader in the text and in the author's argument, and are more overtly interactional; they also however exert a considerable degree of discourse control and convey authority, since the questions asked are the ones that the author chooses to ask and to which he or she has the answers, and are often used in fact to lead the reader in the direction the author wishes. In the RA, questions would be felt to be condescending by many readers, as an egalitarian stance is expected, unlike the unequal social relations of expert-to-novice communication in textbooks. As already pointed out above, however, the writer-reader relation in editorials is also often an unequal one.

What is the specific argumentative role of the conditional question–*if P, Q?*– in the editorial genre? A first point to note is that in this construction, all the P-clauses are initial; the interrogative in Q is therefore performed against the background already set up by P. On analysis, the function of the initial P-clause is found to be that of encapsulating certain assumptions that the writer wishes the reader to make from the preceding stretch of discourse, in order to provide a warrant for the question itself. This encapsulation can be done, however, either with a cooperative intent, or with a critical intent.

An example of the former is:

> Thus, *if* physical examination and radiographic evaluation are unable to provide a reliable and accurate assessment ..., is there a superior alternative? (ED73)

If P sums up the shared writer-reader assumptions from the preceding discourse, and the question in Q is one which the reader is likely to wish to ask at this juncture.

In other cases, however, this encapsulation has the critical intent of enabling the author to question, in Q, the assumptions brought into the discourse in P. The fundamental non-assertiveness of the *if P, Q* construction means that the writer can summon into the text another voice in P, by recalling the claims of others, and then proceed in Q to question these claims, both syntactically and rhetorically speaking :

> After the serious limitations of this analysis are taken into careful consideration, the question remains: *If* a graft-versus-lymphoma effect does exist, why was evidence of it not observed in this analysis? (ED102)

From a polyphonic perspective, it is clear that the author does not take responsibility for the point of view that "a graft-versus-lymphoma effects exists": the co-text is highly negative ("the serious limitations of this analysis"), the use of the *if* operator signifies that the concept evoked is non-assertable, adding the emphatic auxiliary *does* further heightens the doubt cast on the claim, and the negative question in Q directly challenges the contested claim. The *if P, Q?* construction has a clear refutative function here.

The above examples illustrate how the *if P, Q?* structure can be used persuasively to negotiate agreement between writer and reader by a subtle management of polyphony. In other cases, the degree of control exercised by the writer over the dialogue with the reader is much greater. This control can clearly be felt in sequences of two questions, the second of which is a conditional:

> Are such variations the result of differences among surgeons in inherent technical skill or differences in experience or education? *If* the latter, what educational programs would effectively improve technique? (ED4)

The first question ostensibly offers the reader 3 possible answers to the question of why some patients fare better after surgery than others–difference in skill between surgeons, difference in their experience, or differences in education. The first two options however are fake questions–and no doubt very touchy issues–in that the writer, with *if the latter* forecloses or funnels the debate and only considers the third option, while still appearing, through the use of *if*, to respect the reader's freedom of thought.

This funnelling of the debate comes across very clearly also in occurrences where the editorialist either leaves the reader no time to answer the question, or answers it himself, as in:

> *If* "fit elderly" patients can tolerate aggressive multimodality therapy, does this mean that all older patients should be treated this way? The answer is no. (ED79)

The writer can also exercise control by setting up the reader to answer the question in a particular way, by his lexical choices. The only possible answer for the reader to such a question as "Should epratuzumab therefore be used in the same, almost universal (indiscriminate) fashion, in all cell surface $CD22^+$ B-cell malignancies?" is a negative one, given the presence of *indiscriminate*. And indeed, the text continues with "*If not*, what criteria should be used for the clinical development of this and subsequent MAbs?"

5.4.3 Counterfactuals in the Editorials

The confrontation of different voices pointed out in the previous section also comes across clearly in the third and last sub-type of hypotheses that are characteristic of editorials, namely counterfactuals. No occurrences of counterfactuals were found in the other 3 genres studied. Counterfactuals are a prime example of the role of *if* as a space-builder. This hypothetical thinking enables the speaker to envisage the possible consequences of situations which either did not in fact occur in the past or which do not currently hold (Akatsuka and Strauss 2000). The aim of this space-building will often be an evaluative one: if these counterfactual situations are entertained, it is in order to judge, criticise or, more rarely, to commend the actual decisions or behaviour of the actors involved.

The reason why counterfactuals are found exclusively in the editorials and not in the RAs seems to lie in the different rhetorical aims of the two genres. In Knorr-Cetina's words, "[RAs] are not designed to promote an understanding of alternatives, but to foster the impression that what *has been done* is all that *could be done*" (1981: 42; her emphasis). The authors would be shooting themselves in the foot if they gave too much prominence to other hypothetical spaces in which a different set of results might have been obtained, or a different approach seen to be more valid than the one they chose. Despite the necessary presence of hedging, 'alternatives' which are likely to cast serious doubt on their claims are hence downplayed in the RA.

In Editorials, in contrast, the author is not defending his own research claim. Counterfactuals enable him to express criticism of others' work, or regret that a certain avenue was not explored. To illustrate the argumentative and critical potential of this structure, let's look at an extract in which 3 occurrences are found.

> In the context of previous trials in solid tumors that have failed to demonstrate an effect of maintenance therapy on survival, one needs to consider the question of (1) what the likely outcome **would have been** *if* the primary end point of this study **had been** survival, and the study **had been continued** despite the emergence of a statistically significant difference in progression-free survival. (2) *If* the 7-month improvement in progression-free survival **were also associated** with a clinically significant improvement in overall survival, this **would be** the first demonstration that maintenance therapy improves survival (…). However, molecular profiling of ovarian cancer has not identified any factors that would uniquely make ovarian cancer (in contrast to other common solid tumors) a disease for which maintenance chemotherapy leads to an improvement in survival. In addition, the hazard ratio for progression increased after completion of maintenance therapy, indicating that patients still had residual disease despite the prolonged chemotherapy. (3) *Even if* the study **had not been stopped**, it seems unlikely, but not impossible, that maintenance therapy **would have improved** survival compared to a strategy of reinstituting effective therapy at the time of disease progression after initial achievement of a clinical complete remission. (ED49, 50, 51)

The first occurrence is a clear example of an *if*-counterfactual used to build a hypothetical space in order to envisage alternatives (*one needs to consider what the likely outcome would have been if...*). The editorialist is criticising the study, which was stopped too soon to provide data on survival - the primary end-point in oncology - and relativises its positive results (*7-month improvement in progression-free survival*) as it did not go far enough to answer the crucial question of overall survival. The degree of tense backshifting in P indicates the degree of commitment to the likelihood of the counterfactual situation–the more backshifted the verb form, the greater the authorial distance. Occurrences 1 and 3 above are more backshifted, since they hypothesise about known, and therefore irreversible past facts, so the counterevidence is extremely strong; in occurrence 2, in contrast, tense backshifting is less marked as there are no hard facts to go on–it is not known at the time of writing whether survival was better or not. The use of the concessive *even if* in the third occurrence serves to counter potential objections to the criticism by arguing that even in this counterfactual space, the treatment strategy chosen (*maintenance therapy*) would not have improved patient outcome.

This third occurrence brings us to the last sub-category of the refocusing function in the editorials–Concessives and Contrastives.

5.5 Concessives and Contrastives

Concession is one of the most efficient linguistic strategies in argumentative and persuasive discourse, as it enables the enunciator to concede another's voice, thus appearing fair-minded and enhancing his own *ethos*, while in fact prioritising his own voice (Ducrot 2004; Ranger 1998). Concessive conditionals are usually introduced by *even if* : the space-building potential of the *if* operator allows the writer to redraw the boundaries of the argumentative space to include these other voices in P, forestalling possible objections, and creating more space for his own claim; *even* is a scalar operator which introduces "a scale of unlikelihood, or negative expectation, the highest position on which is occupied by the referent of the expression in the scope of *even*" (Dancygier 1998: 161-2).

Concessives are infrequent in the CPs and the RAs (2% of occurrences in each genre). Carter-Thomas, this volume, likewise found very few concessive conditionals in the English-authored RAs in her corpus; they were however far more frequent in the RAs written by French researchers, whether published in English or in French. She concludes that this may indicate a more overtly argumentative stance by the latter. It is therefore interesting to see that in editorials, even when written by English authors, concessives are quite common (10%), indicating that although national academic style and language-related differences influence syntactic choices, the rhetorical aims of the genre also come into play. In editorials, authors need to confront different voices and manage polyphony but still put forward a clear personal opinion, so have recourse to concessives:

> *Even if* health care providers are diligent in keeping current with genetic medicine, the interpretation of the results of genetic testing is often complex. (JCO84)

The editorialist is arguing against DTC (Direct-To-Consumer) marketing of genetic tests by commercial companies, as there is no guarantee of the quality of the follow-up provided to the patient by the company or by the local GP, compared to that provided by specialised centres. The concessive envisages the most favourable situation on the scale - one where the GP does keep up to date with genetic medicine - in an implicit dialogue with this well-informed group of readers whom the author presumably does not wish to alienate. This eventuality is conceded, however, only so that the writer can then assert in Q that the interpretation of test results still remains problematic.

Contrastive conditionals have a rather different argumentative function. The initial P-clause contains some old or given (and hence backgrounded) information with which the new, foregrounded information in Q is contrasted; the *if P, Q* construction acts as a syntactic hinge to introduce the contrast, bridging from one topic to the next. Although this type of *if*-clause is used sparingly in editorials (and not at all in the other genres studied), it serves, intriguingly, to create room for the author to ask a rhetorical question and ram home his point:

> *If* a study of this power [the million-woman study on the link between HRT and breast cancer] creates confusion and panic, what hope is there for communicating uncertain risks about which little is known? (ED157)
> *If* 'fit elderly' patients can tolerate aggressive multimodality therapy, does this mean that *all* older patients should be treated this way? (ED79)

6. Conclusions

This comparison of the same syntactic structure across several genres within a single medical speciality has produced several interesting findings. We have seen, firstly, that *if*-clauses vary considerably in frequency according to genre. Figure 2 diagrams these variations along a cline, from a very low frequency in the case reports at one extreme, to the spoken presentations at the other, with research articles and editorials falling in between.

Fig. 2. Frequency of if-clauses in 4 medical genres per 1000 words

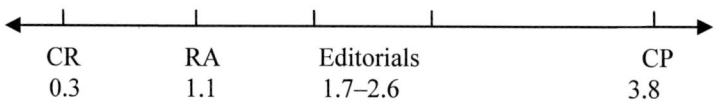

CR	RA	Editorials	CP
0.3	1.1	1.7–2.6	3.8

I have related these differences in frequency to the different rhetorical aims and communicative needs of each genre. Case Reports are short, mainly descriptive, and very limited in the amount of generalisation, hypothesising or recommendation that can be undertaken on the basis of a single, extra-ordinary case-history. As a result, there is little need, or indeed justification, for using *if*-clauses for the Discourse, Factual, or Refocusing functions.

Medical research articles in English restrict their use of *if*-clauses to two main functions: Factual and Refocusing. The dominant, and highly conventionalised, Factual function serves to detail the methodology and patient characteristics by exploiting the circumscribing potential of *if*-clauses to delimit the precise conditions of the research effort. While the rigid IMRD format of the medical RA renders the Discourse function superfluous, *if*-clauses perform the essential functions of presenting the research hypotheses and allowing the syntactic management of hedging in the discussion of results.

The communicative constraints and objectives of the conference presentation genre result in a much lower proportion of Factuals than in the RA. In contrast, the Discourse functions of *if*-clauses–topic-introducing, shifting from verbal to visual spaces, giving polite directives–are frequent, and specific to the spoken mode.

Editorials share with CRs and RAs an almost total absence of this discourse function, but differ from the previous three in that they are not a research genre. Their evaluative and argumentative aims result in a low proportion of Factuals and a very high proportion of refocusing *if*-clauses, which are used to confront diverging points of view, manage polyphony and interact with the reader.

In addition to these functional differences, we have also observed several variations on the basic *if P, Q* constructional pattern with genre. Certain formal elements, such as the preference for initial vs. final positioning of P clauses, the use of the interrogative form in Q, the *if X is to be* pattern, tend to be consistently associated with a given genre, as are certain lexemes such as *then* or *only*, which constrain the semantics of the P-Q link and imply a particular type of writer-reader relation. These constructional and lexical differences appear to be rhetorically motivated, in that each form-meaning correlation is relevant to the specific objectives of the genre in question.

Starting from the basic premise that *if* is a space-builder, we have seen that the types of spaces constructed by *if* vary in a regular way with the genre. In the RA, *if* acts principally to circumscribe the research space by delimiting the precise boundaries or conditions under which the research was conducted, and, to a lesser degree, to open up a space for the research hypotheses; in the CP, in addition, the *if* operator is used to manage the discourse space and guide listeners through the presentation, while in the editorials the role of *if* in managing argumentation and polyphony comes to the fore.

One of the basic postulates of a genre approach is that the communicative aims and context of the discourse will impact on both the overall textual organization and the linguistic / syntactic choices. Interest in the preferred syntactic structures of scientific discourse initially focused on the passive and other impersonal constructions, in the wake of the neo-positivist, objective image of science. More recently, however, there has been growing interest in how claims are persuasively put forward and grounded, and in polyphonic interaction in academic discourse. It therefore seemed an opportune moment to investigate other syntactic constructions which enable this interaction and which illustrate the close connection between argumentation and rhetoric highlighted by theories of informal logic. This study has attempted to address the argumentative and interactional uses to which the *if P, Q* construction is put in one medical specialty. It remains to be seen whether other research disciplines use the structure in the same way, or whether they have recourse to different structures to achieve their rhetorical aims.

7. References

Adams-Smith, Diana E. "Medical discourse: Aspects of author's comment." *The ESP Journal* 3 (1984): 25-36.
Akatsuka, N.M. and S. Strauss. "Counterfactual reasoning and desirability." In *Cause – Condition – Concession – Contrast*, edited by E. Couper-Kuhlen and B. Kortmann, 205-234. Berlin: Mouton de Gruyter, 2000.
Athanasiadou, Angeliki and René Dirven. "Conditionality, hypotheticality, counterfactuality;" In *On Conditionals Again*, edited by A. Athanasiadou and R. Dirven, 61-96. Amsterdam: Benjamins, 1997.
Biber, D., Johansson, S., Leech, G., Conrad, S., & Finegan, E. *Longman Grammar of Spoken and Written English*. Harlow: Pearson Education, 1999.
Carter-Thomas, Shirley. "The 'iffiness' of medical research articles. A comparison of English *if* and French *si*." This volume.
Dancygier, Barbara. *Conditionals and Predictions: Time, Knowledge and Causation in Conditional Constructions*. Cambridge: Cambridge University Press, 1998.
Dancygier, Barbara and Eve Sweetser. "*Then* in conditional constructions." *Cognitive Linguistics* 8/2 (1997): 109-136.
Declerck, Renaat and Susan Reed. *Conditionals: a comprehensive empirical analysis*, Berlin and New York: Mouton de Gruyter, 2001.
Ducrot, Oswald. "Argumentation rhétorique et argumentation linguistique." In *L'Argumentation aujourd'hui*, edited by M. Doury and S. Moirand. 17-34. Paris: Presses Sorbonne Nouvelle, 2004.
Fauconnier, Gilles. *Mental Spaces: Aspects of meaning construction in natural language*. 2nd edition. Cambridge, MA: MIT Press, 1994.
Ferguson, Gibson. "If you pop over there: a corpus-based study of conditionals in medical discourse." *English for Specific Purposes* 20/1 (2001): 61-82.
Ford, Cecilia E. "Speaking Conditionally: Some Contexts for If-clauses in Conversation." In *On Conditionals Again*, edited by A. Athanasiadou and R. Dirven, 387-413. Amsterdam: Benjamins, 1997.

Ford, Cecilia E. and Sandra A. Thompson. "Conditionals in discourse: A text-based study from English." In *On Conditionals*, edited by E. Traugott et al., 353-372. Cambridge: Cambridge University Press, 1986.
Horn, Laurence R. "From *if* to *iff*: Conditional perfection as pragmatic strengthening. " *Journal of Pragmatics* 32 (2000): 289-326.
Hunter, Kathryn Montgomery. *Doctors' Stories: The narrative structure of medical knowledge*. Princeton, NJ: Princeton University Press, 1991.
Hyland, Ken. *Hedging in scientific research articles*. Amsterdam: Benjamins, 1998.
—. "Disciplinary discourses: writer stance in research articles." In *Writing: Texts, processes and practices*, edited by C.N. Candlin and K. Hyland, 99-121. London: Longman, 1999.
—. *Disciplinary discourses. Social interactions in academic writing*. London: Longman, 2000.
—. "What do they mean? Questions in academic writing. " *Text* 22/4 (2002): 529-557.
Knorr-Cetina, K. D. *The manufacture of knowledge*. Oxford: Pergamon, 1981.
Latour, Bruno. *Science in Action*. Cambridge, Mass.: Harvard University Press, 1987.
Nattinger, J. and J. DeCarrico. *Lexical phrases and language teaching*. Oxford: Oxford University Press, 1992.
Perelman, C. and L. Olbrechts-Tyteca. *Traité de l'argumentation. La nouvelle rhétorique*. Bruxelles : Éditions de l'Université, 1958.
Prince, E.F., Frader, R.J., and Bosk, C. "On hedging in physician-physician discourse." In *Linguistics and the professions*, edited by J. di Prieto, 83-97. Norwood, NJ: Ablex, 1982.
Ranger, Graham. *Les Constructions concessives en anglais : une approche énonciative*. Paris: Ophrys, 1998.
Rilling, S. "Lexical phrases as organisational markers in academic lectures: A corpus- and computer-based approach to research and teaching." *The ORTESOL Journal*. 17 (1996): 19-40.
Rowley-Jolivet, E. "Science in the making: Scientific conference presentations and the construction of facts." In *The Language of conferencing*. edited by E. Ventola, C. Shalom & S. Thompson, 95-125. Frankfurt: Peter Lang, 2002.
—. "Different visions, different visuals: a social semiotic analysis of field-specific visual composition in scientific conference presentations." *visual communication* 3/2 (2004): 145-175.
Rowley-Jolivet, Elizabeth and Shirley Carter-Thomas. "Scientific conference Englishes: Epistemic and Language Community Variations." *In Identity, Community, Discourse: English in Intercultural Settings*, edited by Giuseppina Cortese and Anna Duszak, 295-320. Bern: Peter Lang, 2005.

Salager-Meyer, Françoise. "Hedges and textual communicative function in medical English written discourse." *English for Specific Purposes* 13/2 (1994): 149-170.
Salager-Meyer, F., G. Defives, C. Jensen and M. de Filipis. "Communicative function and grammatical variations in medical English scholarly papers: A genre analysis study." In *Special Language: from humans thinking to thinking machines*, edited b y C. Laurén and M. Nordman, 151-160. Philadelphia: Multilingual Matters, 1989.
Swales, John. *Genre Analysis: English in Academic and Research Settings*, Cambridge: Cambridge University Press, 1990.
—. *Research genres*. Cambridge: Cambridge University Press, 2004.
Thompson, S.E. "Presenting research: A study of interaction in academic monologue. " PhD diss., University of Liverpool 1997.
—. "Text-structuring metadiscourse, intonation and the signalling of organisation in academic lectures." *Journal of English for Academic Purposes* 2 (2003): 5-20.
Toulmin, S.E. *The Uses of Argument*. Cambridge: Cambridge University Press, 1958.
Webber, Pauline. "The Function of questions in different medical journal genres." *English for Specific Purposes* 13/3 (1994): 257-268.

CHAPTER TEN

MARKING EVIDENTIALITY IN SCIENTIFIC PAPERS: THE CASE OF EXPECTATION MARKERS

FRANCIS GROSSMANN AND FRANÇOISE WIRTH

1. Introduction

The notion of evidentiality covers all marks signalling what testifies to the validity of the information stated by a speaker or writer. For instance, these marks–which are grammaticalized in some languages–make it possible for the speaker to indicate that he/she received a piece of information through direct perception, inference or hearsay. The literature about evidentiality often tackles the issue of differences and common points between evidentials and epistemic markers (Dendale and Tamsmowski 2001). Although we do not intend to address this issue here, it can be granted that there are close links between these two notions and that both must be considered in an integrated way: while epistemic modalities express the degree of certainty or uncertainty of a statement, it is the role of evidentials to specify the way a piece of information has been collected, particularly by indicating if it is the result of the speaker's inference or if it was passed on to him/her by a third party. Obviously, when specifying the source of a piece of information, the speaker often signals the degree of certainty or uncertainty he/she associates with it, which justifies an integrated treatment.

The same remark is valid for the sub-category we are focusing on in this paper, namely, markers signaling expectations. These markers, which have been classified by some authors in the category of evidentials in the broad sense (e.g. Chafe, 1986), indicate whether a piece of information matches the speaker's expectations or not, presenting it either as expected or surprising. We would argue that the link with evidentiality is mainly based on the fact that the feature of "expectedness" or "unexpectedness" of a piece of information is connected to explicit or implicit inferential schemes that belong to the knowledge of the world or that may be found within the text.

In this paper, we will mostly focus on two questions that specifically relate to evidentiality:
(a) Is there a specificity of these expectation markers in the genre under study, namely the scientific paper?
(b) If yes, how is this specificity made manifest (frequency? meaning and use of markers? existence of specific markers?).
We will also consider two additional questions in closer relation to the general topic of this book:
(c) Is there a specific use of this sub-category of markers according to the disciplines under study (linguistics, economics, medicine)?
(d) Are there differences–on a linguistic and cultural level–in the use of these markers between papers in English and in French and if yes, how do these differences show up?

After some methodological remarks (section 2), we will proceed with a definition of the notion of expectation (section 3) before commenting a list of markers of expectations and analyzing their use according to the language and discipline (section 4). We will then consider the case of *in fact* and *en fait* (section 5) which is particularly interesting in the context of this study.

2. Methodology

Our study is based on a corpus of 150 papers in English and 150 papers in French, in three disciplines (linguistics, economics, medicine)[1]. We first established a list of markers of expectations:
- on the basis of the literature (Chafe 1986, Dendale and Tamsmowski 1994, 2001);
- on the basis of the empirical exploration of the corpus (lexical fields of "surprise" and "expectation") by using a concordancer to find the occurrences;
- by eliminating examples and non-pertinent meanings of markers included in papers. For instance *consistent with* is a marker of expectation in a phrase such as "**consistent with** our findings" but is not in "sixteen children had had conditions **consistent with** the sequelae of meningitis" (Eng-med).

It was not always simple to pinpoint the role of the markers, as some of them have varied values and scopes. In view of such diversity, a mere counting of occurrences is not sufficient to encompass their use in scientific papers[2]. When

---
[1] The KIAP-corpus. We thank Kjersti Fløttum and her team for letting us use their corpus. See Fløttum, Dahl and Kinn 2006.
[2] It is to be noted that while one of the prime interests of Chafe's founding paper, which compares the use of evidentials in English conversation and academic writing, was to show that the marking of evidentiality could vary according to genres, it did not include a qualitative study of the functioning of evidentials within a sub-genre.

in doubt, we checked the use of the marker within its context, by referring to the source article.

The length of papers varying significantly in these disciplines and languages, our counting of the markers is based on the number of occurrences per 1,000 words.

As regards *in fact/ en fait*, we have carried out an additional qualitative study (forty occurrences per language) to analyze their use.

3. The notion of expectation in the scientific genre

While the authors of papers can only guess the expectations of the reader, they need, for their own rhetorical purposes, to introduce as original or new some of their statements or, conversely, to signal some information as well-known or obvious. From a discursive perspective, the author necessarily thinks in terms of textual strategy and takes into consideration the argumentative structure of the paper. In this respect, we want to make a clear distinction between two points. When presenting results, the author positions these in the light of a common stock of knowledge shared by a given community; in this light, the notion of expectation appears as the intersection between the expectations of the scientific community that validates knowledge and the expectations of the researcher himself/herself. The "falsibility" of scientific knowledge, such as described by epistemology, implies a dual process of validation: first by the researcher who assesses the results of his/her research; then by the scientific community. The notion of expectation therefore appears to have a structuring role in the genre under study. While in some other genres, this notion remains loose or fairly general (relating to logic, the knowledge of the world or the compliance with the rules of the genre, etc.), its meaning is much more specific within the field of scientific papers.

As scientific knowledge is often built in contradiction with common sense, the "expectedness" of knowledge is ambiguous in essence. What is expected by common sense is far from coinciding with scientific expectations, the latter claiming to "go beyond". The notion of expectation takes a dual, more complex form, the expectations of the scientist developing against those of the ordinary person[3].

Expectations may also be signaled through the text structure and in particular in the "state of the art" generally summarized at the beginning of the paper. The character of "novelty" can arise from a shift in the questioning (the

---

[3] This does not exclude the possibility of superimposing the two, surprise being for instance expressed from a common sense point of view and results being expected from a scientific point of view.

researcher stating the question in a way that is different from the one typically used); it can also arise from the various degrees of unexpectedness of the results. Finally, according to some models of scientific research, such as the one prototypically illustrated by the experimental approach, hypotheses are used to explicitly express the researcher's expectations, which, in this way, are easily spotted.

4. Markers of expectation: inventory and comparison

As indicated above, the markers taken into consideration signal that the information is presented as more or less expected or more or less surprising. Chafe (1986:271) mentions *of course, oddly enough, actually* and *in fact*. Classifying the markers of expectation as evidentials can be questioned since they do not, as such, signal the means by which the information or knowledge has been obtained. Nevertheless, as already stated above, as they indicate whether the information fits in with the expectations or not, the markers necessarily refer to inferences carried out by the speaker or writer. In scientific papers, in which inferences need to be made as clear as possible, the use of markers of expectation is therefore particularly essential.

When this use is construed in a broad linguistic perspective integrating the discursive aspect, it is necessary to distinguish three levels:
- On a semantic level, some markers have an evidential value by the very nature of their lexical meaning: *of course* or *bien entendu* do signal the expectedness of a statement whereas *surprisingly* marks what is referred to as "mirativity" (DeLancey 1997, 2000);
- On a textual level, these markers can be seen as playing an additional function of textual cohesion (cf. Thompson & Zhou 2001) especially in correlations with *of course...but*. In such cases, the marker prepares the introduction of counter-arguments; in other words, it often introduces a concessive value. However, this concessive value is not always connected to the use of explicit markers such as *but*: this preparatory meaning is often left to the reader to understand;
- The generic level takes even more general characters into account. As has already been mentioned, scientific papers are based on a certain representation of the scientific activity. One of these representations corresponds to the following model: Hypotheses–Verification (experimentation, etc.)–Results–Interpretation of results. Such a model implies a text structure that more or less corresponds to the genre of the scientific paper (or at least one of its implementations). A number of very specific markers are linked to the scientific approach of the genre: *ainsi, conformément à nos hypothèses...., contrairement à nos attentes,* etc.

We decided to take into account both lexical markers that can be considered as more characteristic of the scientific papers (e.g. *in line with our expectations*) and the adverbials (e.g. *of course*) frequently occurring in all kinds of texts. Although this decision can be questioned, both categories including very different linguistic tools, we considered that it would be interesting to compare their use according to the disciplines and languages under study, because they convey two different forms of expectations: expectations based on the very construction of the scientific process and those linked to presuppositions or shared knowledge.

4.1 Markers of congruence

The relation towards expectations can be divided into two main categories: the information or result is either in congruence or non-congruence with the expectations. Table 1 below lists the main lexical markers of congruence that we found in the scientific papers of the corpus, in English and French. Here are a few examples of the use of lexical markers in both languages:

(1) **Conformément aux résultats précédents**, on montre que cette politique n'affecte durablement qu'une partie du système économique, la dynamique de la consommation et de la créance nette de chaque pays. Les soldes de la balance des paiements des deux pays sont alors modifiés. (Fr-eco).

(2) Information-based trade is identified via a positive and significant long-run response of quotations to transaction activity, **in line with the theoretical argument presented in Section 1.** (Eng-eco)

Table 1. Lexical markers of congruence

English	French
Consistent with (our results, findings, with previous reports, the belief, the data, the assumption, the expectations...);	*Conformément à (+ notre hypothèse, notre postulat, nos attentes; conformément à l'intuition, aux données de la littérature, aux prévisions ;*
Not inconsistent with (the literature); in line with our analysis, with the view, with the proposal; in accord with...	*En accord avec (nos résultats précédents...); ces résultats... concordent avec/ sont en concordance avec ; sont compatibles avec ;*
As expected; this is to be expected; as one would expect; as one might expect;	*Comme attendu, comme nous nous y attendions, chose attendue..., comme on pouvait s'y attendre ;*
As predicted (by theory, by the model) the results, the tests confirm... we	*Les résultats confirment ; notre étude permet de confirmer...... a permis de*

confirm the literature's presumptions... Is not surprising, not particularly surprising, is hardly surprising, less surprising	vérifier que... Aussi ne saurait-on être surpris que... ; ce résultat n'est pas surprenant...; sans surprise ; on ne sera pas surpris ; comme cela était prévisible, ces résultats sont prévisibles.

Adverbials marking congruence (Table 2) are less numerous[4].

Table 2. Adverbials marking congruence

English	French
of course	*bien sûr,*
obviously	*bien entendu*
(quite) clearly	*évidemment,*
Naturally	*naturellement*

Here are a few examples of the use of adverbial markers in both languages:

(3) **Although of course Australian English does constitute one of the mixture**, Australians only constituted 7% of immigrants to New Zealand before 1881. (Eng-ling)

(4) **Bien entendu, le terme de "préposition vide" ne doit pas être pris au pied de la lettre**. Il s'agit en fait d'emplois vides de certaines prépositions. Il n'existe pas de préposition toujours vide de sens, du moins si l'on continue à voir un même mot dans le *de* de *la ville de Paris* et celui de *elle vient de Paris*. (Fr-ling)

Example (3) is typical of a reference to shared knowledge which the reader is expected to have; in example (4), *bien entendu* makes it possible for the writer to specify what he/she means by "préposition vide"; although presented as obvious, this knowledge is not necessarily shared by the reader. This illustrates the complexity of the use of this class of markers.

The use of adverbials being more argumentative (they also have a modal value of presupposition), less unique to the scientific paper, we had to judge whether they truly signaled congruence with expectations. Table 3 below indicates the relative frequency of the markers (per thousand words) after filtering.

---

[4] This list is not exhaustive, but rather the result of careful selection: for instance, we chose to exclude adverbials such as *en réalité, effectivement* in French or *actually* in English, which belong to the same micro-system as *in fact* et *en fait*, which are discussed in section 5.

Table 3. Relative frequency of markers of congruence and confirmation

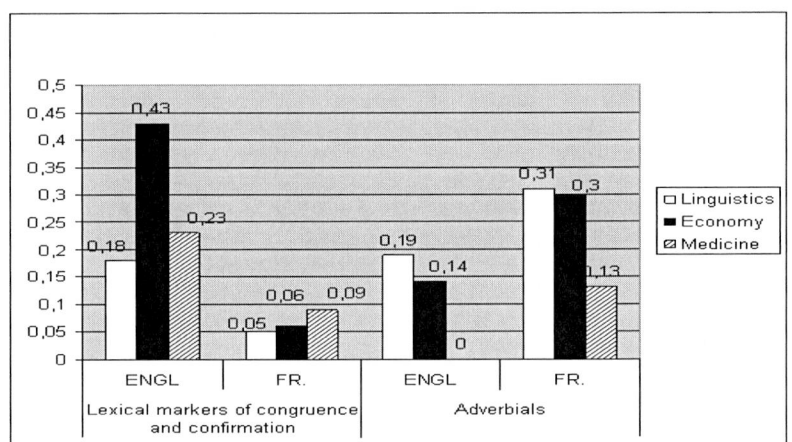

Lexical markers: Engl. = n=349 (for 1,283,868 words); Fr. n= 69 (for 973,495 words).
Adverbials: Engl. n= 180 (for 1,283,868 words); Fr. n= 265 (for 973,495 words).

These results, which must be interpreted with care in view of the limited number of markers under study, yield some interesting indications. As regards lexical markers, we can see from the chart that
- the frequency is significantly higher in English than in French
- in English the frequency is the highest in economy and is higher in medicine than in linguistics
- in French, the frequency is very low for all three disciplines, although somewhat higher in medicine.

Of course, differences between English and French depend on the choice of the respective markers. We tried to minimize this bias by being as exhaustive as possible in our search for equivalent lexical markers in both languages. In English one lexical marker has been found to be particularly productive (*consistent with*), representing more than 75% of the occurrences in economics, close to 55% of the occurrences in medicine and more than 35% in linguistics.

As regards adverbials, we can see from the chart that
- the frequency is significantly higher in French than in English
- in both languages, the frequency is higher in linguistics and economics than in medicine (no occurrences at all in English!).

Medicine distinguishes itself from the other two disciplines, both in English and in French, by a very scarce use of adverbials (none at all in English) and a fairly high number of lexical markers (ranking first in French and second in English).

More generally speaking, it seems that, in English scientific papers, writers tend to express congruence with the expectations more frequently by using terms that are specific to the scientific field (we found a low number of specific lexical markers). Conversely, in French scientific papers, writers tend to use a higher number of adverbials with a more general modal value. We suggest two non-exclusive reasons for this. There could be a cultural explanation (cf. Dahl 2005; Vold 2005) and/or a linguistic explanation (the idea of congruence with the expectations may be conveyed by other linguistic means instead of specific markers).

4.2 Markers of non-congruence and surprise

Table 4 lists the markers studied in this category. It should be noted that we made no distinction between lexical markers and adverbials here, in view of the small number of occurrences found for both kinds. Here are a few examples of the use of these markers in both languages:

(5) Nevertheless, it is true that (1) (3) describe outcomes which are **contrary to our expectations in some way**. (Eng-ling)

(6) Indeed, **rather surprisingly**, adding a text to itself (any number of times) has no effect at all on entropy, which is supposed to reflect vocabulary richness by measuring the disorder or randomness of the text. (Eng-ling)

(7) En effet, les mesures de la phorie sont restées stables, durant la période d'observation de cette étude, dans 93 % des cas. Dans les 7% des cas où elle a évolué, elle a toujours régressé (nous avons même observé deux cas d'inversion). **C'est une constatation un peu surprenante.** Pourquoi n'a-t-elle jamais évolué en augmentant? (Fr-med)

Table 4. Markers of non-congruence and surprise

English	French
Inconsistent with (models, hypotheses, results); not consistent with the expectations… Not expected; less expected, unexpectedly; unexpected… Do not accord with our prior expectations; did not confirm our initial hypothesis… Contrary to (our assumption, a natural intuition …) Paradoxically … Is surprising, all the more surprising, more surprising, somewhat surprising, a surprising finding.	*Contrairement à nos attentes, prévisions, à ce que nous supposions, à nos hypothèses; aux données de la littérature, à une opinion courante De façon surprenante, inattendue, étonnante; un résultat inattendu, étonnant…. Etonnamment… Résultat paradoxal, paradoxalement… Nous remarquons avec surprise; on a la surprise de découvrir…*

We found much fewer markers of non-congruence than congruence (relative frequency from 0.04 to 0.07 in English and from 0.03 to 0.09 in French). With such a low number of occurrences, it is not possible to make any significant comparison between disciplines or languages. It should however be noted that in English various degrees of surprise are expressed with phrases such as *all the more surprising, particularly surprising, somewhat surprising, more surprising, less expected…* French authors do not appear to mark degrees of surprise in the same way.

To summarize, it appears that, in scientific papers, congruence with the expectations is more emphasized than non-congruence. This can be explained by the reasons already stated above: expectation being a constitutive component of scientific activity, it seems logical to find it is more lexicalized than the marking of surprise. However, in view of this very scarcity, it is all the more interesting to identify textual units introducing surprising results or items that do not match expectations.

5. The case of *in fact* and *en fait*

It appeared necessary to conduct a separate study for *in fact* et *en fait*, (a) because of their high frequency in the corpus and (b) because when studying occurrences, we found it difficult to decide whether *in fact/ en fait* should be classified as congruence or non-congruence markers.

5.1 *In fact* and *en fait*: expectation markers?

The connection with the notion of expectation has often been stressed, sometimes in a contradictory way. For instance, *in fact* is listed by Chafe (1986) as a marker of evidentiality in the broad sense, suggesting "that a fact goes beyond what one might have expected". This value of unexpectedness is confirmed by Oh (2000). Oh suggests a common core meaning for *actually* and *in fact,* namely 'unexpectedness'. This value is also highlighted for *en fait* in French (Rossari 1994). Rossari opposes *en fait* and *de fait*, in that the former introduces new information whereas with the latter, the information is presented as already established. The fact that both *en fait* and *in fact* introduce an item that is presented as new or unexpected can explain their adversative interpretation, although, as we will see below, such an interpretation is not compulsory.

According to Halliday & Hasan (1976), "*in fact* introduces a proposition that is contrary to expectation"; Halliday (1985) changes this position, defining *in fact* as an 'elaborative' conjunction introducing some form of clarification. According to Martin (1992), the concessive relation is explicit only in co-occurrence with a contrastive conjunction such as *but*, since "counterexpectation is not part of the meaning". A somewhat different viewpoint is presented by Schwenter and Traugott (2000), who, on the basis of a diachronic study, distinguish 3 values of *in fact*:

In fact$_1$ is the opposite of *in theory*
In fact$_2$ is an adversative adverb with primarily epistemic modal meaning
In fact$_3$ is an adverb that signals that what follows is a stronger argument than what precedes. By highlighting the textual and argumentative role of the marker, this description also minimizes the semantic dimension connected to expectation.

In French, we find the same discussion as in English about the adversative value of *en fait* (Danjou-Flaux 1980; Rossari 1992, 1994; Blumenthal 1996). For Rossari (1994), *en fait* signals a gap but does not go as far as marking an opposition between appearances and reality (contrary to *en réalité*). From a corpus study of press articles, Blumenthal (1996), distinguishes three values of *en fait* according to its distribution. In initial position (IP), *en fait* is nonopposive; in medial position (MP) *en fait* is adversative or, when separate from the verb, modulates the degree of precision of the information[5]. Generally speaking, it appears from the literature that *in fact/en fait* have to be analyzed at two levels. Semantically, they signal a transition towards a deeper level that can convey an explanatory or descriptive aspect going beyond the surface of things; the textual or argumentative value of *in fact/ en fait* derives from this value. When going beyond appearances, one can either contradict a statement presented as superficial or deepen a viewpoint that has already been stated.

5.2 Distribution according to disciplines

The study of the frequencies of *in fact/en fait* according to disciplines shows significant differences as illustrated by the following table.

Table 5. Relative frequency according to disciplines

Discipline	In fact	En fait
Linguistics	0,4	0,21
Economy	0,1	0,16
Medicine	0,01	0,02

In fact: n = 300 (for 1,283, 868 words) ; *en fait:* n= 149 (for 973,495 words).

The very high score of *in fact / en fait* in linguistics (particularly in English with a score twice as high as in French) is significant. In medicine the frequency is very low both in English and in French whereas the figures are average in economics; it should also be noted that *en fait* seems to be more frequent in French economics papers than *in fact* in English economics papers. Their use is consistent with our findings for adverbial markers of congruence; in both languages, the frequency is higher in linguistics and economics than in medicine.

---

[5] We will study the values of both markers according to their position in section 5.1.3.

However, in linguistics, *in fact* is much more productive than *en fait*, which is the opposite of the results obtained with the other adverbials under study, for which French was more productive in linguistics and economics. This is not easy to explain although it could come from a more argumentative tendency of English linguists and/or a larger variety of values assigned to *in fact* as compared with *en fait*.

5.3 *In fact* and *en fait* in initial position (IP)

As the position seems to have a non-negligible impact on the value of both markers in the discourse, it is interesting to compare them from this point of view. Table 6 below gives the distribution observed in the corpus (in percentages).

Table 6. Distribution of *IN FACT* and *EN FAIT* between IP or MP in %

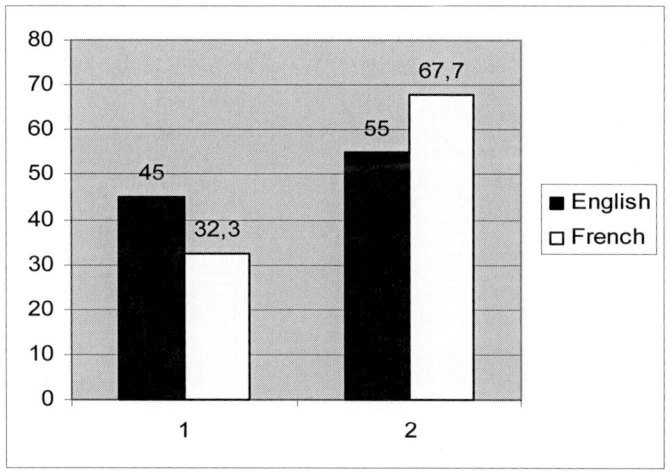

1 = IP; 2 = MP; *In fact* : n = 300 (for 1,283,868 w.), rel.frequ.: 0.23. *En fait:* n = 149 (for 973,495 w.), rel. frequ.: 0.15.

It should be noted that for *in fact*, this distribution corresponds to the figures given by Oh (2000) for the written discourse (55% in medial position, 43% in initial position). For *en fait*, Blumenthal finds about the same number of occurrences in both positions, which is somewhat different from our data (but then Blumenthal's study is based on a corpus of press articles). It seems that *in fact* appears more often in initial position in scientific English than *en fait* in scientific French (often found in medial position).

As emphasized in the literature (Oh 2000; Blumenthal 1996) *en fait/ in fact* have various values according to their position: IP–MP–FP (the final position being almost exclusively used in oral language; we didn't find any occurrences in our corpus, neither in French nor in English). Is it possible to determine specific tendencies for each marker in initial position? Table 7 summarizes the results of a qualitative and more thorough study carried out on some of the papers and involving 40 occurrences for each language.

Table 7. Contrasted values of both markers in IP

Value	Frequency according to the language
REINFORCEMENT/EXPLANATION Strengthening of what has been said previously (the idea is reformulated with more impact) Confirms the expectations = Marker of congruence	Frequent value in English and in French
ADJUSTMENT/RECTIFICATION (restriction) Counterexpectation = Marker of non-congruence	More frequent in French corpus
ADDITION of a new element bringing a piece of evidence that supports the writer's point of view (Figures, Example, Reference) Confirms the expectations = Marker of congruence	High frequency in English, lower in French; Addition of reference not found in French
SHIFT: change in enunciative level, or in type of sequence, e.g. descriptive *vs* explanatory): Presentation of the 'authoritative voice', after other points of view, either in agreement with them or in disagreement with them. Theoretical explanation of data/ information given previously (either by the author or from a different source) No direct link with the expectations?	Frequent value in English and in French

The last value–which we refer to as "shift"–does not seem to be on the same level as the others although it can occur in combination with some of them (reinforcement for instance). It does mark a gap with what has been said before but not necessarily on the level of the expectations. It is very often used by the authors to assert what they want to say, to express "their" truth.

To summarize, in IP, we found that *in fact, en fait* were mainly used to reinforce or explain the meaning in order to support the assertions made by the researcher. This confirms previous results by Oh (2000) for *in fact* and

Blumenthal (1997) for *en fait*. These functions are linked to expectedness rather than unexpectedness. However, differences emerge according to languages. In our English corpus, *in fact* in IP is often used to introduce a piece of evidence:

(8) **In fact**, Wunderlich (1997) presents a similar proposal. (Eng-ling)

(9) **In fact,** only 34% of the data of the preclausal NPs of all LDs are familiar or activated as against 66% of those in TOP. (Eng-ling)

In (8), *in fact* introduces a reference supporting the author's proposal (a use we did not find in the French corpus). Conversely, in IP, the adjustment/ rectification value seems to be less frequent in English than in French:

(10) Reste la troisième variation que nous avons présenté en liaison avec la position de d'ailleurs. **En fait,** cette variation qui concerne la portée de *d'ailleurs* met en jeu d'autres phénomènes que la position de *d'ailleurs*, en particulier les facteurs prosodiques, ainsi que le découpage thématique. (Fr-ling)

5.4 *In fact* and *en fait* in medial position (MP)

In medial position, *En fait / in fact* often provide a way to oppose a more relevant or "truer" point of view to a point of view considered superficial, incomplete or even false; they can therefore easily take on an adversative value in co-occurrence with adversative conjunctions (*mais, but, however...*). In such cases, they often introduce an unexpected element. In English, however, the reinforcement function is quite common, whereas in French, the meaning of *en fait* is more often close to that of *en réalité*.

In the two languages, *in fact* and *en fait* in MP often take part in evaluative assessments or classifications in combination with predicative structures around *be / être* and similar verbs, expressing the "authorial voice":

(11) ... are **in fact** identical; ... is **in fact** connected; ... is **in fact** false; ... is **in fact** strong evidence for its opposite

In these examples, *in fact* (or in French *en fait*) introduces a factual conclusion, which is presented as unexpected. However, in French, more than in English (for *in fact*), *en fait* is sometimes used to introduce a rectifying remark or terminological adjustment:

(12) On est d'abord en droit de se demander, **en fait** on est dans l'obligation de se demander...

6. Conclusion

In our study we have distinguished two very different types of expectation markers:
(a) Lexical markers, specific to the scientific text. We found them, with various frequencies, in the three disciplines. These markers position the research within a scientific frame; they are not very numerous and there are fewer markers signalling non-congruence than congruence;
(b) Adverbial markers, with modal value (*of course, évidemment*). Their frequency is very low in medicine. They are mainly used to signal what the author wants to present as admitted and expected; they can signal results as well as their interpretation and/or any other element of argumentation.

As far as the differences between languages are concerned, it seems from our corpus that English tends to use a higher number of more specific, lexical markers (e.g. *consistent with our findings*) and French a higher number of adverbials, a tendency that can be construed as cultural or as more specifically linguistic.

The analysis of the corpus has shown that these two categories may have a complementary distribution, which is the case in medical papers: the high frequency of the specific lexical markers is coupled with a low frequency of adverbials. In this way, the medical paper tends to develop a system of proof by suppressing the argumentative aspect of expectations. In the other two disciplines, we have a mixed system in which the positioning towards expectations participates in both the argumentative aspect and the establishing of the scientific frame that has been pre-defined. This can be explained by the fact that both linguistics and economics, when assuming the fact that they belong to human sciences, have recourse to shared knowledge and implicit ways of thinking to confirm some of their statements. On the other hand, medicine (at least as represented in our corpus) is exclusively based on empirical results (which are then closely linked to the predictive frame developed for the experimentation). It would be interesting to see, through other disciplines comprising a strong theoretical dimension in addition to this empirical aspect (like physics for instance), whether this obliteration of the argumentative aspect is still verified. Also, in order to deepen such a comparative study, it would be necessary to define sub-categories of the disciplinary corpora. Disciplines such as linguistics, economics or medicine can cover very different fields according to sub-categories. For instance, *theoretical linguistics, experimental phonetics* and *discourse analysis* have very different epistemological bases.

Beyond the differences observed between languages, the study of *in fact* and *en fait* illustrates the flexibility of this marker that can introduce an element supporting a position as well as an element that is contrary to expectations. This ambivalence is a good example of the way in which the reference to facts can be used in the scientific argumentation both to contradict or justify. The case of *in fact* and *en fait* perfectly illustrates the way in which scientific demonstration and the logic of discourse are linked together within the scientific paper.

7. References

Blumenthal, Peter. "Le connecteur *en fait.*" In *Dépendance et intégration syntaxique. Subordination, coordination, connexion,* edited by Claude Muller, 257-269. Tübingen: Max Niemyer Verlag, 1996.
Chafe, Wallace. "Evidentiality in English conversation and academic writing."In *Evidentiality: the Linguistic Coding of Epistemology,* edited by Wallace Chafe and Johanna Nichols, 261-272. Norwood-New Jersey: Ablex Publishing Corporation, 1986.
Chafe, Wallace and Nichols, Johanna, eds. *Evidentiality: The linguistic Coding of Epistemology, Advances in Discourse Processes Vol. XX.* Norwood-New Jersey: Ablex Publishing Corporation, 1986.
Dahl, Trine. "Cultural identity in academic texts."*Akademisk Prosa* 3 (2005): 35–45.
Danjou-Flaux, Nelly. "A propos de *de fait, en fait, en effet* et de *effectivement."* *Le français moderne* 48-2 (1980): 110-139.
—. "*Réellement* et *en réalité* : Données lexicographiques et description sémantique." *Lexique* 1 (1982): 105-150.
DeLancey, Scott. "Mirativity: The grammatical marking of unexpected information." *Linguistic Typology* 1 (1997): 33-52.
—. "The mirative and evidentiality." *Journal of Pragmatics* 33 (2001): 369-382.
Dendale, Patrick and Tamsmowski, Liliane, eds. "Les sources du savoir et leurs marques linguistiques." *Langue Française* 102, 1994.
—. "Introduction: Evidentiality and related notions." *Journal of Pragmatics* 33 (2001): 339-348.
Fløttum, K., T. Dahl and T. Kinn. *Academic Voices - Across languages and disciplines.* Amsterdam/Philadelphia: John Benjamins, 2006.
Halliday, Michael Alexander Kirkwood and Hasan Ruqaiya. *Cohesion in English.* London: Longman, 1976.
Martin, James, R. *English text: system and structure.* Philadelphia: John Benjamins, 1992.
Oh, Sun-Young. "*Actually* and *in fact* in American English: a data based analysis." *English Language and Linguistics* 4.2 (2000): 243-268.
Schwenter, Scott and Traugott, Elizabeth Closs. "Invoking scalarity, The development of *in fact."* *Journal of Historical Pragmatics* 1 (2000): 7-25.

Rossari, Corinne. "*De fait, en fait, en réalité* : Trois marqueurs aux emplois inclusifs." *Verbum* 3 (1992): 139-161.

—. *Les opérations de reformulation. Analyse du processus et des marques dans une perspective contrastive français-italien.* Berne: Peter Lang, 1994.

Thompson, Geoff and Zhou, Jianglin. "Evaluation and Organization in Text: The Structuring Role of Evaluation Disjuncts." In *Evaluation in Text: Authorial Stance and the Construction of Discourse*, edited by Susan Hunston and Geoff Thompson, 121-141. Oxford: Oxford University Press, 2001.

Vold, Eva Thue. "Expressions of uncertainty in scientific research articles." *Akademisk Prosa* 3 (2005): 113–127.

CHAPTER ELEVEN

ACADEMIC DISCOURSE AS SOCIAL CONTROL AND SYSTEM(S), SEEN THROUGH THE USE OF DEMONSTRATIVE NOUN PHRASES IN FRENCH SCIENTIFIC TEXTS

LITA LUNDQUIST

1. Introduction

If we remove 'academic' from 'academic discourse', we are left with 'discourse', a term which in itself has numerous meanings and a host of various applications within academic discourse. In the following, I shall use 'discourse' in its most abstract sense, as introduced by Foucault in his *L'Ordre du discours* (Foucault, 1971) and as later elaborated in system theory by Niklas Luhmann (N. Luhmann, 2003; N. Luhmann, 1995).

I shall also, however, approach academic discourse from another discursive angle by undertaking an empirical analysis of a corpus of French academic discourse, stemming from the three disciplines of economics, linguistics, and medicine. This implies that I also address discourse in its very concrete sense, as *exemplars* of real texts. It is in this sense I shall use the term *text*. Studying a corpus of authentic texts, my approach is rooted in linguistic theory, and more specifically in so-called text linguistics.

The fundamental aim of text linguistics is to investigate how texts are constructed, structured and made into coherent entities by linguistic means (Halliday & Hasan, 1976; L. Lundquist, 1980). An important means of ensuring coherence is through the use of demonstrative noun phrases as anaphors (Corblin, 1987 ch.3; Cornish, 1999, Maes, 1996). I investigate whether a text linguistic analysis of the use of demonstrative anaphors in three different types of texts reveals differences which can be traced back to discourse in its abstract conception.

I explain this specific use of discourse in section 2 before proceeding to my main theme–the use of demonstrative noun phrases in French academic discourse, in sections 3, 4 and 5. I then illustrate differences across types of academic discourse with respect to their use of demonstrative noun phrases in sections 6, 7 and 8. I conclude in section 9 by describing how each type belongs to a specific subsystem within academic discourse.

2. Discourse as control and system

Since I am by no means an expert in social science, I give only a limited presentation of Foucault's and Luhmann's theories on science as *social control* and science as a specific *social system*.

2.1 Foucault on science as social control

Foucault develops the central hypothesis that every society strives to control "la production du discours":

> "Je suppose que dans toute société la production du discours est à la fois contrôlée, sélectionnée, organisée et redistribuée par un certain nombre de procédures qui ont pour rôle d'en conjurer les pouvoirs et les dangers, d'en maîtriser l'événement aléatoire, d'en esquiver la lourde, la redoutable matérialité"" (Foucault, 1971 p.11)

From this assertion, Foucault goes on to consider three external procedures by which control is enforced:

1. *the taboo*, or interdiction. This refers to the exclusion and constraints to what can be said and by whom: "On n'a pas le droit de tout dire, on ne peut pas parler de tout dans n'importe quelle circonstance, n'importe qui ne peut pas parler de n'importe quoi" (Foucault, 1971 p.12)

2. *the rejection*, for instance of views not considered reasonable and as belonging to the mad.

3. *the opposition* between truth and falsity, « the will to truth » ("la volonté de savoir" (Foucault, 1971 p.18)

For our purpose here, the last point, the will to truth, which characterises science and hence scientific discourse, is of special interest. In fact, Foucault emphasises the role of *control* of a given discipline, in which control is exerted not only over the form of discourse, but also over the very object of investigation of a discipline, and over its methods, axioms, techniques and instruments. This occurs because a discipline is a permanent "reactualisation of rules determining a specific organisation" of the discourse in question. Thus, for every discipline there is a kind of *anonymous system of functioning*, as described by Foucault in the following terms:

> « la science est un "système anonyme" de fonctionnement, composé de la définition d'un domaine d'objets, d'un ensemble de méthodes, d'un corpus de propositions considérées comme vraies, d'un jeu de règles et de définitions, de techniques et d'instruments (Foucault, 1971 p.32)

This idea seems central to the investigation of academic discourse. In fact, one can expect that a specific kind of academic discourse will reflect its own *"anonymous system of functioning"* in the way it describes its scientific object, aims, methods, definitions, rules and results, just as one can expect that scientific texts "inside" a specific discipline will reveal similarities as compared to scientific texts "outside", i.e. compared to texts belonging to another discipline. It is my assumption that an investigation of demonstrative anaphors in the scientific texts belonging to three types of academic discourse– economics, linguistics and medicine–will reveal differences in structural patterns that can be traced back to the control and auto-regulation of academic discourse. In Foucault's terms, these differences can be explained by:

> "des procédures internes de contrôle du discours: principes de classification, d'ordonnancement, de distribution » (Foucault, 1971 p.23)

This suggests that a text linguistic analysis can help us mediate between abstract discourse on the one hand and authentic exemplars of texts on the other, by way of disclosing characteristic patterns in the use of demonstrative anaphors.

2.2 Luhmann on science as a social system

Luhmann (N. Luhmann, 2003; N. Luhmann, 1995) also views science as a closed system, in particular as a specific social system. Inspired by theory of autopoietic systems (Maturana & Varela, 1980), Luhmann elaborates an abstract and general theory of systems. In his definition of an autopoietic system as a system which is able to create itself by reproducing its elements while maintaining an organization of these elements that is characteristic of it, we see a reflection of Foucault's argument that a discourse "reactualises its rules determining a specific organisation" again and again, thus exerting a control on the discourse in question, and maintaining it as a specific discourse. Maturana and Luhmann also talk about a system's self-production–its autopoiesis–using the concept of self-reference (N. Luhmann, 1990). Hence, discourse is conceived of as an *"autonomous system"*. I employ this notion of an *autonomous system* as "an autopoietic system (which) produces itself by reproducing its elements while maintaining an organization of these elements that is characteristic of it", and attempt to identify such elements and their organisation characteristic of the three types of academic discourse analysed below.

According to his theory concerning the complexity of modern society, Luhmann distinguishes different social systems, without which "individual persons and organizations can no longer cope with the growing societal mass of information" (Qvortrup, 2003 p.148). This implies a differentiation of knowledge domains, each of which is characterised by a specific set of parameters, first and foremost by its function. For this reason, Luhmann terms them functional systems. I illustrate this idea by describing three functional systems shown in the following table, partly borrowed from Qvortrup (2003, p.148). Economics and politics are selected here to emphasise the characteristics of science. The parameters comprise the *symbolically generalized medium*, which involves the optics through which the social system sees the world; they contain a *binary code* in which the positive pole represents the criterion for success, and the negative pole represents what is to be avoided. The system can only perceive what lies between the two poles. Each system has its *program of reflection* proper, which I regard as related to Foucault's "anonymous system of functioning" mentioned above. Each system is striving towards a specific *function* or goal, which is the creation of new knowledge in science. Science also has its own privileged institutions within which the system reproduces itself.

Table 1. Functional systems

Functional system	Medium	Binary code	Program of reflection	Function	Institutionalising
Economics	Money	+/- profit +/- surplus	Prices Accounting	Reduction of scarcity	Companys and business
Politics	Power	+/- power	Government or party program	Creation of collectively binding decisions	Parties and parliament
Science	Truth	+/- true	Theories and methodologies	Creation of new knowledge	Universities, journals, laboratories

As we see, the medium of science is truth, which corresponds to Foucault's idea of the "will to truth" mentioned above. The code of science is plus or minus true, produced by a program of theories and methods. The goal or function of science is to create new knowledge, which is institutionalised first and foremost in universities, laboratories, journals and other academic settings.

In a much simplified manner, the parallel between Foucault's thesis regarding the control of society over 'la production du discours' and the 'will to truth' in science on the one hand, and Luhmann's theories about functional systems on the other, especially concerning science as a specific functional system with its own medium, code, function, program and institutions, offers an analytical perspective from which to study the relation between academic discourse and academic texts.

According to Luhmann, scientific discourse presents a single subsystem. I put forward the hypothesis that an analysis of the program of reflection, and more specifically of "the linguistic organisation of elements" as Foucault expressed it, will reveal characteristics of and differences between the types of discourse in question, thus supporting the assumption that each constitutes an anonymous system in Foucault's terms and an autonomous system in Luhmann's terms.

3. The text linguistic study of academic discourse

Firstly I explain the main principles of the linguistic investigation carried out below. Text linguistics is a field within linguistics which aims to explain how linguistic expressions contribute to the *wellformedness* of texts. Wellformedness corresponds to *textuality* (Beaugrande & Dressler, 1981), which is the text linguistic counterpart to the linguistic concept of grammaticality, i.e. the grammatical wellformedness of sentences. A key concept within text linguistics is *text coherence* (Halliday & Hasan, 1976; L. Lundquist, 1980), *a sine qua non* of the wellformedness of texts. Indeed, a sequence of sentences without coherence between them would not constitute a text. A text linguistic study thus entails investigation of the linguistic means used to present, order, and link information (or pieces of information) within and especially across sentence boundaries.

Among the linguistic means that convey coherence to a text, the anaphor plays a central role in that it ensures an element contained in preceding text is repeated and maintained over a longer stretch of text. Anaphors mainly consist of noun phrases (L. Lundquist, 2000). They are emphasised in italics in the English example in (1) from a scientific text derived from the discipline of economics. Underlined noun phrases introduce new discourse referents in the text, to which anaphors refer back, thus maintaining them in the text. Noun phrases, shown in bold italics, indicate demonstrative anaphors.

(1) ***This paper*** develops *a* model of information sharing among heterogeneously informed agents and *it* uses *the model* to examine a rationale for intervention in the *foreign exchange market*. *The model* shows that in a partially revealing rational expectations equilibrium, some agents can gain by sharing among themselves private information about transitory exchange rate disturbances. ***In this setting***, a central bank can affect *the exchange rate* by aggregating and disseminating agents' information. *The paper* also illustrates the usefulness of intervention as a way to transmit that information. (…) In ***this paper***, we describe how some of the characteristics of *foreign exchange trading* might give rise to a distinct rationale for intervention in *the market*. ***This emphasis on the market*** enables us to examine carefully one role for intervention and to draw out some of its corresponding implications. (engecon03[1])

I shall focus on one specific type of anaphor, namely *demonstrative anaphors*, i.e. noun phrases which are preceded by the demonstrative determiner (emphasised in bold italics above). French has a neutral form of demonstrative determiner: *ce, cet, cette, ces*, which is neutral with respect to distance and proximity (compared to e.g. English *that* N and *this* N). French examples, representing the three disciplines of economics, linguistics and medicine, are given in (2)-(4):

2. Quels revenus sont nécessaires à une famille avec enfants pour satisfaire les besoins requis pour l'éducation de ***ces derniers*** par rapport à une famille sans enfant ? ***Cette approche*** fonde par exemple les compensations lors d'un divorce. Bien que les économistes n'aiment guère ***cette notion*** de besoins, assez éloignée des préférences, on voit déjà poindre dans ***cette littérature*** la difficulté de réaliser des comparaisons interpersonnelles. NELSON [1990] montre la liaison entre ***ces travaux*** anciens relevant en fait de l'élaboration d'une liste de biens jugés nécessaires à l'éducation des enfants et les développements récents. (Frecon 01)

3. Comme il arrive très souvent dans ***ce type*** de présentation, tout se passe comme si un "bon complot" avait guidé l'évolution historique pour l'amener vers la seule bonne forme normative. Il me semble que ***cette interprétation*** est fondée sur des bases peu solides et qu'on doit accepter l'idée que les trois tournures coexistent actuellement, et qu'elles ont sans doute coexisté à d'autres époques. Dans ***cette perspective***, il faudrait admettre que ***ce phénomène*** de "préposition à éclipses" n'est pas un accident de l'évolution mais que il fait partie de la grammaire. (frling 01)

4. En 1989-1991, les données tirées du SCSAC montraient que pour 9 anomalies sur 14, le Québec enregistrait des prévalences significativement supérieures à la moyenne canadienne (tableau 3). ***Ces résultats*** étaient cependant obtenus à partir de données ne couvrant que 15 % des naissances de l'ensemble du Québec et

---

[1] The number refers to the KIAP corpus, see below.

donc n'étaient pas nécessairement représentatives de la situation québécoise. Les auteurs de l'article de 1995 sur le SCSAC (rapport de la situation) ont expliqué *cette limite* des données (frmed01)

The reason for drawing attention to demonstrative anaphors is that this type of anaphor has special characteristics which, in my view, make them a privileged device for linking analysis of actual texts to assumptions about discourse–discourse in the sense of an anonymous and autonomous social system.

3.1 Demonstrative anaphors

In most linguistic literature (Corblin, 1987; Corblin, 1995; Maes, 1996), demonstrative anaphors are described and explained in contrast to other linguistic means of reference. For instance, *anaphoric* use of demonstratives is compared to *deictic* use of demonstratives, i.e. demonstratives referring to the non-linguistic context (Cornish, 1999). Moreover, demonstrative determiners followed by noun phrases are compared to demonstrative pronouns: *ce problème* compared to *ceci*, *this problem* compared to *this*, a contrast termed "attended" and "unattended this" respectively by John Swales (Swales, 2005). However, the contrast, which is most revealing in the characteristics of demonstrative anaphors, is its comparison with definite anaphors (de Mulder, 1995; Kleiber, 1990). Thus the characteristic feature of demonstrative noun phrases as compared to definite anaphors (see example (1)), is on the one hand that the use of the demonstrative determiner tells the reader to search for an antecedent in the closely preceding context, and on the other hand, that the use of an N as lexical head instructs the reader to see the antecedent in a certain perspective. This perspective may be new with respect to the antecedent, for which reason linguists have argued 're-classification' or 're-categorisation' is an essential function of demonstrative anaphors.

For illustration see (2) above where the third example of a demonstrative anaphor, *cette notion de besoins*, tells the reader to find an antecedent in the preceding context, which has to be perceived as a 'notion of needs'. The antecedent is probably the whole sequence of the first sentence '*satisfaire les besoins requis pour l'éducation de ces derniers par rapport à une famille sans enfant*'. The fourth demonstrative anaphor in (2), *cette littérature,* re-categorises the antecedent *les économistes* from the preceding sentence as "writing economists, whose literature one can refer to".

In (3) above, the demonstrative anaphors *ce type de présentation* and *ce phénomène de "préposition à éclipses"* subsume a former mention or stretch of text under a general term,[2] which classifies *presentation* and *preposition with*

---

[2] Compare with "summary word" (Swales, 2005 p.5).

eclipse, as a *type* and a *phenomenon* respectively. The anaphor *Dans cette perspective* also subsumes the preceding context under a special viewpoint in which the following proposition has to be seen.

Being demonstrative, this specific type of anaphor has another central function in texts. This function is to mark *key-notions*, *central themes* or *strong points* in the text, by pointing out entities which are important enough to be treated further in the text. By demonstrative anaphors, entities are singled out as objects worthy of additional explanation, comments and consideration. Examples of such crucial points in texts are found in (4) above, in the demonstrative anaphors *Ces résultats* and *cette limite des données*. 'Results' constitute a significant point in scientific articles and their line of reasoning, not least in medicine. More specifically, in the text in (4), the fact the results are restricted is crucial.

Characteristics of the use of demonstrative anaphors that:

1. point explicitly to an antecedent in the preceding context
2. (re)categorise the antecedent and place it under a new viewpoint
3. single out crucial moments and strong points in the text

constitute evidence that demonstrative anaphors constitute a privileged linguistic phenomenon with respect to linking scientific texts with scientific discourse.

4. Academic texts in French

The corpus of texts analysed in this study of the relation between the use of demonstrative noun phrases on the one hand, and discourse as a social system and control on the other, consists of a sub-sample of the Kiap corpus.[3] The subcorpus consists of ten texts stemming from the following disciplines: economics (frecon 01-10[4]), linguistics (frling 01-10), and medicine (frmed 01-10). While they contain the same number of articles–ten for each type–the subsubcorpora are of different lengths:

---

[3] The KIAP corpus at the University of Bergen; see www.uib.no/kiap/ and Fløttum, Dahl and Kinn 2006.
[4] Codes refer to KIAP corpus.

Table 2. The three subcorpora of scientific texts

	Words	Units/sentences	Average number of words per text	Average number of words per sentence
10 economic articles	89040	3046	890	29
10 linguistic articles	46136	1528	461	30
10 medical articles	47276	1450	472	32

This first result shows that economic articles are considerably longer than the two other types of scientific articles, which for me suggests the first sign of *social control*, namely the control exerted by the publication guidelines of particular scientific journals.

The texts were all searched with help of the program INTEX (Silberztein, 1999), which makes it possible to define a graph, which is a so-called *local grammar*. A graph was defined that searched for '*ce, ces, cet, cette* + preposed modifier (facultative) + noun'. The numerical result of the search is given in table 3 below.

Table 3. Number of demonstrative anaphors and distribution per sentence

	Total number of demonstrative anaphors	Demonstrative anaphor per sentence
Economics	210	every 5th sentence
Linguistics	338	every 4,5th sentence
Medicine	210	every 7th sentence

Table 3 shows a much higher occurrence of demonstrative anaphors in economics and linguistics than in medicine. This result indicates that the use of demonstrative anaphors represents a recurrent pattern in economics and linguistics, whereas medicine uses other means of conveying coherence. In discourse terms, the difference in frequency of demonstrative anaphors indicates that different control systems prevail for the three disciplines, which therefore respect different "anonymous" and "autonomous" systems, in Foucault's and

Luhmann's terms respectively. The next step of analysis will attempt to clarify this observation.

5. Classes of demonstrative anaphors and academic discipline

In this stage of the analysis, demonstrative anaphors were sorted, firstly according to *frequency*, and secondly according to *type of semantic and pragmatic relation* established with the antecedent. In the first step I concentrated on anaphors with two or more appearances in order to identify recurrent patterns. In the second step I undertook a functional classification of demonstrative anaphors, based on semantic and pragmatic criteria with respect to the sense and function of the demonstrative noun phrase. The categorisation I arrived at comprises the following categories, presented in alphabetical order:

Classifier anaphors
This class comprises demonstrative anaphors, the nominal head of which consists of very general lexical items, such as *type, genre, phenomenon*, etc.; in French expressions such as *ce type de N, ce genre de N, ce phénomène de N*. Such expressions are used to subsume the antecedent under a super-ordinate, general term, which carries little semantic information,[5] but which nevertheless categorises the antecedent as belonging to a special class.

> 5. Dans la conception des panels destinés à mesurer *ce type de comportements*, il apparaît préférable de disposer d'une dimension temporelle suffisante. Trois points paraissent vraiment un minimum pour *ce genre d'exercice* (frecon01)

Example (5) shows that such classifiers are rather vague and imprecise, but still, by using them, the author demonstrates willingness and effort to establish links and emphasise coherence relations in discourse.

Mental space anaphors
This category groups together demonstrative noun phrases which consist of semi-frozen expressions, corresponding to English expressions such as *in this case, from this perspective, for this reason*, etc. They are on the borderline of conjunctions and/or connectives. As they often occupy first position and thus open the information structure of a sentence, linking up tightly to the preceding sentence, I have chosen the designation *mental space builder* (Fauconnier, 1994). In fact, such expressions open up a mental space in which to consider the state-of-affairs exposed in the host sentence.

---

[5] Compare footnote 3.

(6) La production requiert l'utilisation d'inputs particuliers tels que des connaissances, du savoir-faire ou des qualifications spécifiques qui émergent au cours du processus de production. La notion d'apprentissage est alors au cœur de la problématique de l'organisation. ***Dans cette perspective***, le réseau de création de ressources insère la dimension fonctionnelle qui caractérisait le réseau d'allocation de ressources dans le contexte relationnel...(frecon03)

(7) Ce type de modèle permet de répondre à certaines critiques, notamment celle concernant la vision de l'homo oeconomicus comme individu asocial [Ackerman (1997)], dont les préférences ne sont jamais affectées ni par les autres ni par l'environnement. Mais nous retrouvons *dans ce cas* l'objection exposée ci-dessus : une fois donnée, la relation de préférence n'est plus susceptible de changer. (frecon02)

(8) Dit autrement, la fusion de traits morphologiques qui s'épelle son ne contient que des traits nominaux, et exclut donc le trait catégoriel [+P°] (préposition), contrairement, par exemple, à en ou dont, comme en témoignent la forme intrinsèquement non fléchie de ces mots. ***Pour cette raison-même*** son refuse d'accueillir tout argument indirect. (frling05)

From a discourse perspective, mental space building demonstrative expressions are of course crucial in that they point to the kind of mental space–which is often also an argumentative space–which the author sets as a frame for the reader's evaluation of the content of the host sentence. Mental space expressions may also disclose important aspects of academic discourse ruling the three types of scientific texts analysed here. The first aspect is that medicine uses no mental space building demonstratives (in the present subcorpus), which I discuss in section 6.

Method anaphors
This type of demonstrative anaphor refers to the methodology used in the investigation described in the article. It covers terms such as *caractéristique, chiffre, conclusion, constat, description, définition, différence, dimension, résultat, scenario*. Such terms refer directly to what was called 'theories and methodologies' in Table 1, showing the specific 'program of reflection' for the social subsystem of science. Examples of demonstrative anaphors referring to methodology in the three different disciplines hint at what is considered important in the specific program of reflection of each discipline:

(9) D'après ce qui précède, de nombreux éléments sont susceptibles d'expliquer ***cette plus grande robustesse*** des résultats : réflexion approfondie sur la définition des variables de la régression, évolution des techniques économétriques associées à une plus grande rigueur au niveau de la mise en œuvre empirique, ... La faiblesse de ***cet impact***, conjuguée aux signes positifs

parfois trouvés, relativise toutefois la portée de *ce résultat* et ne permet toujours pas de clôturer définitivement un débat vieux de plus de trente ans. (frecon04)

(10) À moins qu'on ne se résolve à considérer que *jusqu'à* fonctionne ici comme un adverbe, argumentatif ou paradigmatisant, *ces exemples* constituent une violation tant de la caractéristique de catégorisation - le sujet est considéré comme un groupe nominal - que de celle de dépendance ... (frling08)

(11) La variation en fonction du sexe observée dans la proportion d'utilisateurs de corticostéroïdes en inhalation était toujours manifeste chez les bénéficiaires SR lorsque l'utilisation de ces médicaments était considérée en association avec celle de sympathomimétiques en inhalation; *cette variation* pourrait surtout s'expliquer par la proportion de personnes qui consomment des corticostéroïdes en inhalation à dosage plus élevé. (frmed03)

Key words here are *robustness*, *impact* and *result* in economics, *examples* in linguistics, and *variation* in medicine. We return to these key words in section 8.

Reference anaphors
With this type of demonstrative noun phrase, the author refers back to an antecedent, which consists of a (bibliographical) reference to an author, a theory, an article, etc. I distinguish two types of reference: 1) 'self-reference', i.e. reference to the article presented, *In this article I want to ...*, and 2) 'other-reference', which refers to theoretical work of scholars in the discipline in question.

1. 'Self-reference' anaphors
The first type, *dans cet article je présenterai...*, can also be considered a *deictic* use of the demonstrative determiner. It refers to the article presented, written 'by me' 'in front of you' and 'read by you'. It is however also a very conventional expression, which, in its different variations, occurs in all 30 articles, i.e. for every discipline, in the abstract section, the introduction and/or the conclusion.

(12) Nous proposons *dans cet article* d'analyser les possibilités d'un développement durable à partir du comportement des consommateurs. L'analyse économique souligne en effet la subordination des producteurs: aux consommateurs, dont les préférences constituent la justification ultime du système économique. Il nous semble donc intéressant de revenir aux fondements de la micro-économie du consommateur et d'interroger cette dernière à la lumière de la soutenabilité. Ceci constitue la première partie de *cet article.*
(frecon02, Introduction)

Cet article is used 19 times in the economic text corpus, 7 times in linguistics, where the variations *cette étude* and *cette analyse* are also frequent (6 and 5 times respectively), and only twice in medicine, where the expression *cette étude* is most frequent (16 times).

2. Other reference anaphors
Bibliographical references to the works of colleagues in the field and instantiated by means of demonstrative anaphors will be called 'other reference'. The following is an example (13):

> (13) Un parcours des principaux ouvrages de grammaire utilisés actuellement dans les universités françaises, sous l'angle des syntagmes prépositionnels prédicatifs (Gardes-Tamines, 1990 ; Le Goffic, 1993 ; Riegel, Pellat, Rioul, 1994 ; Vargas, 1995; Denis, Sancier-Château, 1994 ; Tomassone, 1996 ; Wilmet, 1996) montre que l'analyse fonctionnelle de la phrase et la distinction "compléments d'objet indirects" vs "compléments circonstanciels" sont des préoccupations communes à tous *ces ouvrages*. (frling02)

Resumptive anaphors
Resumptive demonstrative anaphors summarize, or sum up, a part or sequence of the preceding sentence or text. They are also called 'encapsulating' anaphors (Conte, 1989), because they may encapsulate a proposition or a verbal phrase into a noun phrase. In a syntactic perspective, this is seen as 'hypostatising', which means that a second or third order entity (a quality, property or proposition, respectively) is 'lifted' and 'promoted' to a first order entity, such as an NP (Lyons, 1977 p.445). Examples in English would be *this question, this conception*, etc, also called "summary words" (Swales, 2005), which while encapsulating also re-categorise.

> (14) Le réseau est alors conçu comme une forme de coordination spécifique qui privilégie les relations entre acteurs. ***Cette conception*** emprunte à l'approche évolutionniste …(frecon03)

> (15) Il n'existe pas de préposition toujours vide de sens, du moins si l'on continue à voir dans un même mot dans le de 'de la ville de Paris' et celui de 'elle vient de Paris'. Mais certains parlent ici d'homonymie, et donc casent les deux 'de' dans deux classes différentes. Notons que *ce problème* ne se pose pas pour les locutions prépositives, jamais vides de sens. (frling04)

Specialised anaphors
Under this heading, I group demonstrative anaphors which are either specific to the discipline as such, e.g. *cette société* and *ce secteur* for economics, *cette grammaire* and *ce dictionnaire* for linguistics, and *cette maladie* and *ce patient* for medicine, or, which are specific to the particular topic treated in the article, such as *préposition* for a linguistic article on prepositions.

(16) l'économie rentre dans un régime de croissance mixte (il est évident que **ce saut** de régime ne se fait pas à la même date pour les deux valeurs de k). ***Dans ce régime***, le stock de pollution continue à croître ... (frecon05)

(17) Cet article étudie deux prépositions composées: au sujet de et à propos de. Nous analyserons tout d'abord ***ces prépositions*** d'un point de vue lexicographique ... (frling10)

(18) Une infection par le VIH a été suspectée à plusieurs reprises, mais la PCR pour le VIH est restée négative. Depuis Janvier 1997, le patient a accepté des perfusions mensuelles de gammaglobulines à la dose de 0,4 g/kg/mois. ***Ce traitement*** a permis d'obtenir un dosage résiduel de gammaglobulines supérieur à 5 g/l. (frmed07)

In addition to these six classes of demonstrative anaphors:

1. classifier anaphors
2. mental space anaphor
3. method anaphors
4. reference anaphors
5. resumptive anaphors
6. specialised anaphors

two more classes can be distinguished which appear almost exclusively within one subcorpus. The first is *temporal anaphors*, of the type *cette (même) période* (seven times in medicine) and *cette date* (twice in economics), while the second consists of noun phrases where an adjective constitutes the head: *ce dernier/ces derniers*, which appear 14 times in the economic subcorpus (twice in linguistics and three times in medicine). This construction is used to single out the last-mentioned of two (or more) discourse referents in the preceding text:

(19) Aussi idéalisées qu'elles paraissent, les hypothèses correspondants aux inégalités (5) reflètent assez bien l'esprit de la législation française. Pour chaque licenciement, ***cette dernière*** impose, en effet, des indemnités proportionnelles aux salaires (le taux d'indemnisation étant d'autant plus grand que le salarié est ancien). (frecon07)

This appears to be a preferred type of anaphor in economics as compared to the other two disciplines, which I believe is related to the focus on close local coherence.

The above classification of different functional types of demonstrative anaphors helps us distinguish between different sorts of demonstrative anaphors used in the three scientific disciplines. In a second step of analysis, the different categories will serve as *tertiae comparationis* in comparing the three disciplines.

However, the classification is not without problems, for it is less rigid and clear-cut than suggested above. Rather than distinct classes of demonstrative anaphors, we are dealing with a graduation of expressions, some of which are very close and partly overlap. Thus method and domain specific anaphors may in certain cases be difficult to discriminate, just as resumptive and mental space anaphors are often close. For this reason, in the next step of my analysis I consider the following three super-ordinate groups of demonstrative anaphors as they are used in scientific texts:

1) method indicating and domain specific demonstrative anaphors
2) classifying, resumptive and mental space demonstrative anaphors
3) reference demonstrative anaphors

6. Distribution of types of demonstrative anaphors across scientific disciplines

The distribution of the different types of demonstrative anaphors across scientific disciplines is shown in Table 4 according to percentage of the total use of demonstrative anaphors in each subcorpus. Only demonstrative noun phrases occurring in identical form twice or more than twice are shown, given my aim of determining *patterns* of linguistic structure that can be considered typical of the texts in question, and controlled by some sort of "anonymous" and "autonomous" social system.

I now discuss the most significant differences that can be deduced from Table 4.[6] The most noticeable finding is that the discipline of medicine does not use demonstrative noun phrases as demonstrative mental space anaphors *at all* (of the type *dans ce cas, dans ce sens, dans cette perspective*, etc.), as opposed to economics and linguistics, in which they account for 14% and 11% respectively. Considering mental space constructions as a very specific linking

---

[6] Given the small text corpus, we can by no means talk about statistically valid differences.

Table 4: Distribution of types of demonstrative anaphors across disciplines

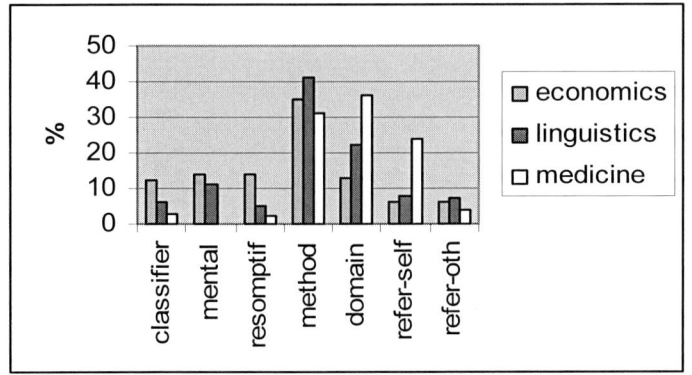

device which establishes an explicit coherence with the preceding sentence (or text sequence) while putting the content of the host sentence in an often argumentative view, it is crucial to note the fact that medicine texts do not employ this type of argumentative coherence whatsoever. Mental space openers are close to frozen, lexicalised expressions, functioning as simple connectives. Nevertheless, they reflect a choice made by the author of the scientific article–or imposed on the scientific actor by a controlling discursive instance.

The same observation goes for the use of demonstrative classifiers (*ce type de, ce genre de*, etc.) and resumptive demonstrative noun phrases (*cette conception, cette démarche, cette question*, etc.), which medicine uses remarkably less than the two other disciplines: only 3% and 2% respectively as opposed to 12% and 14% for economics and 6% and 5% for linguistics. Economics shows a particularly high frequency of these two types of demonstrative noun phrases, which, as we saw above, indicate the crucial point of a text. I therefore consider this an indication of a difference within the system of scientific discourse: economics uses demonstrative anaphors in order to build mental spaces, to classify and encapsulate preceding content, i.e. as key linking devices in its argumentative structure, whereas linguistics does less so, and medicine does not at all. In contrast, medicine seems inclined to focus on, via the use of demonstrative anaphors, domain specific key concepts and themes (*cette intervention, ce médicament*, etc.). Here, medicine rates higher than economics and linguistics: 36% as compared to 13% and 22%, i.e. by almost three and two times respectively. When it comes to reference, medicine is also considerably higher than the other two, especially with respect to self-reference (*dans cette étude, dans cette enquête*, etc.): 24% as opposed to 6% and 8% respectively. In reference to others (*dans ces travaux, ces auteurs*, etc.), on the other hand, economics and linguistics are slightly higher (6% and 7% compared to 4%). I interpret this as indication that in medicine, scientific actors are keen on singling out the study presented as crucial in the scientific argumentation. In fact, argumentation in medicine can be seen as founded to a high degree (almost a quarter of total use of demonstrative anaphors), and to a higher degree than the two other disciplines, on the investigation carried out, including methods, instruments and techniques employed. The two other disciplines instead use demonstrative anaphors to refer to other scientific 'voices' as key actors in the argumentation, which may indicate that argumentation within these last two disciplines is more polemic.[7] As for demonstrative anaphors used to make comments on the scientific method applied, the difference is less noticeable. Linguistics score a little higher than economics, which scores higher than medicine (41% > 35% > 31%).

The observations above are summarised in Table 5, in which classifiers, mental space and resumptive demonstrative anaphors are shown grouped together in one bar, method and domain specific anaphors in another, and reference anaphors in a third. Table 5 also includes the occurrences of 'single' demonstrative anaphors, i.e. forms which occur only once in a text corpus.

These 'singles' represent for all three text corpuses about a third of the total number of demonstrative noun phrases, which means that 'repeated demonstrative anaphors' are very common (2/3). 'Singles' appear most frequently as method anaphors (*ce chiffrement, ce critère, ces calculs*, etc.) and domain specific anaphors (*ce contrat, ce connecteur, ce malade*, etc.).

Table 5: Super-ordinate groups of demonstrative anaphors, frequent and singles

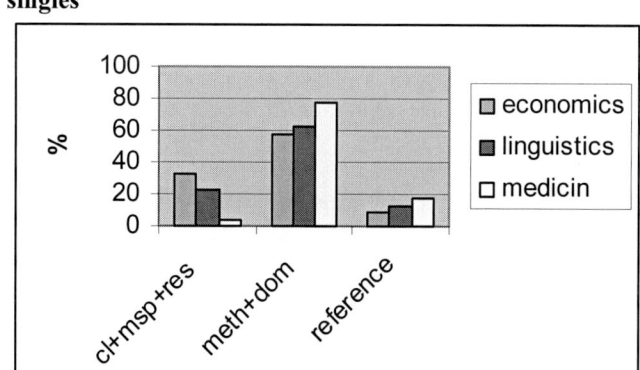

---

[7] This does not mean that medicine does not refer to the work of others, far from it. My study only shows that this is not done with the use of demonstrative anaphors.

7. Summary of results

Keeping in mind that demonstrative anaphors create a privileged type of coherence not only in linking sentences but also in pointing out central themes worthy of additional comments and observations, an obvious interpretation of the results above is that in the discipline of medicine, scientists use domain specific and methodological topics to present the main line of text coherence– the backbone and strong points of their scientific reasoning, so to speak. In Halliday's functional terms (Halliday & Matthiessen, 2004), demonstrative coherence in medical texts seems to be based mainly on the *ideational function* of language. In addition is the frequent demonstrative reference to the scientific study itself, to its methods, techniques and results. I suggest the function of these demonstrative anaphors is to create an "ideational coherence based on scientific validation" or "scientific argumentation".

Researchers in the disciplines of economics and linguistics, as shown in Table 5, also focus on "scientific coherence", though to a lesser degree than researchers in medicine. Rather, linguists and especially economists rely to a higher degree upon demonstrative classifiers, mental space anaphors and resumptive anaphors. As we have seen from the examples above, these types of demonstrative anaphors have a more local function, in that they serve to link sentences locally and tightly: classifiers subsume an antecedent under a general term, such as *this type of N*; mental space builders create a new space in the host sentence on the basis of what was said in the preceding sentence or sentences (*in this perspective…*); and resumptive anaphors sum up and abbreviate content from often large stretches of text in a single term (*this problem*), which, promoted to a discourse referent on its own, can receive a new predication, a new qualification. Using Halliday's functional framework again, demonstrative coherence in economics and linguistics thus seems to be founded to a larger extent on the *interpersonal* and *textual* functions of language. The kind of intersential relations created by classifying, resumptive and mental space demonstratives, is also close to the so-called "rhetorical relations" of specification, elaboration, etc. (Mann & Thompson, 1992). I therefore suggest that the overall function of this group of demonstrative anaphors is to create a local "interpersonal, rhetorical coherence", which is often also an "interpretive coherence" (Swales, 2005 p.6). In economics, demonstrative anaphors create such interpersonal, rhetorical and interpretive coherence in a third of cases (33%), and in linguistics in a fifth of cases (21%).

8. Lexical differences

The difference in the use of types of demonstrative anaphors across scientific disciplines is further corroborated by a closer study of the lexical material used as nominal head in anaphors referring to method. Such an analysis brings us closer to Foucault's definition of scientific discourse as consisting of a specific object domain, a unity of methods, a corpus of propositions considered true, and an interplay of rules and definitions, of techniques and instruments.

Surprisingly few lexemes appear as head in demonstrative anaphors across the three academic disciplines, as represented in the present subcorpus. Only two lexemes are common to all three subcorpuses (*hypothèse* and *résultat*), and only five lexemes are common to two of them, as shown in Table 6:

Table 6: Lexemes as head in demonstrative anaphors, common to two or three disciplines

	Economics	Linguistics	Medicine
Hypothèse	X	X	X
Résultat	X	X	X
Conclusion	X	X	-
Différence	X	X	-
Donnée	X	-	X
Test	-	X	X
Variation	X	-	X

Instead one finds a great variation between the terms used as lexical head in demonstrative anaphors within a single discipline (see Table 7). What is striking in the below list is that medicine has the exclusivity of four lexemes only, as opposed to 21 for both economics and linguistics. These last two disciplines thus seem to have a much greater variety in what they consider to be crucial points in their methods, techniques and instruments. This finding could also, on a general level, be said to indicate that there is less focus on the "idea" *per se* in economics and linguistics, and more focus on re-naming and re-classifying.

Table 7. Lexical heads appearing in one discipline only in method demonstrative anaphors

Economics	Linguistics	Medicine
Biais	Constituant	Chiffre
Constat	Construction	Enquête
Critique	Contrainte	Taux
Définition	Description	Tendance
Dimension	Disjonction	
Effet	Dissociation	
Ensemble	Distinction	
Equation	Elément	
Estimation	Emploi	
Fonction	Exemple	
Impact	Groupe	
Mesure	Inventaire	
Méthode	Item	
Modèle	Lecture	
Modélisation	Particularité	
Niveau	Position	
Relation	Présentation	
Restriction	Solution	
Scénario	Structure	
Variable	Suggestion	
Variance	Valeur	

For economics, it seems essential to refer demonstratively to models and methods: *modèle* appears 13 times,[8] *modélisation* and *méthode* twice each. In addition to this is *scénario* which occurs six times. This shows that economics, as a scientific subsystem, has a great propensity to refer explicitly to its own models and methods, a sign of the 'self-reference' characteristic of "autopoietic systems" in Luhmann's terms. Regarding methods in economics, *équation* (4 times) and *estimation* (twice) are also found.

In linguistics, method, i.e. scientific reasoning, is based on linguistic examples: *exemple* appears 9 times. Linguistic examples are used to distinguish (*distinction* 3 times) between the use (*emploi* 7 times) of items (*item* 5 times) and elements (*élément* twice), to describe (*description* twice) and interpret (*lecture* twice) particularities (*particularité* three times), constraints (*contrainte* twice), and value (*valeur* twice), and to suggest (*suggestion* twice) solutions

---

[8] Plus seven times *ce type de modèle*.

(*solutions* twice). The "self-reference" of this discipline thus seems to be founded on comparing and describing characteristics of examples stemming from within the discipline. This is a sign of the internal self-reference of linguistics where object domain and description are founded–and confounded–in language.

Medicine reveals only four crucial points particular to this discipline: *chiffre* (4 times), *tendance* (3 times), *manifestation* (twice) and *taux* (twice), with the help of demonstrative anaphors. The method itself is not singled out by demonstrative anaphors, only the manifestations of it and the results of mathematical procedures (numbers, tendencies and rates). The scientific manifestations stem from the survey carried out (and reported in the article), which I counted as self-reference demonstrative anaphors: *cette étude* and *cette enquête* (19 times). The "self-reference" of medicine thus seems to depend on visible and/or mathematical manifestations.

9. Conclusion: Demonstrative anaphors, scientific discipline(s) and discourse

I conclude the analysis by relating the above findings concerning the use of demonstrative anaphors in the three subcorpuses of scientific texts to the ideas about *discourse as social control* introduced at the start, especially those describing scientific discourse as having specific internal control procedures. Let us recall that according to Foucault there is an "anonymous system" monitoring a given discourse, and that this *anonymous system* has the effect of re-actualising the rules which determine the specific discourse in question (see p. 221 above). This idea is similar to Luhmann's characterisation of discourse as constituting functional systems, which are also *autonomous systems*, because each of them has individual rules of re-production and self-reference. In this view, the results from the text linguistic analysis of demonstrative anaphors above suggest it is reasonable to consider the disciplines of economics, linguistics and medicine as three sub-systems within the functional system of science, as described in Luhmannian terms in Table 1 above. The differentiation, I claim, belongs to the parameter of 'program of reflection', as illustrated in Table 8 below,[9] in which I have added the main results found above; namely both the specific type of coherence and lexemes which frequently occur as lexical head in demonstrative method anaphors. 'Reflect' in 'program of reflection' is here intended in the sense of both thinking (about), reproducing and revealing. Economics reflects via *models* from which results

---

[9] The parameters of medium (truth), binary code (truth/false), function (creation of new knowledge) and institution (universities) are kept constant.

are equated and estimated, and linguistics reflects upon *examples*, which are compared and described, and for which solutions are suggested. Medicine reflects via *surveys* and mathematical operations.

Table 8. The three disciplines as functional subsystems

Functional sub-systems in science	Program of reflection
Economics	Interpersonal, interpretive, rhetorical coherence Models–equate and estimate
Linguistics	Interpersonal, interpretive, rhetorical coherence Examples–compare and describe
Medicine	Ideational scientific coherence Surveys–treat mathematically

The differences revealed above may be another way of describing the distinction between so-called hard science, such as medicine, and soft science, to which linguistics and economics belong.

The text linguistic study carried out in this paper calls for elaborations and developments in different directions. Firstly analysis should be performed on a larger corpus of texts in order to draw statistically valid conclusions. Secondly, it would be interesting to involve other types of academic discourse in order to identify other subsystems of science in Foucault's and Luhmann's sense. Thirdly, it would be most appealing to transfer the analysis of demonstrative anaphors to discourse stemming from other functional systems, such as literature. A small research project on the use of demonstrative anaphors used in a novel by Balzac, *Une femme de 30 ans*, already indicates that demonstrative anaphors used here are of a quite different type than the ones found in academic discourse, namely of the *qualifying* type: *cette femme douce et silencieuse, cette fatale campagne, cette épouvantable catastrophe, ce maudit enfant, ce belliqueux appel*. Fourthly, and most importantly, a cross-linguistic study is called for, which could shed light on whether differences and similarities found in the use of demonstrative anaphors in the same academic discipline but in different languages can be traced to systematic typological differences between the languages in question (as has been shown for the use of associative and 'unfaithful' anaphors in French and Danish (L. Lundquist, 2006; L. Lundquist, 2003; L. Lundquist, 2005), or whether linguistically predicted differences are neutralised by the control of a–globalised and international–academic discourse. A preliminary step in this direction has been taken with a comparison of demonstrative anaphors in French and Norwegian scientific texts (L. Lundquist, in press), the first results of which show significant differences that can apparently be explained only by fundamental differences between the two languages and two language types–romance and Germanic language types respectively. Hence, a cross-linguistic perspective would add a third and linguistic dimension to the twin perspective involving discourse and text developed in this study.

10. References

Beaugrande, R. D., & Dressler, W. U. *Introduction to text linguistics.* London: Longman, 1981.
Conte, M. *La linguistica testuale.* Milano: Feltrinelli, 1989.
Corblin, F. *Les formes de reprise dans le discours : Anaphores et chaînes de référence.* Rennes: Presses universitaires de Rennes, 1995.
—. *Indéfini, défini et démonstratif. Constructions linguistiques de la référence.* Genève : Droz, 1987.
Cornish, F. *Anaphora, discourse, and understanding evidence from English and French.* Oxford: Clarendon Press, 1999.
de Mulder, W. Anaphore définie versus anaphore démonstrative: Un problème sémantique? In *L'anaphore et ses domaines*, edited by G. Kleiber, & J. Tyvaert,143-158). Paris: Klincksieck, 1995.
Fauconnier, G. *Mental spaces aspects of meaning construction in natural language.* Cambridge: Cambridge University Press, 1994.
Fløttum, K., T. Dahl and T. Kinn. *Academic Voices - Across languages and disciplines.* Amsterdam/Philadelphia: John Benjamins, 2006.
Foucault, M. *L'ordre du discours: Leçon inaugurale au collège de France prononcée le 2 décembre 1970.* Paris: Gallimard, 1971.
Halliday, M. A. K., & Hasan, R. *Cohesion in English.* London: Longman, 1976.
—., & Matthiessen, C. M. I. M. *An introduction to functional grammar* (3rd ed.). London: Arnold, 2004.
Kleiber, G. Article défini et démonstratif: Approche sémantique versus approche cognitive. Une réponse à Walter de Mulder. In *L'anaphore et ses domaines*, edited by G. Kleiber, and J. Tyvaert, 199-227. Paris: Klincksieck, 1990.
Luhmann, N. The autopoiesis of social systems. In *Systems thinking, vol.3*, edited by G. Midgley, 65-79. London: Sage Publications Ltd, 2003.
—. *Social systems* [Soziale Systeme.]. Stanford, Calif.: Stanford University Press, 1995.
—. *Essays on self-reference.* New York: Columbia University Press, 1990.

Lundquist, L. Anaphores lexicales démonstratives et discours scientifiques. *Scolia,* Strasbourg, in press.
—. Lexical anaphors, information packing, and grammaticalisation of textual relations. In *Grammatica. Festschrift in honour of Michael Herslund,* edited by H. Nølke, I. Baron, H. Korzen, I. Korzen & H. H. Müller, 311–323. Bern: Peter Lang, 2006.
—. Noms, verbes et anaphores (in)fidèles. Pourquoi les Danois sont plus fidèles que les Français. *Langue française,* edited by M. Herslund, and I. Baron, 145 (2005): 73–91.
—. L'anaphore associative en danois et en français, sur quoi roule-t-elle? Etude contrastive et expérimentale. In *Aspects linguistiques de la traduction,* edited by Michael Herslund, 105–124, 2003.
—. Knowledge, events and anaphors in texts for specific purposes. In *Language, text and knowledge,* edited by L. Lundquist, and R. Jarvella, 97–125. Berlin/New York: Mouton deGruyter, 2000.
—. *La cohérence textuelle: Syntaxe, sémantique, pragmatique.* København: Nyt Nordisk Forlag, 1980.
Lyons, J. *Semantics. vol. 2.* Cambridge: Cambridge University Press, 1977.
Maes, A. A. *Nominal anaphors, markedness and the coherence of discourse.* Leuven: Peeters, 1996.
Mann, W. C., & Thompson, S. A. *Discourse description, Diverse linguistic analysis of a fund-raising text.* Amsterdam: John Benjamins, 1992.
Maturana, H. R., & Varela, F. J. *Autopoiesis and cognition: The realization of the living.* Dordrecht, Holland ; Boston: D. Reidel Pub. Co., 1980.
Qvortrup, L. *The hypercomplex society.* New York: Peter Lang, 2003.
Silberztein, M. Text indexing with INTEX. *Computers and the Humanities,* 33 (1999):3.
Swales, J. M. Attended and unattened "this" in academic writing: A long and unfinished story. *ESP Malaysia,* 11 (2005), 1–15.

CHAPTER TWELVE

HYBRID VOICES:
ENGLISH AS THE LINGUA FRANCA OF ACADEMICS

ANNA MAURANEN

Academic communities have been mobile from the start. From this perspective European universities are now back where they started from: ambitious future professionals and academics obtain their education from good universities in different countries. In the process they establish useful contact networks. The resulting academic communities are thoroughly international and highly mobile. What has changed from the Middle Ages is the speed of communication, the scale of the phenomenon–and the common language.

Mediaeval universities were just as international as ours are today, but the recent mobility at all levels of study takes place on a mass scale not seen before. Efficient mobility requires easy communication, which means that the movers must be able to count on a language which they already know and do not have to start to learn from the beginning every time they change places. In mediaeval universities the default language was of course Latin, and today it is English. It is true that foreign students also happily spend time in universities which operate in local languages, especially in large European countries whose languages are known outside the country like France or Spain, but English is the only alternative for many other countries. Small European countries are rapidly expanding their international degree programmes, which they generally offer in English to attract as many students as possible. It is also more economical to limit the selection to one international language.

Apart from degree courses, today's Europeans spend time abroad in student and staff exchange without much intention to learn the local language or to integrate in the local community, let alone immigrate. For most of these mobile academics and future professionals English is an instrument, not an object of study; they do not go to the Netherlands or Denmark to learn English, but to prepare themselves for an international career.

The position of English in these circumstances is thus radically different from that of English-speaking countries. English is used as a lingua franca in present-day Europe also extends the traditional domain English has had as the language of scholarly publications. Everyday use among non-natives in spoken interaction puts a great deal more pressure on the language to adapt to the circumstances of use than the slow and conservative process of publishing in English where native speakers act as gatekeepers and protectors of their mother tongue.

This paper looks into the use of English as a lingua franca in university discourses. The speakers come from diverse backgrounds, mostly Europe, and are recorded in typical speech events in degree programmes, conferences, thesis defences or guest lectures. It is hypothesised that the social context of the discourses favours strategies of communicative explicitness. Manifestations of explicitness strategies are explored and also compared to native speakers' English in comparable circumstances.

1. Background

The academic communities using English as a lingua franca (ELF) are typically international and they are much more like networks than stable local or regional communities. The networks are multi-faceted, comprising entities like universities, collegial networks of the same discipline or school of thought without local restrictions, and personal acquaintances and friendships as well as large impersonal communities of "members of the discipline" or "the scientific community". Clearly, some of these social groups are concrete and consist of individuals actually encountered, while others could be likened to what Anderson (1991) termed "imagined communities" in that the communities are not tangible but people see themselves as members of such groups. These networks or communities are characterised by mobility and relatively weak social ties, which have been associated with linguistic change (Granovetter 1973; Milroy 2002). The fundamental feature of the situation where English is used as an academic lingua franca is diversity: socio-cultural, conceptual and linguistic.

ELF speakers come from a wide range of sociocultural backgrounds; people from many nationalities, minority subcultures and ethnic origins meet in academic settings and speak English as the default lingua franca. The cultural context of ELF speaking is therefore a hybrid of many backgrounds and a local setting. Successful communication in such culturally complex situations requires adaptability and intercultural negotiation skills.

By conceptual diversity I mean the local intellectual traditions that people have grown up in and internalised in the course of their earlier education. As the papers in this volume illustrate, local and national intellectual traditions remain strong and diverse despite the ubiquitous use of English as the language of international publication. These intellectual traditions come together in face-to-face encounters, and give rise to negotiations of conceptual meanings and interpretations, even when seemingly the same input is being dealt with as in seminar or conference discussions.

Linguistic variety, which is of primary interest here, is inevitable in a situation where, despite a lingua franca, speakers have different mother tongues. The situation can be likened to dialect contact, because speakers have their own ways of speaking English, which tend to show similarities within first language boundaries. The dialect comparison does not hold in all respects, though. Varieties of English spoken by people with different first languages are unlike regional dialects in that there is no speech community which would use and regulate these varieties in its internal communication. When English is learned as a foreign language, it is not used for communication among speakers who share a first language. Even though the similar language backgrounds of, say, Dutch speakers influence their English, the similarities have not arisen in mutual communication. What we have here is more like a group of independently developed idiolects with a number of similarities.

A different kind of linguistic diversity results from speakers' proficiency levels: even though the speakers in demanding speech situations like university contexts are more proficient in English than is necessary for the average package tour tourist or a holiday resort street vendor, a wide range of fluency levels is manifest among the speakers. Their linguistic proficiency can be seen as a result of "variable learning" (Mauranen 2003). Speakers who have learned English as a foreign language are likely to have had very different experiences: in academic contexts we can assume a comparatively good acquaintance with formal written varieties, but speakers' experiences from schooling vary in duration and focus. Communicative skills and colloquial language are not equally appreciated in all cultures, and skills in grammar, phonology and lexis receive different emphases. First-hand experience of speaking English also varies among ELF speakers, and has been acquired in diverse circumstances in different parts of the world. Variable learning is a term which captures more appropriately the ELF reality than "imperfect learning", which is traditionally used in language contact studies (see, e.g. Winford 2003). Imperfect learning seems to imply that there is a single dimension of mastery of a target language along which speakers can be placed. ELF contexts also quite often include the presence of native speakers, which further expands the proficiency range.

ELF speakers can thus make few assumptions about shared cultural background or about their interlocutors' command of the language; such unpredictability is a permanent and salient feature of the situation. As I have noted before (Mauranen 2006), speakers seem to be aware of this. They expect comprehension to be hard to achieve in purely linguistic terms, and engage in various strategies to offset the problems that might ensue. Misunderstandings are not common because speakers prevent them: they try to converge towards a shared middle ground on account of the uncertainties involved.

A central concern in academic settings is negotiating the conceptual domain, that is, seeking to increase the participants' shared knowledge. At the same time, spoken face-to-face interaction foregrounds interpersonal relations: participants have to manage turn-taking, and respond to others' contributions on the spot, with all the concerns for face, status, and other social parameters which come into play.

Social interaction can be seen as constantly resolving a tension between cooperation and competition, as participants engage with each other in negotiating meanings and positions. This does not depend on whether the speakers happen to be using their mother tongue or not. International academic encounters are run everywhere with little concern for the language abilities or difficulties that people might experience. The events or programmes or projects are dominated by the nature of the task at hand, and it is considered normal that the lingua franca is a foreign language to some. But when the events actually take place, the participants who come together engage in a good deal of mutual adaptation; the negotiation of the language takes place in face-to-face encounters.

In the face of this diversity, participants' adaptive strategies must lean heavily on cooperation. Gaps in shared knowledge can be bridged by strategies of enhanced clarity and explicitness. Thus the demand for cooperativeness and explicitness can be expected to rise in comparison to stable local discourse or speech communities.

I would like to hypothesise that in the culturally and linguistically hybrid context that academic ELF speaking takes place, cooperation and explicitness are foregrounded as strategies of social interaction. Below, I explore explicitness in ELF discourse, and operationalise it as (1) rephrasing (...*we're bec- not becoming we're considered to be Europeans because we are in Europe*...), (2) topic negotiation (...*the Russians they didn't care*...), and (3) discourse reflexivity (...*what I would like to ask you*...).

2. Data

The present study is based on a corpus of spoken ELF, the ELFA corpus, which has mainly been compiled at the University of Tampere (English as a Lingua Franca in Academic Settings: www.uta.fi/ laitokset/kielet/engf/ research/ elfa/), and consists of 0.6 million transcribed words. All of the data is naturally-occurring discourse, recorded in authentic situations, and consists of complete individual speech events. The compilation was based on "external" criteria, that is, not determined by language-internal considerations, but by socially-based recognition of the genres of the discourse communities. Native speakers of English are sometimes present; they have not been recorded giving monologues or playing dominant roles in dialogues like doctoral defences, but appear as participants in multi-party discussions. No sessions with speakers who all share a L1 are included, neither are courses where English is the object of study—English language courses have thus not been recorded. The speech events cover many different kinds of university discourses: lectures, seminars, thesis defences, and conference presentations. The largest type of event are courses in international degree programmes run in English. Most events involve dialogue or polylogue: interactive, multi-participant events constitute the bulk of the data (for more on the compilation principles, see Mauranen 2003).

As a reference corpus of comparable native speaker data I have used the 1.8 million-word Michigan Corpus of Spoken Academic English (MICASE: www.hti.umich.edu/m/micase/). Just as ELFA is not entirely confined to non-native speakers, MICASE does not exclude other than native speakers entirely, even though the proportion of non-natives is small.

3. Rephrasing

Repetition and rephrasing are basic ways of saying the same thing more than once; they can be kept separate by limiting repetition to verbatim cases, and leaving modified paraphrases to the larger category of "rephrasing". This simplification causes problems if we want to be precise about drawing the borderlines–how much variation to allow in repetition is hard to tell exactly: do pitch or loudness count, for example, or small morphological modifications? At the other end, how far can rephrasing and paraphrasing go and still be regarded as variations of the "same", in terms of meaning or effect? Does it matter if the speaker makes it explicit that he or she intends her meaning to stay the same despite new phrasing (by saying things like *in other words, what I mean is...*) but hearers find it so mean something different? We could dwell on such matters for a long time but here I want to take a simple route and to accept anything as rephrases which either the speaker marks as a rephrase or the analyst can reasonably recognise as a reformulation of an immediately preceding utterance. I have tried to be conservative rather than liberal in regarding expressions as rephrases of the same, and required that the reformulation follows the first formulation immediately, that is, the discourse does not move on before the rephrasing. I have further limited rephrasing to self-rephrasing and excluded the kinds of single-word repetitions (... *of of of...*) which Biber et al. (1999) call "repeats". Clearly, other-rephrasing and self-repetition after the discourse has moved on are important features of discourse as well, but my present concern is with speaker's own reformulations.

Repetition and reformulation are often seen as signs of "dysfluency" (e.g. Biber et al., 1999), especially in foreign language speakers (e.g. Skehan 2005), but I see them as important means of coping with the exigencies of spoken language (Mauranen forthcoming). They can be seen as giving both speakers and hearers more space for processing, and rephrasing is an important means for speakers to make themselves clear. In foreign language contexts, the benefits of reformulation include improving the chances that at least one of the formulations will get across to the hearers.

I illustrate self-rephrasing from two angles: first, as "rephrase markers", which concentrate on the speaker's expressed anticipation of a self-rephrase, and secondly as rephrasing appears in running text, with or without prior marking.

3.1 Rephrase markers

Marx and Swales (http://www.lsa.umich.edu/eli/micase/kibbitzer.htm) have studied the MICASE corpus for what they call "Announced self-repairs", and placed it as a "kibbitzer" on the MICASE homepage. I took this investigation as a point of departure to see to what extent ELF speakers do similar things. This opens up an exploration of rephrasing from the explicit end, since announcing self-rephrasing borders on discourse reflexivity, albeit at the "low explicitness" end (see, Mauranen 1993). I do not adopt their term, though, because "self-repair" is unnecessarily negative and implies that a perfectly ordinary spoken tactic is somehow problematic, drawn upon when speakers have got themselves into trouble. It is one of those terms frequently used for spoken language which subtly hint that speech is a corrupt version of language proper, which is carefully polished writing. This negative interpretation is unlikely to have been the express purpose of Marx and Swales, because, as they say themselves, they were looking for

> "phrases that a speaker might use when he or she wanted to tell the interlocutors that an attempt to fix a speech mistake, clarify an idea, or rephrase an ambiguous utterance was coming up" (ibid.).

A "speech mistake" is thus just only one of the possibilities, even though the term seems to suggest primarily these. I therefore suggest "rephrase markers" as an alternative term in simple analogy with "discourse markers", which is well established in discourse analysis. Marx and Swales began their study by consulting their own and other informants' intuitions about what might be used as expressions of the desired kind, and after searching for them in the corpus, presented their findings in quantitative terms. The quantitative approach lends itself nicely to comparisons, and I therefore searched my own data for the same expressions. Clearly, straightforward comparisons of this kind are not without their problems: when we start from L1 forms, we may leave out typical ELF uses, which danger is exacerbated by beginning from the intuitions of a group of native speaker linguists. There is also the technical problem that ELF speakers' output includes more variability than current concordancers can properly capture. Thus, the caveats are that this is somewhat arbitrary and disadvantageous to ELF speakers, but the advantage is that the comparison is objective in simple quantitative terms.

The findings are listed in Table 1, with the rank order based on MICASE. The lists illustrate rephrase markers, not just raw figures of the expressions, so for example in the case of (*I*) *mean,* instances like *you know what I mean, you understand what I mean* and *for example I mean X* were excluded. To count as self-rephrasing, the subject was normally first person singular, even though the lists show shorter forms (*mean* rather than *I mean, trying to say* rather than *I am/was trying to say,* etc.).

Table 1. Rephrase markers in MICASE and ELFA		
	MICASE	ELFA
in other words	224	9
mean	50	438
trying to say	19	4
another way	18	-
that is to say	16	3
namely	15	17
i.e.	14	-
meant	11	1
what I'm saying is	7	-
clarify	4	-
rephrase	4	1
more specifically	2	-
misspoke	1	-
Σ	385	473
/ 100,000 words	2.26	139.12

Table 1 shows a striking difference. The signals for self-rephrasing are so much more frequent in ELFA as to be of a different order of magnitude altogether. If we look at the distributions, it is immediately obvious that the ELF speakers use a small variety of expressions, but those extremely often. This is no less than we would expect on the basis of SLA research: it is an economical strategy to resort to one expression for one meaning or function, and this is what many language learners do. Like learners, non-native speakers need to make good use of the items they have in their repertoire.

What is not so obvious is that the expression which is the overwhelming favourite among ELF speakers is not the most frequent one among natives. Moreover, it is not the most bookish one, as might be expected in an academic, text-dominated environment, but one which is typical of everyday speech. This would seem to point to spontaneous acquisition in social interaction rather than classroom learning or a strong written language bias. It would also seem to indicate that sensitivity to repertoires–levels of formality, register or mode differences, etc. are not limited to mother tongue usage.

3.2 Self-rephrasing in running text

Although rephrase markers give a good preliminary glimpse at explicitness in self-rephrasing, it is a good idea to counterbalance this by taking a sample of running text just to see how speakers go about rephrasing in continuous speech. On the face of it, rephrasing without marking or prefacing seem to be relatively common, but this cannot be captured by automatic search procedures.

The following brief extract is from a lecture of roughly average fluency, picked at random to stand for ordinary ELF discourse. The rephrases are italicised and numbered.

Extract 1. ELFA lecture

the fertility and mortality rates were high which meant that people had many children but **most of not most of them but about 30 40 percent of the children**[1] died before their first year. because of **the poor nutrition level this poor diet**[2] the whole standard of living was poor in in modern standards, low literacy rate means that most of the people could not read , and only few could write (COUGH) , and it's typical for that kind of so- that kind of society[3] that administration is also autocratic **there was no idea it's not even idea of democracy**[4] in those days (P:04) and **there was minimum social and (career) mobility which meant, or we could say that poor people had no chance for (career) mobility**[5] even though there are some exceptions of course . Finland was exporting something . **in in in purpose to be in purpose to import**[6] grain and what was exported was raw materials like raw timber butter and tar , timber and tar were exported to mostly to Britain and to Netherlands and **butter was impor- exported**[7] to er Stockholm and and St. Petersburg

Extract 1 has seven rephrases in 191 words, which means a proportion of about three and a half per cent. This sounds high, but then the figure only describes a little snippet from one speaker. It is interesting that most reformulation does not seem to affect the meaning of the initial phrasing, which we see if we look at each one in turn.

(1) *many children but most of not most of them but about 30 40 percent of the children*
This is clearly a case where the speaker has second thoughts about the contents of what he is saying, and we can put it down as rephrasing with a change of meaning.

(2) *the poor nutrition level this poor diet*
Here the speaker clearly reformulates the phrase but retains meaning; one would expect clarifications of this kind in pedagogical discourses generally.

(3) *for that kind of so- that kind of society*
Minor adjustments of this kind occur in speech in any circumstances; nothing is really changed the second time around. Something has caused the speaker to stop without completing the structure the first time the utterance was composed, but what it was is lost to later reconstruction. We can only say that the structure was interrupted and then picked up again. The reformulation retains both structure and meaning.

(4) *there was no idea it's not even idea of democracy*
In this instance we can see syntactic rephrasing; the meaning is clearly retained but it sounds as if the first attempt at phrasing the structure was not to the satisfaction of the speaker so he has a new take on it. To the outside observer the first start is more satisfactory; it also illustrates the inappropriateness of the "repair" term: rephrasing does not necessarily improve on the first formulation, or mend its problems. An initial formulation can be just as good or better than the new one.

(5) *there was minimum social and (career) mobility which meant, or we could say that poor people had no chance for (career) mobility*
The speaker makes explicit his intention to rephrase by using a marker (*or we could say that*). There is a change of meaning: the speaker puts the matter more bluntly, specifying that it is in fact the poor that are affected by minimal social and career.

(6) *in in purpose to be in purpose to import grain*
Technically this example could be described as a case of lexical replacement: *be* is replaced by *import*. However, it looks equally likely to be a structural impasse: the speaker interrupts the structure after *be*, and we could speculate that he does this because he cannot think of a good way of continuing (such as *be in a position to import...*) and takes a shortcut with a simpler structure. It is of

course also possible that he has second thoughts about the verb *be* with respect to his intended meaning and notices *be* is not doing the job.

(7) *butter was impor- exported to er Stockholm*
The last rephrasing looks like a slip of tongue; although again it could be classified mechanically as a lexical replacement affecting meaning–it does reverse the sense–it is not at all likely that the speaker changed his mind about what he wanted to say. He knows whether butter was imported from or exported to Stockholm, but he is talking about both imports and exports, so both terms are salient and active in the ongoing processing.

It seems that self-rephrasing operates in two dimensions: adjustment of structure and adjustment of meaning. When the speaker is concerned with the hearer's interpretation of the contents, that is, when his or her contribution to shared knowledge is deemed to be important, the speaker modifies the contents. Reformulation of this kind was seen above in the first rephrase (*most of not most of them but about 30 40 percent of the children*) and in the fifth one (*or we could say that poor people had no chance for (career) mobility*). The wish to affect interpretation is particularly prominent when the force of an utterance is modified by a rephrase, as when hedges are added or removed, as in *or would you_do you want the ninety-three seven kind of, ratio to stand* (MICASE), where the second formulation makes the question more direct and challenging.

On the other hand, as was already noted, a typical motivation behind rephrasing seems to be a desire to improve clarity. For this, the original meaning is to be retained, and the form changed so as to improve the chances that at least one of the formulations will get through to the hearer. This is common tactics in pedagogy, and it appears to be frequent in ELF discourse, as we saw in Extract 1 above. Frequent self-rephrasing is typical in non-native speech in institutional settings when interacting with native speakers, as Kurhila (2003) found: despite non-natives' tendency to reformulate, native speakers oriented to the contents, not form of what they were saying, and did not correct non-native attempts at grammatical formulation. It is hard to say in quantitative terms whether there are major differences between native and non-native speakers in the quantity or the quality of reformulations, because most studies have focused on one or the other only. From my very tentative explorations into small comparable samples of ELFA and MICASE so far, it would seem that rephrasings focus on form, particularly among ELF speakers, and that most of them are very minor and not preceded by rephrase markers.

4. Negotiating topic

An important facet of clarity and explicitness in discourse is ensuring that interlocutors follow each other's train of thought, which is intertwined with the topic at hand. Changes in topic referents need to be made clear. There are many ways of introducing referents to discourse as illustrated in the following instances from the ELFA corpus:

(i) th- **this is about multiculturalism** I I would like to know if ...
(ii) **about Stalin** I heard I heard that er during the 70's they...
(iii) **a couple of questions** erm **this citizenship** how much does **it** influence the people...
(iv) at first I thought it was oh god **this psychoanalysis** I hate **it** because I sort of resent Freud's some some of his theories...

Speakers thus have available to them a number of possibilities for referent introduction: for example they can announce what they are on about with the help of the preposition *about* as in (i) and (ii) above, resort to reflexive discourse (*a couple of questions*), as in (iii); or they can use a strategy of introducing a topic by first launching a noun phrase, and following it with a clause where a pronoun reference stands for the noun phrase (iii and iv). It is the last type which is of particular interest here, because it has been treated rather dismissively by many kinds of grammatical description, and is certainly not one that is taught as part of English courses in formal schooling, because it is not a normal feature of written discourse.

This kind of fronting is a typical feature of spoken language, which may be the reason why it has been treated rather negatively in formal grammar, as the commonly used term "left dislocation" reveals. Spoken discourse analysis has noted its frequency, and seen it mostly as a way of highlighting or foregrounding the topic. More than that, from a social interactionist perspective it has been shown to be situationally motivated (Pekarek Doehler 2001), which is in line with work on spoken language grammar such as that of Carter and McCarthy (e.g. Carter and McCarthy 2006, McCarthy and Carter 1997, McCarthy 1998). Carter and McCarthy (1997) call it "head", or "topic slot", and later (2006) "header". They see it as the speaker's means of orientating the listener, and characterise it as an "act of consideration to the listener" (McCarthy 1998:77). Ford et al. (2003) term this kind of fronting "negotiating referent", which highlights their observation that a central role of this structure is to ensure that interlocutors have the same topic in mind before going on. I adapt their term a little, and use "negotiating topic" or "topic negotiation" for this, seeking to capture the interactive potential, while eliminating the implication that there is a syntactic problem of something being "dislocated" or out of joint. Interaction-based perspectives show the importance and wide range of uses of this structure; like so many grammatical structures it can be shown to be shaped by the needs of face-to-face interaction. Here confine myself to topic negotiation as an explicitness strategy.

The basic pattern for the topic negotiation structure is this: (Demonstrative +) noun phrase$_1$ + coreferential subject pronoun$_1$, and in the ELFA data the variable slots are filled mostly as follows:

The	+ noun phrase	+	*he*
This			*she*
These			*it*
Those			*they*

A search of all seminar data in ELFA yielded a distribution where *it* combined with conceptual referents, *he/she* with person referents, and *they* combined with a broad range of referents. *They* references were also the commonest, and therefore give the best illustration of the range of referents the structure was used with: groups of people, institutional bodies, and physical or abstract objects. These are undoubtedly common topics in university discussions. Here are examples of each group:

Groups of people:
 in this case politicians **they** had a mission but is there any missi
 worker [unions] [mhm-hm] **they** cannot do do anything becau
 acute hepati -tis and almost almost all of them **they** die , and the
 but people , peasants , **they** fought for the Swedish king for
 mean there are still many people mhm **they** are saying that this
 [these] [mhm-hm] trade unions **they** mainly exist in a er bi- big factories [and]
 John F Kennedy and Kruchev er i hope i i premier yes yes Kruchev yeah those two **they** compromised within 13 days

Institutional bodies:
 Estonia and Latvia **they** have this problem with Russian minority
 those superpowers in the EU like Germany and France **they** decided anything and
 the Estonian government **they** made some kind of simplifying towards
 most specifically local government **they** try to apply e-government the local
 while the others countries **they** do have so you think it's so easy t

Physical objects:
 the fat drops they **they** can be like very small vesicles or then they can be
 these er circles **they** er present areas which are strategically important
 when these kind of kidneys **they** are put into an adult patient
 the pediatric kidneys **they** can be that's more, and when
 alright the door **they** are @@ not like , just yeah it's a it

Abstract objects:
the Ottoman heritage and historical background **they** have been like close together for a for a long time
and these institutional expressions **they** er are not out of this problem like NATO European Union
these different layers of identity **they** are by no means mutually exclusive so you can
many of these project projects **they** just go somewhere because erm the ability is not well er the public sector salaries **they** are open you know e- everybody can
so these differences **they** are , important but anyway if at this point
i think the- these er two perceptions **they** contradict somewhat each other all the time

As can be seen in the examples, ELF speakers use this structure quite comfortably to negotiate topics. This feature of spoken English grammar is so fundamental to interaction that it has made its way into the ELF speaking community even though it is highly unlikely that most (if any) of the speakers have been taught to use it in their grammar lessons. It is a salient discourse feature also because apparently it is shared by many languages, even typologically distant from English, such as Finnish. The topic negotiation structure is therefore a good candidate for a discourse universal.

5. Discourse reflexivity

The final type of explicitness to be addressed in this paper is discourse reflexivity (also known as "metadiscourse"), which was already touched upon above. Discourse reflexivity is discourse about discourse, and it could reasonably be hypothesised that this is such a basic, indispensable property of language communication that it is very likely to be a discourse universal. All languages have means of talking about language itself. In spoken discourse specifically, this is necessary for organising the ongoing interaction, in addition to organising the flow of language itself. For both of these functions, discourse reflexivity is vital, and it is hard to imagine successful linguistic interaction without it. We can safely expect to find discourse reflexivity in ELF, and any casual look at the data amply fulfils such expectations. I exemplify the function here briefly with a small set of related expressions, namely those involving the items *ask*, *answer*, and *question*.

These three items participate in an activity which is quite central in academic seminars and other polylogic situations: asking questions and answering them. These activities need to be prefaced and labelled for referential and evaluative acts during discussions. While many other means can also be employed to this effect, the most direct language items themselves are also in frequent use. The most common is *question* (7.2/100,000w). It is typically used in an introductory capacity, that is, prefacing a question. The most recurrent forms are *one question, my question is,* and *I have/ I've got a (kind of) question.* Some examples of *one question*:

> and **one question** when you say that er , that when European allies prefer to spend m
> okay well I have **one question** it's not exactly yeah on this essay
> I had just **one question** [because] [yeah] I was reading so
> okay er , so one **one question** about those er choosing
> I'd like to raise **one question** and , and er they are so exc
> erm yeah **one question** what about educating boys [I've

Ask was also relatively common (3.6/100,000w). Its dominant pattern is *I would like to ask (you),* followed by *I want(ed) to ask (you).* Both of the common patterns thus include a distancing element, *would like, want* or *wanted.* This is again similar to native speaker preferences, and probably has its origins in the nature of social interaction. Discourse reflexivity in the MICASE corpus tends to be heavily hedged– probably because discourse reflexivity imposes the speaker's order on the discourse and is in need of redressing the power balance (Mauranen 2001). This is, then, a case where a relatively small and closed set of linguistic expressions (reflexivity) co-occurs with a set of pragmatic expressions (hedges), as can be seen in the following examples of *I would like to* with discourse reflexive expressions:

> so **I would like** to **ask** about what do you mean about e-governisation can you
> **I would like to ask** erm about the concept information society er erm are we are
> the last question **I would like to ask** it was the second page and the the last
> to come back to your paper **I would like to ask** why performativity is not used in
> are , @@ er writing **I would like to address two questions** i i mean , you
> m i do like the essay **I would like to bring up**, an issue that like could be in- i
> n the bibliography so **I would like to draw your attention** that er at the master
> wo countries and here **I would like to** especially erm **discuss** the problem of
> ho would like to start **I would like to make** a very very short **comment** mhm
> h] mhm er so at first **I would like to say** that er for instance in lithuania as i
> ely put mhm-hm then **I would like to show** you something more of er from f
> member in the group **I would like you to** s- you to yeah tell tell m- **tell us** a l

The frame *I would like to* is used about half of the time with such discourse reflexive expressions, which means that this is one of its important functions. The rest of its uses are not far from this either–such as cognitive verbs which on many occasions are indirect questions (...*so i would like to know maybe if the information society*...).

The last search word in this group, *answer*, turned out to occur too rarely for patterning to be discernible; the only repeated sequence was *did I answer your question*, but even this was infrequent.

We might, again, hypothesise that since this connection between discourse reflexivity and polite tentativeness occurs in both ELF and native speaker English, it is a response to the demands of social interaction rather than a particular set of items which collocate in native speakers' repertoires. It also goes well beyond the normal teaching curriculum, so that the expressions are likely to have been spontaneously acquired in interaction by both native and ELF speakers.

6. Conclusion

ELF speakers need to negotiate diversity on different planes simultaneously. To cope with this they engage in a variety of adaptive strategies, among which cooperation and explicitness hold an important place. Other researchers have noted the cooperativeness of ELF speakers (Firth 1996; Meierkord 2000), which is not unlike encounters between native and non-native speakers (Kurhila 2003). Non-natives tend to let difficult points in conversation pass (Firth 1996), co-construct expressions and signal comprehension very frequently. In addition, Kurhila's (2003) study on native and non-native speakers of Finnish found that non-natives frequently resorted to grammatical reformulations of their own talk.

Self-rephrasing was very common among the ELF speakers in this study: rephrase markers were several times more frequent than in the Michigan corpus of chiefly native speakers, and most rephrases appear to go unannounced, i.e. without preceding markers. The findings here also suggest that most rephrasing is concerned with form rather than meaning. If the speaker rephrases an utterance so that the contents are affected, he or she manipulates the way in which the meaning is interpreted. This is very clear in the readjustment of pragmatic force. Rephrasing form, in contrast, affects clarity: the more formulations are given to the same sense, the better the chances that the contribution is understood. This is a common pedagogical tactic, too, with teachers rephrasing themselves as they speak. From ELF speakers' tendency to rephrase form we could conclude that their primary concern is with the clarity and comprehensibility of their expression–a way of overcoming linguistic and cultural barriers in the situation. Reformulations thus work towards clarity and help avoid misunderstanding.

Topic negotiation was a frequent means of raising the level of explicitness in the discourse. It is easy to agree with the interpretations of Carter and McCarthy (1997) and Ford et al. (2003) and see this as a considerate, collaborative strategy on the part of the speaker. It results from interactional needs rather than a desire to achieve grammatical correctness. As a typical feature of spoken grammar it is not a normal foreign language teaching point, but possibly easy to pick up in use because it is salient and an apparently widespread phenomenon in different languages. Insofar as it is familiar to speakers from a number of linguistic backgrounds, it is likely to work well in communication and be strengthened further.

Discourse reflexivity is a well-known non-grammatical means of managing discourse, which helps organise contributions to content as well as interaction. It supports clarity and explicitness in discourse organisation. The present findings suggest that it tends to co-occur with hedging expressions among ELF speakers in the same way as it does in native speaker discourse. This is a very tentative finding and requires more work, but interestingly it supports the observation that situational and interactive factors select and shape the language that is adopted in lingua franca use.

All the language items studied here were interactively salient and promoted communicative clarity by making utterances more explicit. The motivation for adopting such uses of language arises from the needs of the interactive situation, where shared knowledge is relatively low and many aspects highly unpredictable. The interlocutors share English, but the qualitative and quantitative differences in commanding it are considerable. They also share knowledge of a disciplinary area and of university settings, but must expect diversity in these as well, given the different traditions they come from. There are many socio-cultural and conceptual meanings to be negotiated, and the language, which is only partly shared, needs to adapt to the complexities of the situation. It seems that the speakers manage this quite successfully: seminars and conferences are run, theses examined, and degrees obtained. English is employed efficiently to meet these demands, but it does not remain intact in the process. We must expect English to accept new usages along with new user groups.

7. References

Anderson, Benedict. *Imagined Communities. Reflections on the Origin and Spread of Nationalism*. London: Verso, 1991.
Biber, Douglas, Stig Johansson, Geoffrey Leech, Susan Conrad and Edward Finegan. *The Longman Grammar of Spoken and Written English*. London: Pearson Education, 1999.
Carter, Ronald and Michael McCarthy. *Cambridge Grammar of English*. Cambridge: Cambridge University Press, 2006.
Firth, Alan. "The discursive accomplishment of 'normality'. On Conversation Analysis and 'Lingua Franca'". *Journal of Pragmatics* 26 (1996): 237-259.
Ford, Cecilia, Barbara Fox and Sandra Thompson. "Social Interaction and Grammar" In *The New Psychology of Language*. [Vol. 2], edited by M. Tomasello, 119-143. Mahwah, NJ: Lawrence Erlbaum, 2003.

Granovetter, M. "The strength of weak ties." *American Journal of Sociology* 78 (1973):1360-80.
Kurhila, Salla. *Co-constructing Understanding in Second Language Conversation*. Helsinki: University of Helsinki, 2003.
Marx, Stephanie and John M. Swales. "Announcements of Self-Repair: "all i'm trying to say is, you're under an illusion". http://www.lsa.umich.edu/eli/micase/kibbitzer.htm
Mauranen, Anna. *Cultural Differences in Academic Rhetoric. A Textlinguistic Study*. Frankfurt: Peter Lang, 1993.
—. "Reflexive Academic Talk: Observations from MICASE." In *Corpus Linguistics in North America*, edited by Rita Simpson and J.M. Swales, 165-178. Ann Arbor: University of Michigan Press, 2001.
—."The Corpus of English as Lingua Franca in Academic Settings". *TESOL Quarterly* 37 (2003): 513-527.
—. "Signalling and preventing misunderstanding in English as lingua franca communication." *International Journal of the Sociology of Language,* 177 (2006); 123-150.
—. "Spoken Rhetoric: How do natives and non-natives fare?" In *Proceedings of the Conference on Cross-linguistic and Cross-Cultural Perspectives on Academic Discourse*, edited by Eija Suomela-Salmi. Turku: Turku University Press, forthcoming.
McCarthy, Michael. *Spoken Language and Applied Linguistics*. Cambridge: Cambridge University Press, 1998.
McCarthy, Michael and Ronald Carter. "Grammar, tails and affect: constructing expressive choices in discourse". *Text* 17 (1997): 405–29.
Meierkord, Christiane. Interpreting successful lingua franca interaction. An analysis of non-native/non-native small talk conversations in English. In *Conversation Analysis: New Developments*, edited by A. Fetzer and K. Pittner, *Linguistics Online* 5 (2000), Special Issue. http://www.linguistik-online.com.
Milroy, Leslie. "Social Networks." In *The Handbook of Language Variation and Change*, edited by J.K. Chambers, Peter Trudgill and Natalie Schilling-Estes, 549-572. Oxford: Blackwell, 2002.
Pekarek Doehler, Simona. "Dislocation à gauche et organisation interactionnelle" *Marges Linguistiques* 2 (2001), 177-194. www.marges-linguistiques.com
Skehan, Peter. "Understanding fluency in second language performance." Paper presented at the IATEFL Conference, April 5-9 2005, Cardiff.
Winford, Donald. *An Introduction to Contact Linguistics*. Oxford: Blackwell, 2003.

CHAPTER THIRTEEN

SIMILARITIES AND DIFFERENCES IN FRENCH AND ENGLISH EAP RESEARCH ARTICLE ABSTRACTS: THE CASE OF ASP

JOHN M. SWALES AND SARAH VAN BONN

1. Background to the data

GERAS is the acronym for Groupe d'Etude et de Recherche en Anglais de Spécialité (the Group for study and research in specialized Englishes). Since its first conference in 1977, GERAS has become probably the most active and widely recognized English for Academic Purposes association in France (and the French dependencies), much of its prominence being due to the long-standing and energetic leadership of Professor Michel Perrin, who eventually retired as president of GERAS in 2000. The first publication of the *Groupe* was the 1983 proceedings of the 3rd European Symposium on LSP held at Michel Perrin's home institution—Université Victor Segalan Bordeaux 2—and edited by him. The first volume of *Asp: La Revue de GERAS* ("Asp" being an acronym of Anglais de Spécialité) appeared in 1992—a substantial volume of close to 600 pages—and annual volumes have appeared regularly ever since. However, in 1994 the numbering system changed to reflect the size of each volume, larger annual or semi-annual volumes having multiple numbers. For example, the 1997 volume is labeled 15-18 and contains 47 articles (35 in French and 12 in English).

The GERAS website (http://www.langues-vivantes.u-bordeaux2.fr/GERAS) describes its main journal *ASp* as follows:

> La revue publie des articles, de synthèse ou de recherche, des notes, de recherche, de pédagogie, d'orientation, des recensions et comptes rendus relatifs à l'anglais de spécialité conçu comme secteur d'enseignement et domaine de recherche. Les contributions visent à éclairer la spécificité de l'objet anglais de spécialité, notamment dans ses dimensions linguistiques, culturelles, didactiques, et à élargir la connaissance de l'anglais des diverses spécialités.

(The journal publishes review and research articles, research, pedagogical and guidance notes, reviews and summaries relative to specialized Englishes conceived as both a teaching activity and a research area. Contributions aim at clarifying the nature of specialized Englishes, especially in its linguistic, cultural and didactic dimensions, and in increasing understanding of English for various Specific Purposes.)

According to Ray Cooke, the long-time secretary of GERAS, the members of GERAS generally number about 130, and each receive a copy of *ASp* and periodically *La lettre de GERAS*, which typically contains an editorial by the president, news of those who have recently completed doctoral degrees in the field, EAP job announcements in France, information on upcoming conferences, and news of the activities of the four sub-groups of GERAS covering law, business and economics, health, and the human sciences. Around 200 copies of *ASp* are printed, some of the extras being for sale to non-members. The annual totals of *ASp* articles in English and French (through 2004) are listed in Table 1.

Table 1. Totals of *ASp* articles in English and French (2004)

Year	Total articles	In English	in French
1992	37	7	30
1993	27	5	22
1994	48	17	31
1995	38	14	24
1996	40	7	33
1997	47	12	35
1998	35	6	29
1999	42	12	30
2000	40	16	24
2001	20	8	12
2002*	20	3	17
2003	14	2	12
2004	29	8	21
Totals	437	117	320

* The page for #35/36 could not be found on the website on June 30, 2006.

As the figures show, over the 13-year 1992-2004 period, a regular majority of papers in *ASp* were written in French, averaging around 73% of the overall total. The papers in English were consistently in a minority averaging just over a quarter of the total, with the highest percentage in 2000 (40%); and here it is perhaps interesting that the proportion of papers in English has not increased over time—in contrast to many developments elsewhere. Most of these English-language papers appear to be written by Anglophone members of GERAS living in France, although some came from elsewhere, including those written by invited speakers at GERAS colloquia, such as Tony Dudley-Evans and Ann Johns. A few of the English papers were written by French scholars; two regular contributors, Catharine Resche and Claude Sionis, write in both languages. As expected, the great majority of the French papers were written by Francophone members of GERAS, although occasionally Anglophone authors, such as Shirley Thomas and Chris Gledhill, published in French.

In general, we see here a small but vibrant national EAP/ESP discourse community consisting of a majority of French scholars and a minority of Anglophone expatriates making their academic careers in French institutions of higher education. Since this is a community devoted to "Anglais de spécialité", it is reasonable to assume that both the French and English L1 writers have very high command of the other language as an L2; indeed, many will be near bilinguals—the Francophones by education, study, teaching ESP, as well as periods of residence in Anglophone environments, the Anglophones by immersion and integration into French academic and social life. As the above intimates, *ASp* is a bilingual journal. More importantly for our purposes, irrespective of whether an article is written in French or English, each article is fronted by two abstracts, one in French and one in English. Because of the high degree of content similarity between the abstract pairs, the *ASp* data potentially offers an unusually controlled comparison of similarities and differences between the two academic languages in terms of linguistic, rhetorical and informational choices, especially when it is remembered that the authors' professional interests and experiences likely make them experts in those two languages.

We selected for our corpus the abstracts from 15 research-oriented articles written in French by Francophone authors and 15 similar articles written in English with author names connoting Anglophone status. Although using author names to determine L1 status can be an unreliable procedure in a country like the U.S., in France it is much less so, especially as the first author had some familiarity with the GERAS discourse community. The 15 paired Francophone abstracts were all taken from the 1999 volume. For the Anglophone paired abstracts, we had to look a little further, taking nine from 1999, four from 1996 (the only two volumes available to us in their entirety), while the last two were obtained electronically from the 2002 volume. (A list of the articles from which the abstracts were drawn is given in the appendix.)

2. Background to the analysis

In 1990, Swales concluded that abstracts were an under-researched genre from a discourse-analytic perspective. In these terms, he instanced only an unpublished study by Rounds (1982) showing an unexpected amount of hedging, and a 1985 chapter by Graetz, who, *inter alia* concluded "The abstract is characterized by the use of the past tense, third person, passive, and the non-use of negatives" (p. 125). A decade and a half later, the situation has radically changed. In a recent overview entitled "Recent linguistic research into author abstracts", Montesi and Urdiciain (2005) cite 28 studies of research article abstracts since 1990, to which we can add a further half dozen or so. Montesi & Urdiciain also discuss another six studies dealing with conference abstracts. The conference abstract, however, is arguably a different genre because it is a stand-alone text (rather than operating as an accompanying part-genre), with the consequence that it will be accepted or rejected entirely on its own merits. The high-stakes competitive environment of the conference abstract typically means that, in terms of Yakhontova's (2002) distinction, the ensuing text will be more concerned with "selling" rather than "telling".

The abstracts used in this literature have been mostly drawn from biology, linguistics, and medicine, although both Hyland (2000) and Stotesbury (2003) offer elaborate multi-disciplinary studies covering many fields. Equally selective has been the comparative work between English and other languages: There are single papers dealing with German (Busch-Lauer, 1995), Swedish (Melander et al, 1994), Norwegian (the KIAP Project), Portuguese (Johns, 1992), Arabic (Al-Harbi, in press.); on the other hand, there are at least eight investigations comparing Spanish and English abstracts, some of the more accessible being Lorés (2004), Martín Martín (2003) and Valero Garcés & Calle Martínez (1997). In this context, it is significant that we have been unable to find any previous studies that have investigated features of *French-language* abstracts, despite the continuing academic importance of that language. This striking discrepancy between the absence of French studies and the proliferation of Spanish ones may reflect a relative lack of interest in discourse and genre analysis among French EAP practitioners, and its enthusiastic adoption by their Spanish counterparts over the last decade.

As we turn to the major themes and the major findings in the previous literature, it is important to note that wide disciplinary variation in abstracts has been consistently reported (e.g. Hyland, 2000; Stotesbury, 2003). Given this heterogeneity, we have restricted our review to work that has examined RA abstracts in applied linguistics; specifically we focus on the relevant portion of Melander et al. (1997), Bittencourt dos Santos (1996), aspects of Hyland (2000), and those sections of Lorés (2004) that deal with the *Applied Linguistics* journal.

We feel that such a limitation is not overly narrow because of the widely recognized "broad tent" nature of the language sciences. Martín Martín (2003) analyzed abstracts from experimental phonetics, but this field is more closely allied with the natural sciences rather than the humanities. Comparably, Dahl (2004) investigated the abstracts for the kind of "argumentative" papers found in formal and theoretical linguistics. *Ceteris paribus*, we can expect strong sub-disciplinary differences and particularities in various branches of the language sciences.

Both Bittencourt dos Santos and Hyland offer comparable five-part moves for applied linguistics abstracts. The major difference in categorization appears at first sight to concern the second move, glossed by Bittencourt dos Santos as "presenting the research" and by Hyland as "purpose". Although an overt *purpose* move has now become obligatory in the structured abstracts in the medical field (Hartley and Sydes, 1997), such a precise "In order to..." formulation is not *de rigeur* in applied linguistics. In fact, Hyland's one example of a "purpose" move from this field, would seem to be just as easily classifiable as "presenting the research":

> "In this article we a) argue that mainstream composition studies is at present too narrow in its scope and limited in its perspective and b) offer some thoughts, from our unique interdisciplinary position, that we feel could help mainstream compositional professionals improve this situation". (2000: 72)

Percentages of uptake of these moves are shown in Table 2.

Table 2. Percentage of uptake of moves

	Bittencourt	Hyland
Move 1 (Situating/Introduction)	43	46
Move 2 (Presenting/Purpose)	98	97
Move 3 (Methodology)	98	42
Move 4 (Results/Product)	80	96
Move 5 (Discussion/Conclusion)	62	19

Factors that might have influenced differences between these two sets of findings include the fact that Bittencourt dos Santos' data is from the early 1990s while Hyland's is drawn from 1997, and that Bittencourt dos Santos chose a set of three journals, two of which have a strong APA-style, while Hyland had much broader coverage. The disparity in the prevalence of a Methods move in the two studies might reflect the nature of the two corpora, or might even, following Berkenkotter & Huckin's (1995) finding of some downplaying of methodological accounts in recent years, the time difference between the two sets of data. The contrasts in the uptake of Moves 4 and 5 may in part be ascribable to difficulties in disentangling in these short texts *Results* from *Discussion*. But overall, it would seem that applied linguistics RA abstracts are generally expected to present the research being undertaken and to provide some information about the findings. An account of methodology is likely in empirical papers, while introductory contextualizations and concluding remarks are options available to those with a more promotional/rhetorical bent.

Lorés had only nine abstracts in her applied linguistics sub-corpus, seven of them she ascribed to the IMRD pattern discussed above, but two classified as following the CARS model for article introductions (Swales, 1990). She interestingly noted that these CARS-structure introduction-like abstracts would likely be classified by information scientists as "indicative" rather than "informative" in the sense they focused on what was done (and perhaps why), rather than on what was found. Finally, Melander et al. (1997) found a clear difference between the Swedish linguists writing in Scandinavian journals and the Americans writing in international ones. The former focused heavily on the methods and the results with little in the way of scene-setting or concluding remarks. An opening typical of this sub-corpus is the following:

> The article deals with Themes (the function associated with left-dislocated structures) and Tails (the function associated with right-dislocated structures) in English conversation.

On the other hand, the Anglophones offered full IMRD type abstracts with considerable rhetorical work undertaken in the opening sentences, as in: "A crucial event in the historical evolution of scientific English was the birth of the scientific article".

3. The *ASp* Corpus: Results

One might assume that the 30 abstract pairs from *ASp*, because they are summaries of the same paper, would be very similar to each other. In many cases they are; consider the following English and French sentences from Abstract 1 (see the appendix for further details).

> The project presented here stems from two observations: firstly, an essential skill for students in science and engineering is acquiring visual literacy, to enable

them to read and interpret iconographic material; secondly, because of hyperspecialization in a narrow field, their general scientific culture is often impoverished.

Le projet présenté ici est motivé par un double constat: d'une part, la nécessité, pour les étudiants scientifiques et élèves-ingénieurs, d'acquérir une 'culture visuelle' leur permettant de lire et d'interpréter des documents iconographiques; d'autre part, l'appauvrissement de leur culture scientifique générale, en raison d'une hyperspécialisation.

It is true that there are some attestable differences: *stems from* (which could not be directly translated into French and retain the same metaphorical meaning) is translated as *est motivé par*; what follows the colon in English are two full sentences separated by a semicolon, while in French we have two long noun phrases on either side of the semicolon. However, the two textual extracts generally correspond. Both serve the same rhetorical purpose (introducing the subject and situating the research). Both follow the same general sentence structure (Full sentence: transition word, list item; transition word, list item). And most importantly, the language is generally the same "The project presented here" is directly translated as "Le projet présenté ici"; "an essential skill [...] is acquiring" appears as "la nécessité d'acquérir," the word *impoverished* is retained in the translation (though it is a different part of speech) as *appauvrissement*; the list goes on. In sum they are quite similar.

We independently coded the 30 abstract pairs into "broadly similar" and "sufficiently different to be a reconceptualization". We agreed that six (20%) fell into the latter category, all (interestingly) written by Francophone authors. Here are the opening sentences to one such pair (Abstract pair 18):

> Enseigner l'anglais dans le secteur LANSAD ne doit pas faire perdre de vue la langue générale dans laquelle la langue spécialisée est enracinée, même s'il est évident qu'il faut s'attacher à donner aux étudiants la possibilité d'aborder un secteur spécialisé et d'en maîtriser les moyens d'expression.
>
> It is now widely acknowledged that ESP should not be considered as a sub-language for it is deeply-rooted in general-purpose English indeed.

A first obvious difference is that the French version of the sentence is much longer. In consequence, at this juncture one might expect the next sentence in the English version to correspond to the subordinate clause appearing in the French version. However, this is not the case; the second sentence of the English version actually corresponds (more or less) to the beginning of the second sentence of the French version:

Teaching ESP therefore implies a wide range of access routes, which the present paper offers to explore..

La présente étude passe précisément en revue plusieurs techniques qui sont autant de voies d'accès à la langue spécialisé [...].

So, it seems that the subordinate clause of the first French sentence never makes it into the English translation of the abstract. In addition, there are other differences. The French version uses a local acronym probably unknown to outsiders ("le sector LANSAD), while the English version adopts an internationally accepted term. More importantly the English "It is now widely acknowledged" opens with an argument about general theoretical knowledge, while the French version ("Enseigner l''Anglais") dives straight into a world of practical pedagogy. In fact, a general concern with selecting the right theoretical approach prevails throughout the English abstract; in contrast, the French counterpart stresses the need to do things in such a manner that university students will be helped. This pair of abstracts can thus be contrasted not only linguistically but also in the way the study being reported has been situated.

As mentioned, one interesting factor that seems to be at work here is that all six non-corresponding abstract pairs were written by Francophone authors. In fact, it was relatively easy to follow the translation process for the Anglophone authors producing French-language abstracts (despite the occurrence of interesting, smaller linguistic differences). However, this was not at all the case for the Francophone "reconceptualizing" authors, where it was nearly impossible to detect a clear process of translation. Morover, if we take non-direct translation as an indication of increased adoption of the discourse style of the language the text is being translated into, we see a tendency among a minority of the Francophone authors to re-conceptualize their research in terms of their understanding of the rhetorical traditions and discourse conventions of Anglophone text on ESP/Applied Linguistics. And here we can again recall that these writers are all English specialists. Thus, the changes observed in the *ASp* corpus are likely not indications of L2 problem areas, but rather changes which reflect salient differences in the Francophone and Anglophone ways of constructing academic text.

In contrast to a study comparing *The Journal of Linguistics* with *Le Bulletin de la Société de Linguistique de Paris* (Van Bonn, 2005), surface differences were much less marked—as might be expected—in the *ASp* corpus. The number of sentences in the two *ASp* sub-corpora was very similar, even though the French sentences seemed to be a little longer. (Word counts between English and French are unreliable because of the latter's penchant for apostrophes and elision.) In terms of paragraph structure, most of the abstracts pairs (20 out of 30—two-thirds of the total) do not employ any paragraph separation. There are also six total abstract pairs, three for French articles and three for English ones, for which both versions make use of paragraph separation. However, there remain four abstracts where the paragraph demarcation does not correspond; more specifically, three abstract pairs have paragraph breaks in French but not English, and one abstract pair has paragraphs in the English version but not in the French version. It is also worth noting that the only instances where the use of paragraphs does not correspond for abstract pairs are in the abstracts written by Francophone authors. The fact that the majority of the non-corresponding abstract pairs have paragraph demarcation in the French version but not in the English version is perhaps reflective of the tendency of French prose in general to use more paragraphs than English (as discussed in Régent 1985). Secondly, the fact that the Francophone authors were the only ones to choose to use paragraph separation in a non-corresponding manner perhaps indicates that they are more comfortable changing this feature from one abstract to another.

In some ways, a greater difference was found in first person pronoun use. The French abstracts contained 32 such pronouns, the English only 23—a finding that is in contrast to both Fløttum (2003) and Van Bonn (2005). Another notable finding, given that all the abstracts are single-authored, was that only five of the 55 total pronouns were singular and these five occur in just two abstract pairs, both of which written by Anglophone authors. Most Anglophone *Asp* authors who opted for a personal-pronoun approach seemed to have absorbed from their working environment a French avoidance of *I/je* and applied that reluctance not only to their French prose, but to their English academic writing as well!

Metatext also tended to show difference. Twenty-one of the 30 *ASp* abstract pairs (71%) use some overt metatextual expression in one abstract, in the other, or both to refer to the text being summarized in the abstract. However, there were four occasions when only the English version opted for this rhetorical device, and in general there was more metatext in the English subcorpus (25 instances as opposed to 14). Further, the English metatextual terms showed considerably less variation:

Table 3. Number of metatexual expressions

English		*French*	
paper 20	20	article	9
article	4	etude	3
study	1	communication	1
		presentation	1
		document	1
		contribution	1

Doubtless part of the explanation for this difference lies in the fact that there is no obvious French equivalent for that common *utility* metatextual term, "paper".

Another difference that showed up between abstract pairs is that often part of one tends to be more detailed or specific than part of another, particularly in those that we classified as *reconceptualizations*. However, there do not seem to be any systematic patterns here for why these differences occur, as is suggested by the very fact that the numbers of instances where the French abstract has more detail or some added information is about equal to the number of instances where the English abstract has more detail or information. There are 17 examples of some piece of information being present in English and not in French, and 16 examples where something is present in French and not in English. There are even instances where one abstract uses more detail in French for one section of the abstract and more detail in English for another part. Abstract-pair 22 (one of the reconceptualizing ones) illustrates this. The sentence which appears in the French version as

> Avec la firme «Orange» la métonymie apparaît comme constitutive de l'éxpérience téléphonique

appears in the English version as

> The firm « Orange » has chosen to materialise the wave carrying the words of a phone talk from speaker to listener via a humorous cartoon, stressing the inherent metonymic character of the telephone experience.

However, later on in the same abstract, the English sentence

> The firm Vodaphone has decided to […] concentrate instead on the social networks which spur the development of the telecom industry

appears in the French version as

> L'entreprise Vodaphone a clairement mis en valeur un glissement métonymique de la connexion physique au lien social dans sa publicité pour les conversations au tarif de deux pence par minute en faisant se succéder trois scènes riches, sans y inclure l'ombre d'un téléphone

In both of these cases, it is difficult to perceive why the author has chosen a detailed explanation in one place and a more general account in the other.

Sometimes further detail is added in one version, as in Abstract pair 16 where the French phrase "ce projet" appears once in the English version as "this online educational project" and later on as "the content of this telecommunication-based course." A summary noun explaining the relationship being discussed can be given, as in Abstract pair 4, where the French explanatory noun phrase "la relation entre" does not appear in the English version; or in Abstract 2 where the summary noun phrase "the question of" appears only in the English version. Sometimes too just an adjective is included in one version of the abstract but not the other, as in Abstract pair 19 where "different" in the noun phrase "different notions" appears in English but not in French. Further examples of similar shifts could be given, but the above should suffice to indicate that there seems to be no trend for abstracts in one language or for authors of one L1 group to use, add, or leave out specific types of information. Rather, at this level of detail we see further evidence that stylistic preferences of individual authors are influencing their decisions when reworking an abstract from one language into the other.

In contrast, the French abstracts do give a general impression of using a greater amount of nominal and nominalizing language. Consider for example, this elaborate prepositional construction in the French version of Abstract pair 18:

> au travers de l'initiation à l'observation des néologismes, des dictons et des proverbes, des nombreux réseaux de métaphores, sans oublier les références à la littérature

In effect, it is noticeable that, at times, what appears as a verbal phrase of some kind in English appears as a noun phrase in the French equivalent. Twelve of the abstract pairs provide an instance of noun-like language in the French text appearing as verb-like language in the English abstracts, and there are a total of 13 instances, indicating that one pair of abstracts has more than one instance of this linguistic feature (Abstract pair 1). Of these 12 abstracts, half belong to the Anglophone group and half belong to the Francophone group, so L1 does not seem to be a significant factor here. The use of nouns in French where they do not appear in English occurs for the most part in one of two linguistic contexts in English: either for a list of verb phrases/complete sentences or for a gerund phrase. Abstracts 1 provide an example of full sentences in English appearing as noun phrases in French. The English version reads

> The project presented here stems from two observations: firstly, an essential skill for students in science and engineering is acquiring visual literacy […]; secondly, because of hyperspecialisation in a narrow field, their general scientific culture is often impoverished.

While the French version uses *apprauvrissment* (impoverishment) for *is often impoverished*:

> Le projet présenté ici est motivé par un double constat: d'une part, la nécessité, pour les étudiants scientifiques et élèves-ingénieurs, d'acquérir une 'culture

visuelle' [...]; d'autre part, l'appauvrissement de leur culture scientifique générale, en raison d'une hyperspécialisation

For an example of a gerund phrase in English which appears as a simple noun phrase in French, we can turn to Abstracts 22, where the French sentence beginning

L'hypothèse selon laquelle

appears in English as

Starting from the assumption

The other linguistic features we explored produced much more similarity than difference. We found little of significance when comparing tenses, or when studying the use of transition words or connectives such as *therefore* or *cependant*. There were some notable differences in the choice of voice. Indeed, nearly 70% of all passive uses occurred in the English sub-corpus, there being 31 instances of a finite clause appearing as passive in English but active in French (with only two counter-examples). However, it would be well to recognize that these are minor stylistic variations primarily attributable to the greater propensity for impersonal and reflexive options in the French verb.

In conclusion, in this paper we have examined some of the features exhibited by the bilingual abstracts in the annual or biannual volumes of *ASp*, the main scholarly organ of GERAS, an ESP/EAP association based in France. To summarize the more interesting findings, we note that the French versions of the abstracts often have slightly longer sentences, use more first person personal pronouns, opt more for the active voice, incorporate a smaller number but a greater variation of metatextual expressions, and select more nominal language than their English counterparts.

4. Discussion

We began our review of the literature with summaries of the work on RA applied linguistic abstracts by Hyland and Bittencourt dos Santos. This work is valuable from a number of perspectives, such as indicating the level of social science maturity of the field, and in Hyland's case, in also showing an increase in introductory and conclusionary moves over the 1980-1997 timespan, partly as a result of concomitantly recognizing greater competitiveness for readership and partly due to a heightened sense of need to interact with that readership. However, this kind of macro-level analysis turned out to be less discriminatory when applied to the *ASp* corpus. This is because the differences between the English and French versions of the abstracts lie below the level of move or do not involve changes in the ordering of moves. Nor is it the case, following up on Lorés' perception, that one member of an abstract pair opts for an informative IMRD structure, while the other proffers an indicative CARS-type summary. However, at greater levels of delicacy that target sub-move or within-move linguistic realizations, differences do emerge. The French version's methodology may be more or may be less explicit than the methodology described in the English version. The members of the abstract pair may "situate" the research rather differently, placing the emphases, for example, in one member of the pair on theory and on educational practice in the other.

As might have been anticipated, the differences we have uncovered are somewhat infrequent in number and somewhat small in scale, at least outside of the 20% of the abstract pairs we identified as *reconceptualizations*. Even so, there may be larger lessons for all those of us who attempt cross-linguistic and cross-discoursal comparisons of texts, for here lurks in the undergrowth an untidy mass of confounding variables. Today, this is particularly the case when an attempt is made to construct a comparative corpus of English texts and those in another language. With the growing dominance of English in the research world, it becomes increasingly difficult to control for variables such as equivalent status of the two journals, an equivalency in the size and expectations of the intended readership, and some comparability in manuscript acceptance rates and level of reviewing and editorial gatekeeping. Burgess's (2002) study of introductions in English and Spanish journals is exemplary in its focus on the linguistic and rhetorical consequences of writing for a small national local audience (many members of whom may be personally known to the author), as opposed to an international one. It is worth noting that the first part of Burgess's (2002) title is "Packed houses and intimate gatherings"; doubtless all discourse analysts are well aware of the consequences of such audience features.

There would seem to be two kinds of solution to what we might now call "the discourse community problem" in contrastive studies. One, advocated by Swales (2004), is to search out sufficiently small, regional, and low-impact English-language journals so that a fair comparison with the other-language journals can be made. Melander et al. (1997) note that they had to search for departmental "working papers" in order to find adequate numbers of Swedish-language linguistics articles; hindsight suggests that they might have done better by searching out English-language "working papers" from Anglophone universities in order to strengthen the validity of the comparison.

The other solution is the one we have adopted here. We identify a bilingual community—indeed one also fully immersed in language and linguistic concerns—that has for its members an open and neutral bilingual publication policy for its main journal. At least as far as the abstracts are concerned, we now have closely matched texts, and ones which are likely to be read by GERAS members with approximately equal facility and interest in whichever of the two languages they opt for. In this way, we suggest that "the discourse community problem" has at least been reduced to manageable proportions. Indeed, we suggest that it would be worth conducting studies on other bilingual applied linguistics journals such as *Ibérica* in Spain or the *Especialist* in Brazil. And finally, we note that our findings are not dramatic, indeed, as with personal pronoun use, somewhat unexpected (c.f. Fløttum, 2003). It may turn out that, when discourse community effects are neutralized, differences among academic languages will not be so striking and so significant as the contrastive rhetoric literature might have us believe; rather, those differences will likely be subtle and nuanced and occur within the details of the realizations of particular moves.

5. References

Al-Harbi, Lafi. "Arabic Research Article Abstracts: A Writer's License". *Journal of Pragmatics* (in press).
Berkenkotter, Carol and Thomas N. Huckin. *Genre Knowledge in Disciplinary Communication: Cognition/Culture/Power.* Hillsdale, NJ: Lawrence Erlbaum, 1995.
Bittencourt dos Santos, Mauro. "The Textual Organization of Research Paper Abstracts in Applied Linguistics". *Text* 16 (1996): 481–99.
Burgess, Sally. "Packed Houses and Intimate Gatherings: Audience and Rhetorical Structure. In *Academic Discourse*, edited By John Flowerdew, 196–215. Harlow, UK: Longman, 2002.
Busch-Lauer, Ines A. "Textual organization in English and German Abstracts". *Anglicana Turkuensia* 14 (1995): 175–186.
Dahl, Trine. "Some Characteristics of Argumentative Abstracts". *Akademisk Prosa,* 2 (2004): 49–67.
Fløttum, Kjersti. "Personal English, Indefinite French and Plural Norwegian Scientific Authors? Pronominal Author Manifestation in Research Articles". *Norsk Lingvistisk Tidsskrift,* 21 (2003): 21–55.
Graetz, Naomi. "Teaching EFL Students to Extract Structural Information from Abstracts. In Ulign J. M and Pugh A. K. (Eds) *Reading for Professional Purposes: Methods and Materials in Teaching Languages*, edited by Jan Ulijn and Anthony K. Pugh, 123–135. Leuven: Acco, 1985.
Hartley, James and M. Sydes. "Are Structured Abstracts Easier to Read than Traditional Ones?" *Journal of Research into Reading* 20 (1997) 122–136.
Hyland, Ken. *Disciplinary Discourses: Social Interactions in Academic Writing.* London: Longman, 2000.

Johns, Tim. "It is presented initially": Linear Dislocation & Inter-language Strategies in Brazilian Academic Abstracts in English and Portuguese. *Ilha do Desterro*, 27 (1992): 9–32.
Lorés, Rosa. On RA abstracts: From Rhetorical Structure to Thematic Organization. *English for Specific Purposes,* 23 (2004): 280–302.
Martín-Martín., Pedro. "A Genre Analysis of English and Spanish Research Paper Abstracts in Experimental Social Sciences". *English for Specific Purposes* 22 (2003): 25–43.
Melander, Bjorn, John M. Swales, and Kirstin M. Fredrickson. "Journal Abstracts from Three Academic Fields in the United States and Sweden: National or Disciplinary proclivities?" In *Culture and Styles of Academic Discourse*, edited by Anna Duszak, 251–272. New York: Mouton de Gruyter, 1997.
Montesi, Michela and Blanca G. Urdiciain. "Recent Linguistics Research into Author Abstracts". *Knowledge Organization* 32 (2005): 64–78.
Régent, O. "A Comparative Approach to the Learning of Specialized Written Discourse". In *Discourse and Learning: Papers in Applied Linguistics and Language Learning from the Centre de Recherches et d'Applications Pédagogiques en Langues*, 105–120. New York: Longman, 1985.
Rounds, Patricia L. "Hedging in Written Academic Discourse: Precision and Flexibility" (mimeo). Department of Linguistics, The University of Michigan, 1982.
Stotesbury, Hilkka. "Evaluation in Research Article Abstracts in the Narrative and Hard Sciences." *Journal of English for Academic Purposes* 2 (2003): 327–341.
Swales, John. M. *Genre Analysis: English in Academic and Research Settings*. Cambridge, UK: Cambridge University Press, 1990.
—. *Research Genres: Explorations and Applications*. Cambridge, UK: Cambridge University Press, 2004.
Valero Garcés, C. and C. M. Calle Martínez. "Contrastive Rhetoric in ESP : A Cross-linguistic Analysis of Finite Verb Profiles in English and Spanish Medical Abstracts". *UNESCO ALSED-LSP Newsletter* 20:2 (1997): 22–36.
Van Bonn, Sarah. "French and English Journal Article Abstracts from General and Applied Linguistics: A Comparative Study". Unpublished Honors Thesis. Department of Linguistics, University of Michigan, Ann Arbor, 2005.
Yakhontova, Tatyana. "'Selling' or 'telling'"? The Issue of Cultural Variation in Research Genres. In *Academic Discourse*, edited by John Flowerdew, 216–232. Harlow, England: Pearson Education, 2002.

Appendix

ASp. 1999. 23-26.
Abstracts 1. Elizabeth Rowley-Jolivet. Designing Posters
Abstracts 2. Elizabeth Rowley-Jolivet. The pivotal role of conference papers in the network of scientific communication
Abstracts 3. Ray Cooke & Sue Birch-Bécaas. From the defective to the effective: exploiting fortuitous errors in non-native speakers' written productions
Abstracts 4. Nigel Bruce. Classification and hierarchy in the discourse of wine: Émile Peynaud's *The Taste of Wine*
Abstracts 5. Shirley Thomas. Thematic networks and text types
Abstracts 6. David Banks. Becoming part of the network: French scientists and the use of English at conferences
Abstracts 7. John Mullen. Creating networks, creating in-groups: choice of vocabulary in *The Economist* editorials
Abstracts 8. Jonathan Upjohn. Exit proficiency: The proof of the pudding
Abstracts 9. David Rees. Using Internal and External Computer Networks as a Language-Learning Resources for Students

ASp. 1996. 11-14.
Abstracts 10. Pauline Tee Anderson. The Use of Cartoons in Teaching Commercial English
Abstracts 11. Kathryn English, Tina Mc Donnell, & Shirley Thomas. Can Old Dogs Learn New Tricks? An Account of an Experimental Course Using the Internet in the Classroom
Abstracts 12. Jonathan Upjohn, Diana Amedeis, & Marie Hélène Fries. Speaking Skills in Scientific English: Intelligibility, Redundancy and Composition Strategies
Abstracts 13. Susan Birch. French Researchers Publishing in English: An analysis of a corpus of first drafts

ASp. 2002. 35-36.
Abstracts 14. David Banks. System Functional Linguistics as a model for text analysis.
Abstracts 15. Ray Cooke. Helping scientists to write scientific English: Challenges and issues

Asp. 1999. 23-26.
Abstracts 16. Sonia Lacabanne. De la théorie à la pratique: Internet, source d'informations, et de réflexions dans un cours d'Anglais pour les physiciens de l'E.N.S.-Lyon
Abstracts 17. Alain Cazade. De l'expérimentation multimédia à l'analyse. Quelques pistes pour tirer parti d'un parcours apprenant en langues
Abstracts 18. Catherine Resche. Un réseau de voies d'accès à la langue spécialisée en anglais L2
Abstracts 19. Alex Boulton. Anciennes et nouvelles technologies : métaphores de l'esprit linguistique
Abstracts 20. Sylvie Monin. L'emprunt en anglais médical contemporain
Abstracts 21. Jacqueline Percebois. L'*Interconnector* : un réseau de transmission de gaz européen : Approche lexicologique comparative du français et de l'anglais des réseaux et contrats gaziers
Abstracts 22. Marie-Hélène Fries-Verdeil. La vraie vie est ailleurs…fonction métonymique des réseaux dans quelques publicités britanniques pour le téléphone
Abstracts 23. Catherine Resche. De l'utilité d'une approche syntaxique en langue spécialisée : exemple de l'anglais économique
Abstracts 24. Anne Magnet. Réseaux de cohérence et de cohésion dans la pratique de l'anglais scientifique
Abstracts 25. Pierre Cotte. Réélaboration et structure : L'héritage dans la langue et en linguistique
Abstracts 26. Michel Petit. La fiction à substrat professionnel : une autre voie d'accès à l'anglais de spécialité
Abstracts 27. Jean-Louis Vidalenc. Faisabilité d'un enseignement à distance de phénomènes lexicaux et syntaxiques : analyse d'un corpus de documents internet présentant un des traitements du cancer de la prostate
Abstracts 28. Claire Bourguignon. LSP : une langue ou un langage
Abstracts 29. Jean-Claude Barbaron. Emacs et Windows : quelques outils et interfaces destinés aux chercheurs
Abstracts 30. Joseph Rézeau. La maille et le nœud : apprendre en réseau

LIST OF CONTRIBUTORS

Kjell Lars Berge is Professor of Textual Science at the Department of Linguistics and Scandinavian Studies, University of Oslo. He has published theoretical as well as empirical studies. His main theoretical contribution is a theory on the diachronic of textual norms. His main empirical work has been on the development of textual norms and cultures in 18th century Scandinavian, and on pupils' writing at schools. Currently Berge is president of The Norwegian Non-fiction Writers and Translators Association.

Marina Bondi is Professor of English at the University of Modena and Reggio Emilia, Italy. She has published on various aspects of discourse analysis and EAP, with particular reference to the argumentative features of academic discourse and to the role of metadiscourse and evaluative language. Her recent work centers on language variation across genres, disciplines and cultures through the analysis of small specialized corpora.

Shirley Carter-Thomas is Senior Lecturer in English at the Institut National des Télécommunications (INT/GET) in Evry, France and member of the CNRS research team LATTICE (Langues, Textes, Traitement Informatique, Cognition). Her research interests revolve around functional linguistics, information structure, writing pedagogy *(La cohérence textuelle – pour une nouvelle pédagogie de l'écrit*, L'Harmattan, 2000) and genre analysis of academic discourse – with publications in *English for Specific Purposes*, *International Journal of Applied Linguistics* and *ASp* (Anglais de Spécialité).

Trine Dahl is Associate Professor of English linguistics at the Norwegian School of Economics and Business Administration (NHH) in Bergen. Her main research focus within academic discourse is on the language of economics. More specifically, she has studied abstracts as well as the use of metadiscourse within that discipline. She is currently investigating how knowledge claims are presented in economics and linguistics research articles. She has published papers in international journals such as Journal of Pragmatics and International Journal of Applied Linguistics, and is co-author of *Academic Voices* (Benjamins 2006).

List of Contributors

Kjersti Fløttum is Professor of French linguistics at the Department of Romance studies and Vice-Rector for international relations at the University of Bergen, Norway. Her general research fields are text linguistics, discourse analysis, semantics and pragmatics. More specifically her research and publications are related to genre theory, linguistic polyphony, academic discourse and political discourse. She is co-author of *ScaPoLine. La théorie scandinave de la polyphonie linguistique* (Kimé 2004) and *Academic Voices* (John Benjamins 2006). She is currently head of the KIAP project on academic discourse (www.uib.no/kiap) and of the multidisciplinary project EURUN, studying European political discourse.

Anje Müller Gjesdal is Research fellow in French linguistics at the Department of Romance studies at the University of Bergen, working on pronominal semantics in research articles. She is affiliated with the KIAP-project (Cultural Identity in Academic Prose) and the Norwegian PhD Research School in Linguistics and Philology. Gjesdal's research interests include semantics, pragmatics and corpus linguistics.

Francis Grossmann is Professor of Linguistics at the University Stendhal in Grenoble, France. His major research interests and major works involve literacy in early childhood (e.g. *Enfances de la lecture. Manières de faire, manières de lire à l'Ecole Maternelle*, Peter Lang) and academic writing (e.g. La surénonciation comme norme du genre: l'exemple de l'article de recherche et du dictionnaire en linguistique, in Langages, 156, 2004, with F. Rinck) as well as lexical semantics of the French language.

Ken Hyland is Professor of Education and director of the Centre for Academic and Professional Literacies at the Institute of Education, University of London. He has taught applied linguistics for almost 30 years on 3 continents. He has published 11 books and over 100 articles and chapters. His most recent work includes Metadiscourse (Continuum, 2005), English for Academic Purposes (Routledge, 2006) and Feedback on writing (edited with Fiona Hyland for CUP, 2006). He is co-editor of the Journal of English for Academic Purposes.

Torodd Kinn is Associate Professor of Scandinavian linguistics at the University of Bergen. In the field of academic discourse, his interests lie primarily in pronominal usage and author-reader interaction. His research has a second focus on synchronic and diachronic aspects of Scandinavian grammar. He is co-author of *Academic Voices* (Benjamins 2006).

Lita Lundquist is Professor of Language for Specific Purposes at the Copenhagen Business School. She has written several books and articles on the topic of text linguistics and text coherence, especially on the use of anaphors in different languages and language types, and in different texts and text types. Focus has been on language and cognition, and in more recent work on language use and society, a relation captured in the notion of discourse.

Anna Mauranen is Professor of English at the University of Helsinki. Her research and publications focus on corpus linguistics, contrastive rhetoric, academic discourses, speech corpora, applied linguistics and translation studies. Her major publications include *Linear Unit Grammar* (co-authored with John Sinclair; 2006), *Translation Universals - Do They Exist* (2004), *Academic Writing. Intercultural and Textual Issues* (1996), *Cultural Differences in Academic Rhetoric* (1993). She is currently running a corpus-based research project on spoken English as a lingua franca (the ELFA corpus).

Elizabeth Rowley-Jolivet is Senior Lecturer in English at the Ecole Polytechnique, University of Orleans, France. Her research interests cover epistemology, genre analysis, spoken and written communication in science, and multimodality. She has compiled a sizeable corpus of multi-disciplinary presentations given in English at international scientific conferences, which has formed the basis for publications on visual discourse in science (*English for Specific Purposes* 2002, *Visual communication* 2004), disciplinary textual patterns *(Text and Texture*, L'Harmattan 2004), the construction of scientific facts (*The Language of Conferencing*, Peter Lang 2002), syntactic analysis (*English for Specific Purposes*, 2004), and scientific rhetoric (*International Journal of Applied Linguistics*, 2005).

Françoise Salager-Meyer is Professor at the University of the Andes (Mérida, Venezuela). She was educated at the University of Lyon, France, and the University of Texas, Austin. She is currently teaching ESP and Russian at the University of the Andes. She is the author of numerous publications on the analysis of written medical discourse, her latest research mainly adopting a diachronic and cross- linguistic perspective. In 1994 and in 2003, she was awarded the H*orowitz Prize.*
Salager-Meyer's co-authors are María Angeles Alcaraz Ariza from Universidad de Alicante, Spain, and Maryelis Pabón from Universidad de Los Andes, Mérida.

Philip Shaw is Professor in the Department of English at Stockholm University and the Language Unit of the Royal Technical Institute, Stockholm. He has degrees from Oxford, Reading, and Newcastle upon Tyne universities. He has taught at universities in Thailand, Germany (Bonn), England, and Denmark. He is co-author (with Gunnel Melchers) of *World Englishes: an Introduction* (Arnold 2003). He is interested in uses of English, mainly in business and academic settings, particularly across cultures and from a genre-analytic standpoint.

John M. Swales is Professor Emeritus of Linguistics at the University of Michigan, where he was also Director of the English Language Institute from 1985-2001. Recent book-length publications include "Other Floors, Other Voices (1998), "English in Today's Research World" (with Chris Feak) (2000), and "Research Genres: Explorations and Applications" (2004). Although retired, he remains active with visiting scholars and with the MICASE project.
Swales' co-author, Sarah Van Bonn, is a Research Assistant in the English Language Institute at the University of Michigan. She graduated with highest honors in Linguistics and Comparative Literature in 2005.

Johan L. Tønnesson is Professor in "sakprosa", i.e. subject oriented prose, at the University of Oslo. He has published two books and several articles, most of them in Norwegian, on academic history writing. Theoretically he works in the broad field of dialogism, theory of multi-vocalism, social semiotics, rhetoric and text linguistics. His main contribution to this field is an operational definition of Eco's concept *Model Reader*, which is integrated with related concepts into a "score" model for text analysis.

Eva Thue Vold is Research fellow in French linguistics at the Department of Romance studies, University of Bergen, Norway. Her main research interests include academic discourse, epistemic modality, evidentiality and corpus linguistics. She is currently working on a project concerning the use of epistemic modality in academic discourse, with a particular focus on cross-disciplinary and cross-linguistic variation. Since 2003, she has been affiliated to the KIAP-project.

Françoise Wirth is Translator, working from English and German into French. She is a graduate from Paris Ecole Supérieure d'Interprètes et de Traducteurs (Sorbonne nouvelle). Many of her translations have been published in various Human Sciences journals (Actes de la Recherche en Sciences sociales, Le mouvement social, etc.). She also teaches translation to English-speaking students at University Stendhal (CUEF).